Forecasting
Interest Rates

Forecasting Interest Rates

John B. Schwartzman

McGraw-Hill, Inc.

New York St. Louis San Francisco Auckland Bogotá
Caracas Lisbon London Madrid Mexico Milan
Montreal New Delhi Paris San Juan São Paulo
Singapore Sydney Tokyo Toronto

Library of Congress Cataloging-in-Publication Data

Schwartzman, John B.
    Forecasting interest rates / John B. Schwartzman.
        p.   cm.
    Includes bibliographical references and index.
    ISBN 0-07-055967-8
    1. Interest rates—Forecasting—Handbooks, manuals, etc.
I. Title.
HG1622.S39   1992
332.8'2'0112—dc20   92-12092
                                                          CIP

1 2 3 4 5 6 7 8 9 0   DOC/DOC   9 8 7 6 5 4 3 2

ISBN 0-07-055967-8

The sponsoring editor for this book was David Conti, the editing supervisor
was Stephen M. Smith, and the production supervisor was Donald F. Schmidt.
It was set in Palatino by Carol Woolverton, Lexington, Massachusetts.

Printed and bound by R. R. Donnelley & Sons Company.

This publication is designed to provide accurate and authoritative information in regard to the subject matter covered. It is sold with the understanding that the publisher is not engaged in rendering legal, accounting or
other professional service. If legal advice or other expert assistance is required, the services of a competent professional person should be sought.

—From the declaration of principles jointly adopted by a committee of the
American Bar Association and a committee of publishers.

To Sheila

Contents

Preface

What This Book Is About

Forecasting Interest Rates describes a carefully thought-out process by which the reader can learn how to track the movement of interest rates weekly, monthly, and quarterly in order to ascertain a trend and thereby make a forecast. The process is used not only to track today's interest rate movements but also those for any time in the future. The method for tracking interest rates is to examine the current factors that influence the movement of interest rates. These factors can be incorporated into the process of tracking. The basic factors that will be discussed include economic, inflation, monetary, fiscal, global, political, and psychological factors. The means for executing the process is to fill out a weekly interest rate chart that includes selected short- and long-term interest rates and common indicators such as the yen in dollars, the Commodity Research Bureau's futures index, and the price of West Texas Intermediate Crude oil, all of which will at some time or another react to the movement of interest rates. Spaces at the top of the chart allow the user to enter economic and inflation factors published by various federal agencies and private associations that are always reported during a particular week. Each space on the chart represents a specific day, Monday through Friday. Finally, the weekly interest rate chart also includes a large space in which to write an abbreviated summation of a particular factor and symbols to show in which way the factor influenced the movement of interest rates—up, down, or neither way. Other spaces allow you to write in the trend of interest rates based on the data gathered and interpreted on the chart, overlooked factors that might affect interest rates in the future, and a comments section in which to include any thoughts you may have concerning the future trend and forecast in interest rates.

The weekly interest rate chart is a matrix created to show how certain factors move interest rates and to allow you to interpret these factors in terms of how they influence interest rates. By using the weekly interest rate chart, you can make assumptions about the movement of interest rates that lead to a possible trend and forecast. Further, a monthly interest rate chart and a quarterly interest rate chart, based on the weekly interest rate chart, allow you to continue summarizing the important factors that will influence the movement of interest rates over a longer period of time. All the charts taken together provide an array of data and interpretations to help in making a forecast.

Because interest rates react to psychological interpretations of many factors, we can only attempt to elucidate those factors that will, when viewed and linked together with many other factors, move interest rates in one direction or another. Today's interest rate factors may well be different from tomorrow's, but the process of tracking them as described in this book will remain the same. The process you will learn from this book can be adapted to future changes that will occur in both domestic and foreign interest rate analysis. By using this process, you will be able to obtain an understanding of how economic, inflation, monetary, global, and political factors influence the movement of interest rates today and tomorrow.

The principal pieces of information used are obtained from four well-recognized, publicly accessible publications: *The New York Times, The Wall Street Journal, Investor's Business Daily,* and *Barron's.* Other publications can be used, but these four are among those commonly read by people in many businesses, the investment community, government, and academe. The active interaction of the weekly interest rate chart, these publicly accessible sources, and an understanding of the key factors that can move interest rates fulfill the process described in this book in order that you can establish a workable basis for making a reasonable interest rate forecast.

The entire process has been designed to minimize the time needed to put the data in the weekly interest rate chart while allowing an appropriate amount of time in which to interpret the data without disrupting the day's activities. Initially the system takes time to set up, to learn where to find the requisite information from the applicable sources and how to use the weekly interest rate chart. Once all of these ingredients are understood, however, the actual process takes little time to execute, and is both easy and fun to perform. Most important, the user will find that he or she is observing history as it is being made, both in the United States and all over the world. There are many interest rate factors that constantly interact throughout the world. By using the weekly interest rate chart, you can keep abreast of these changes and see how they affect the movement of interest rates.

Audiences This Book Serves

Various audiences can use this book. Both beginning and experienced investment professionals, including bond, stock, commodity, and currency portfolio managers, traders, and research analysts, can use it, as can individuals involved in marketing these investment products, whether for banks, insurance companies, investment companies, or others. A second audience includes business executives involved in purchasing, budgeting, and investing company funds. These executives might include the company treasurer, the investment manager, and the chief financial officer. A third audience is salespersons in a variety of businesses, including account officers in real estate firms and mortgage banking companies who participate in building residential, commercial, or industrial structures. A fourth audience is bank loan officers involved in lending funds for personal and business uses, such as buying new equipment and materials, expanding a business, making construction loans, and establishing home mortgages or auto loans. A fifth audience includes business, finance, and economics students at either the undergraduate or the graduate level seeking to gain a more complete understanding of how interest rates reflect both national and foreign economic, inflation, and monetary policies. This book can help students learn a "hands-on" approach not only to understand the factors that influence the movement of interest rates but also to integrate this understanding with courses in economics, finance, management, and investments in order to gain greater insight. A sixth audience is local, state, and national officials who need to understand how interest rates can affect their fiscal, economic, and monetary decisions as they carry out their responsibilities, whether they are budgeting, creating fiscal reforms such as tax laws, or developing economic and housing programs. Lastly, the most important audience is the individual who has to make decisions about home mortgage rates, auto loans, college tuition loans, and personal investments.

Benefits of Using This Book

The principal benefit of using this book is that since the process of tracking interest rates leads to determination of a trend and then allows you to make a reasonable forecast as to the movement of interest rates, you can use it to aid in making specific personal and business decisions. Since the process is adaptable to both domestic and foreign economic, monetary, inflationary, and geopolitical changes, the process will change as the times and factors change. A particular benefit is that the weekly, monthly, and quarterly interest rate charts can be computerized so that graphs can be drawn and information stored and researched when needed for further analysis. Another benefit is that because publicly accessible information, including the four newspapers mentioned above, is used as the primary source of information, you can continue to keep abreast of changes as reported in these and other newspapers and journals. These changes are then entered in the interest rate charts to help determine the direction of interest rates.

Composition of This Book

This book is divided into three parts. The first part consists of three chapters that discuss the practical applications of interest rates, definitions of yields and interest rates, and where to locate the important interest rate information. Chapter 1 defines four types of interest rates, namely personal interest rates, business interest rates, investment interest rates, and governmental interest rates. Then the chapter defines interest rates and ends with a discussion of three major goals of this book. These are (1) the process; (2) understanding the factors that influence interest rates, including economic, inflation, fiscal, monetary, global, and political factors; and (3) understanding how these factors can lead to determining interest rate trends. Chapter 2 defines the difference between yields and interest rates. This distinction is critical in understanding how interest rates move in one direction as opposed to another. In this chapter, the subjects of yield, interest, and rate are presented, and, finally, an overall definition of interest rates is analyzed. In addition, you will learn what makes a reliable interest rate factor and how to link various factors together to establish a trend. In Chap. 3 you learn how to find interest rate information quickly by using four major newspapers: *The Wall Street Journal, The New York Times, Investor's Business Daily,* and *Barron's.* This chapter gives an overview of the location of important interest rate information in the above publications so that the data can be placed on the interest rate charts.

The second part of this book, comprising Chaps. 4 through 10, describes the various factors that influence interest rates, including factors dealing with the economy, inflation, monetary and fiscal policies, global issues and the U.S. trade deficit, the dollar, and political issues. As each indicator or factor is discussed, you will learn not only what the factor and its component parts are, but also key interpretations and problems of each of these factors. In each case, how the factors influence interest rates will be discussed.

The third part represents the working process of this book. Chapter 11 describes how to set up the weekly interest rate chart. The precise location of information needed for the chart is shown by indicating where the information is in each of the four newspapers that were discussed in general in Chap. 3. In addition, the monthly and quarterly interest rate charts are discussed as a means to track interest rates over a longer time period. Reproductions of each of these copyrighted charts are included. In Chap. 12 an actual week, 3 months, and quarter are described in order for the reader to see how I use the process to track interest rates. The actual filled-out charts are included to aid understanding.

I have set out to create an easy-to-use process for readers working in many professions and jobs that is both current and adaptable for the future. Because time is always a critical element in performing your day-to-day activities, I have created a process that is as efficient as it is easy to execute, allowing plenty of time for interpretation of all the data. The process described in this book will allow you to understand the various factors that influence the movement of interest rates in a particular direction, thus establishing a trend that leads to a forecast. The process will permit you to make better personal and business decisions.

John B. Schwartzman

Acknowledgments

There are professional colleagues, friends, and family too numerous to mention who I would like to thank, and to whom I am particularly indebted for their support and encouragement throughout this venture. I want to thank all the students I have been privileged to teach at The American Institute of Banking for the past 8 years, who have provided me with evaluations of my course "Interest Rates: Influences and Trends," from which much of this book is drawn, and many enthusiastic class discussions. Special thanks go to my colleagues at The Bank of New York, with whom I have had the pleasure of working and discussing interest rates and sundry things for more than 10 years.

Several business friends and members of my family read the manuscript and provided many valuable comments: Lowell A. Kleiman, President, Scientific Industries Inc.; Priscilla Kleiman; Steven E. Adler, President, Belwool Corporation; Richard Dodd, vice president and senior portfolio manager in the tax-exempt bond management department at The Bank of New York; Peter A. Schwartzman, hospital analyst at Moody's Investor's Service; Terese Stryker, former student and trust portfolio manager at The Bank of New York; and Robert Pucciariello, vice president and foreign currency trader at Farr Man Capital Inc. In addition, I would like to thank my agent, Paul M. von Freihofer, for his determined efforts on behalf of this project; David Conti, my editor at McGraw-Hill, for his advice; and Stephen Smith, also at McGraw-Hill, for immeasurably improving the readibility of the text.

Special thanks must be given to James J. Cooner, senior vice president at

The Bank of New York, for his encouragement, counsel, and invaluable comments from when this book was just an idea to when the final touches were put on the manuscript.

Finally, I take full responsibility for any errors of interpretation or omission.

1
What Are Interest Rates?

Practical Aspects of Interest Rates

Changing interest rates affect personal, business, investment, and governmental decision making. The movement of interest rates in one direction or another is influenced by a multitude of factors, including economic, inflationary, monetary, fiscal, global, and political factors. The confluence of these factors into a particular direction over a period of time establishes an interest rate trend. The decision by either individuals or organizations to take an action depends not only on the level of interest rates at the time but also on the judgment that interest rates will continue to rise or fall in the future. Let us view a number of typical personal, business, investment, or political decisions that are based at least in part on interest rates.

Personal Interest Rates

Interest rates affect an individual's personal life in many ways. When a person decides to take a particular action will often depend on the level of interest rates. If interest rates are high, the individual may not wish to borrow funds to build an addition to his or her home. If interest rates are low, the individual might decide to purchase a vacation home because borrowing costs are now lower than they were several months ago. Following are some additional examples of personal decisions that are based on interest rates.

When someone buys a new car, part of the financing is usually provided by a loan from either the automobile company or a bank. The amount the buyer pays over a specified period of years is based on a particular interest rate or car loan rate. If the person wants to buy a new house, a mortgage will have to be obtained; the mortgage payment is based on a specified interest rate or mortgage rate. If a homeowner wants to expand and renovate his or her kitchen, taking out a personal loan at a specified interest rate is a means for doing it. Sending a second child to college often means that a tuition loan from a local bank is needed. That loan carries a specified interest rate. If a couple wants to take a special vacation trip to celebrate an anniversary, borrowing funds from a bank at a particular interest rate is a good way to do it. If an individual wants a personal home computer in order to write a book or perform additional office work at home, a personal loan to help finance it carries an interest rate charged by the bank. Or suppose that your refrigerator suddenly breaks down. If you decide to buy a new one using a credit card so that you can pay off the large amount over several months, the credit card company charges a specified interest rate for any outstanding balance on your account. These are just a few examples of the types of interest rates that individuals use for personal activities. When the individual decides to make a particular decision often depends on the level of interest rates.

Business Interest Rates

An important part of running a business involves the use of interest rates. If a company decides to expand its facilities, a loan from the local bank carries a specified interest rate. During certain periods of the year, a company may have to replenish its inventory. Using a loan at a determined interest rate is one method of financing the purchases. A company that wishes to replace worn-out equipment with new, state-of-the-art equipment may take out a loan from a bank at a particular interest rate. Perhaps the company has grown enough to warrant building a new plant in another location. Again, a loan from a bank at a certain interest rate can be used to finance the building of a new plant.

Investment Interest Rates

Return on investment is always of great concern to the investor. Interest rates play a key role in obtaining the maximum return on specific types of investment, such as U.S. Treasury securities, municipal bonds, corporate bonds, pool or collateralized single-family mortgage bonds, and foreign bonds. Investment in short-term instruments for a good return can possibly be obtained from commercial paper of major finance companies and corporations, certificates of deposit from many banks, bankers' acceptances, and many other types of short-term investments. For the individual, obtaining a high interest rate on savings deposits, or investing in certificates of deposit or municipal bonds, can provide a good return on the monies invested. If interest rates are higher than they were 6 months ago, an individual may want to purchase municipal securities because they now yield a higher return than they would have 6 months ago. All of these investment types have a particular interest rate which becomes part of the total return.

The return on investment of financial assets is important not only to individuals and families but also to nonprofit institutions including college pension funds, helping agencies that provide many services to disadvantaged persons and families, philanthropic groups, and religious institutions. Trust departments, specialized investment companies that manage certain types of investments such as municipal bonds or high-technology stocks, use the level of interest rates to determine their investment strategy.

Governmental Interest Rates

The nation's bank or central bank has as its goals to maintain a growing economy and to keep inflation low. In order to accomplish these goals, interest rates fixed by the nation's central bank attempt to sustain these goals. For example, if the U.S. economy is growing too fast with the result of rising inflation, the central bank may decide to increase short-term interest rates to stem the inflation and cool off the economy. Or if the economy is in a recession, the central bank may lower interest rates to encourage more bank loans to stimulate business in order to spark a recovery. What the central bank does is related directly to what institutions such as the major depository banks do in terms of raising or lowering their interest rates. All of these effects filter down to the individual who wants to buy a house, the nonprofit institution looking for a good return on its investments in order to help its constituency, and the company anxious to purchase new equipment.

During times of economic stress, politicians call for the lowering of interest rates, particularly if the nation is heading toward a presidential election. The assumption is that if interest rates are lower, the U.S. economy will grow, people will be hired, and personal income will increase so that more money will be spent to purchase goods and services. The politics of interest rates is an important factor in determining their level and the effect on the voting public that puts people in office or removes them.

Foreign governmental interest rates are also an important factor in industrialized economies, particularly Germany and Japan. The rise and fall of foreign interest rates can affect the level of U.S. interest rates. In a constantly changing world whose economies are closely tied together, the effect of another major nation's central bank raising or lowering its interest rates to quell inflation or stimulate its economy can directly affect U.S. interest rates. For example, if Germany raises its interest rates to stem rising inflation in that country, it would put pressure on U.S. interest rates to increase in order to encourage foreign investors to purchase U.S. Treasury securities, which are used to fund our budget deficits.

Definition of Interest Rates

All the above examples define the practical world of interest rates as they affect personal, business, investment, and governmental decision making. When these interest rate decisions are made depends on both the current level of interest rates as well as a forecast of future levels.

In my view, interest rates reflect psychological reactions to a multitude of domestic and foreign economic, inflationary, monetary, fiscal, and political factors that influence what goes on in the world. Sidney Homer and Richard Sylla, the authors of one of the major references on the history of interest rates, had this comment on interest rates:

> In the charts and tables of interest rates over long periods, students of history may see mirrored the rise and fall of nations and civilizations, the exertions and tragedies of war, and the enjoyments and the abuses of peace. They may be able to trace in the fluctuations the progress of knowledge and technology, the successes and failures of political forms, and the long, hard, and never-ending struggle of democracy with the rule of tyrants and elites.*

They went on to say the following:

> Students of economics may read in the ebb and flow of interest rates the success of some communities and the failure of others to develop effective commercial ethics and laws and suitable monetary and fiscal techniques and policies. They may recognize the effects of economic growth and of economic decline as these two forces alternate over the dimensions of time and space.†

These quotations constitute what I believe to be my philosophy of interest rates, which is that the history of interest rates reflects both subtle and

---

*Sidney Homer and Richard Sylla, *A History of Interest Rates: 2,000 B.C. to the Present*, 3d ed., Rutgers University Press, New Brunswick, NJ, 1992, p. 1.

†Ibid.

overt changes in world events. Even a cursory reading of Homer and Sylla's book on the history of interest rates will tell you that. Sometimes we recognize these changes, sometimes we do not. A major thrust of this book is to encourage readers both to think about and to try to understand the factors that influence interest rates. By understanding why interest rates move in a particular direction in order to determine a trend, the reader—whether an individual, a corporate executive, a money manager, or a governmental official—will feel more comfortable in making personal, business, investment, and governmental decisions.

Homer and Sylla also had a poignant wit. They noted that "around the turn of the last century, a famous Austrian economist . . . declared that the cultural level of a nation is mirrored by its rate of interest: The higher a people's intelligence and moral strength, the lower the rate of interest."*

Goals of This Book

There are three major goals of this book: (1) to create a process by which the reader can continuously track the movement of interest rates today as well in 5 years from now; (2) to understand the various factors that influence the direction of interest rates; and (3) to determine the trends that define the movement of interest rates in order to make a forecast of the direction in which interest rates are heading.

Goal One: The Process

The process is one by which the reader can track interest rates in order to see the trend. By using simply constructed weekly, monthly, and quarterly interest rate charts and by obtaining the requisite information from publicly accessible newspapers and weekly publications, the reader can keep abreast of the factors that influence the constantly changing direction of interest rates. More important, the factors that influence interest rates will change over time as the world changes. By using the chart and publications that are available to the public, the reader will be able to follow the changes in a way that can be easily put onto the interest rate charts. Once the user learns the process, the time needed to put the information into the chart will take no more than 15 minutes. That will leave additional time in which to think about interpreting these factors as they affect the movement of interest rates.

*Ibid.

Goal Two: Understanding the Factors That Influence Interest Rates

What Makes a Reliable Factor? In order to understand the factors that influence interest rates, one must first understand what makes a reliable interest rate factor. These factors are reported by various federal agencies, university research centers, and nonprofit companies specializing in business economic research, including the Department of Commerce, the Department of Labor Statistics, the Federal Reserve Board, the University of Michigan, and the Conference Board of business executives. One other factor, politics, is difficult to quantify but is nevertheless very important in determining the movement of interest rates.

Characteristics of a reliable interest rate factor as reported by private, nonprofit, and governmental institutions include the following.

1. It should indicate trends in U.S. interest rates by reflecting economic, inflation, monetary, fiscal, and political factors, both domestic and foreign.

2. It should be statistically sound.

3. It should have a history of use.

4. It should be able to alter its component parts periodically to reflect structural changes in the U.S. economy.

5. It should be reported on a regular basis within a specific time period, such as a certain week, month, or quarter during the year.

6. It should be promptly available to the general public through various media including local and national newspapers, business magazines and journals, and radio and television programs.

These characteristics of a reliable factor suggest why certain specific factors have been chosen for use in our process. As demographic, social, and economic changes occur not only within the United States but also in other parts of the world, many of these factors will change. New factors will then be reported as those institutions that report this information to the public absorb the new information. By understanding the process, the user will be able to incorporate these changes.

The discussion of interest rate factors has been divided into several areas, including economic, inflationary, monetary, fiscal, political, and global factors. Economic factors include reports on U.S. industrial production, employment numbers, new housing starts and permits, durable goods orders, factory orders, auto and retail sales; inflation factors such as the producer price index, the consumer price index, and personal income;

monetary factors such as the federal funds rate and the discount rate; fiscal factors such as the U.S. federal budget deficit and tax policies; global factors such as foreign interest rates, the U.S. trade deficit, the value of the U.S. dollar against foreign currencies, and international interest rate cooperation; and political factors such as speeches by important domestic and foreign leaders and domestic and foreign banking officials concerning U.S. and foreign economies and global inflation and interest rates.

Linking the Factors Together. An important aspect of understanding these factors is linking them together to determine a trend. The individual factors in the selected areas can be linked together to establish a trend in the U.S. economy, which in turn will be affected by the movement of interest rates. For example, if interest rates remain high over a sustained period of time, they will begin to slow down the U.S. economy. One can observe the reaction of specific interest rates by tracking a number of these factors. Further, high interest rates will lead to a fall in new housing starts, which is linked to declines in industrial production, which is linked to rising claims for unemployment insurance, which is linked to increases in the unemployment rate, and so on.

Another example of linkage is that if inflation continues to rise, it will be reflected in the producer price index, which is linked to increases in the consumer price index, which is linked to declines in auto and retail sales. All these individual factors will lead to changes in the movement of interest rates. For example, if the Federal Reserve Board feels that inflation is pushing interest rates too high, it will raise short-term interest rates to quell the inflationary flame, even if that may mean a temporary cooling of the U.S. economy. The precise time at which the Fed implements a decline in interest rates is a matter of a thousand guesses. As we learn how to track these factors, we will also learn how to assess them. One essential rule is that one month's number does not indicate a trend. But over a period of months, linkages of factors do point to a trend, and that is when interest rates begin to change. When interest rates reach a certain level, often a perceived level and one that is not easily predictable, interest rates will affect the U.S. economy and other foreign industrial economies as well. The economic and inflation factors that affect major foreign industrialized countries such as Germany, Japan, Taiwan, Mexico, and Canada directly affect the same U.S. factors. The linkages between these countries are vitally important in understanding the movement of U.S. interest rates.

The linkages among similar factors that explain what is happening to foreign economies such as those of Japan and Germany in relation to that of the United States are vitally important in understanding the movement of U.S. interest rates. The split-second exchange of information that flies in computer bits all over the world into a mass of individual terminals requires considerable and thoughtful effort on analysts' part to put these factors into perspective. These interpretations are always found in the publications we will discuss in Chap. 3.

Goal Three: Understanding Trends and Forecasting

To forecast or not to forecast, that is always the question. A key goal of this book is to use the process to understand trends in interest rates in order to make informed decisions about the movement of interest rates. Paraphrasing Webster's dictionary, trend is defined as a general direction.* If interest rates are moving in a general direction, then that direction establishes a trend. Again paraphrasing Webster's, the definition of a forecast is a prediction.† If the chart we use to track interest rates is clearly showing a direction or a trend, then it is possible to make a reasonable guess or prediction as to the future direction of interest rates. Many people sincerely believe that it is impossible to predict or forecast the movement of interest rates because of the uncertainty of determining what domestic and global factors influence interest rates. But people still forecast interest rates because their responsibilities demand taking the risk of making personal, business, investment, and governmental decisions no matter how difficult it may be to determine the direction of interest rates. The individual might want to decide whether to purchase a new house based on the current low mortgage rates or wait to see if they will move still lower. A company president has to decide when to build a new plant, in large part based on the cost of financing it (the interest rate charged on the loan needed to build it). The chief investment officer of a major investment house has to provide a reasoned prediction or forecast of the direction of interest rates over a 6-month period in order to establish an investment policy for stocks, bonds, and cash. Clearly, making such forecasts is fraught with uncertainty, but it is done. Let us consider some comments about forecasting to see why.

Forecasting interest rates is more art than science. This book looks at interest rate movements on the basis of why they are moving in one direction or another in order to determine a trend. Charting the information, thinking the information through, and using one's intuition based on the assembling of various significant factors can provide an opportunity to see the effects that these factors have on the direction of interest rates. Clearly, once an understanding of what moves interest rates is obtained, one can gauge what direction interest rates might move in the future. But

---

*Webster's Ninth New Collegiate Dictionary, Merriam-Webster, Springfield, MA, 1984, p. 1258.

†Ibid., p. 402.

the determination is still a personal judgment by an individual to make a decision to purchase a new home or the view of a chief investment officer attempting to create an investment strategy to earn a profitable return on the financial assets invested for clients. Both of these decisions are based on a perception that interest rates will move in a particular direction over time. Business, investment, and personal financial and political decisions are based on this understanding.

Forecasting interest rates is no less difficult than predicting the direction of the U.S. economy or the future success of your local sports team. As the Israeli economist Shlomo Maital noted in his book, *Minds, Markets & Money*:

> If Americans have trouble making sense of what they read, hear, and see about the economy, they are in good company. So do the experts. In the last decade [he means the 1970s but the same is true for any decade; just witness the extraordinary changes in the last decade] the economic world has been literally turned upside down. Markets behave perversely. Prices jump erratically. Causal arrows reverse direction. Eternal truths become falsehoods. And forecasters run for cover and hope for better days.*

As John Kenneth Galbraith, the distinguished economist, professor, former ambassador, presidential advisor, and noted wit said when asked about forecasting, "there are only two kinds of interest rate forecasters: those who don't know where rates are going, and those who don't know that they don't know."† If one can understand why interest rates have been moving in a particular direction, then, possibly, one can determine a trend and make a forecast. The risk is great, however, that the forecast will be wrong, because events happening in this world are incredibly uncertain and often amazingly surprising.

No less an authority than Dr. Seuss stated his view of forecasting as follows:

> As our graph shows, Trends are trending.
> This is good, Yet, nevertheless,
> the destination of the trendings
> is not simple to assess.

> As of now, the Uppers are upping
> and the Downers are droobling down
> excepting on alternate Thursdays
> when it works the other way round.

---

*Shlomo Maital, *Minds, Markets & Money: The Psychological Foundations of Economic Behavior*, Basic Books, New York, 1982, p. 3.

†John Kenneth Galbraith, quoted by Tom Herman, in "Newsletters Buck the Bullish Bond Trend," *The Wall Street Journal*, November 12, 1990, p. C17. Reprinted by permission of *The Wall Street Journal*, © 1990 Dow Jones & Company, Inc. All rights reserved worldwide.

And there occasionally are occasions
when some Upper comes a cropper
and bottoms out at the bottom
Then . . .
some bottomer is the Topper.

Consequently, on the other hand,
I believe this can be said:
you'll be wise if you step gently
whilst you tread on your neighbor's head.*

The Overall Goal of This Book

If any guess is as good as another, the reader should be able to make an informed guess or forecast based on observing a trend. That informed guess or forecast, based on an understanding of the factors that influence the movement of interest rates, is the overall goal of this book.

*Theodor S. Geisel, "The Economic Situation Clarified: A Prognostic Evaluation by the Dr. Seuss Surveys," *The New York Times Magazine,* June 15, 1975, p. 71. Copyright © 1975 by The New York Times Company; reprinted by permission. Also, reprinted by permission of the Estate of Theodor S. Geisel; copyright © 1975.

2
Yields and Interest Rates

Introduction

In this book I refer to "yields" as much as I do to "interest rates." It is important to understand the difference. *Yields* are reactions to daily market conditions, which are influenced by the psychological reactions of securities traders who buy and sell fixed-income securities or bonds based on a multitude of factors, including economic, inflation, monetary, fiscal, political, and global factors. When these factors produce a trend, market conditions move not only yields but ultimately interest rates. The interest rate of a bond reflects other interest rates, including mortgage rates, credit card rates, business loan rates, and automobile loan rates, all of which are collectively called interest rates. As a proxy for understanding the movement of interest rates, I use several U.S. Treasury securities including the 3-month Treasury bill, the 2-year Treasury note, the 10-year Treasury note, and the 30-year Treasury bond. For example, if the U.S. economy begins to slow down, yields begin to decline. Two-year Treasury notes are auctioned or sold to the public every month. So if yields have been moving downward in reaction to a slowdown in the U.S. economy, the auction of the new 2-year Treasury note will have a lower interest or coupon rate. During this period, mortgage rates will also begin to decline as they react to the same factors and interpretations. On the other hand, if the U.S. economy continues to rapidly grow and inflation increases, yields on the same 2-year Treasury note will also rise. So at the next monthly auction of the 2-year Treasury note, the original coupon or interest rate will be higher. Again, mortgage rates as well as a host of other interest rates will also rise as they react the same way to the same factors.

The daily movement in yields is caused by market conditions which in part reflect the psychological reaction of both buyers and sellers to the groups of factors we have mentioned earlier. In turn, these U.S. Treasury securities move up and down in both yields and interest rates. The financial markets of Wall Street, as well as financial markets across the world, speak in terms of both yields and interest rates. In order to understand why interest rates change, one must also understand why yields change. More important, what is the relationship between yields and interest rates in terms of the factors that affect them? My definition of yields is based on the psychological influences that affect these and other types of securities on a daily basis. Over a period of time, the rise or fall of yields will increase or decrease the level of interest rates. And at the same time, all the other interest rates tend to move in the same direction because they are also reacting to the same set of factors.

Mathematically, a change in bond yields directly affects the price of a bond, because the composition of a bond consists of its stated maturity, its price, and its coupon or interest rate. For example, a municipal bond could have a coupon or interest rate of 7.00%, a face value of par or $1000 in most cases, and a maturity of 5 years. The 7.00% is the *coupon rate*, or the interest the borrower will pay to the bondholder on the face value of the bond for use of that money. The price *at par* means the face value of the bond, which in terms of percentage means 100 and in terms of dollars $1000.

All bonds are expressed as a *yield to maturity*, based on the assumption that the bondholder will keep the bond until it matures. An investor buys one bond at $1000 or a price of par or $1000 of face value. If the investor buys 25 bonds, the cost is $25,000. As the yields on a bond rise, the price of that bond falls. Investors speak of yields as the total return or rate of return for holding an investment until its stated maturity based on receiving periodic coupon payments (usually semiannually) and the original face value of the bond when it matures. For example, assume that a 7.00% bond bought for $1000 rises in yield to 7.48%, reflecting a drop in the bond price to $980. The key concept is that as yields rise, the price of the bond falls. Yields are always expressed in *basis points*, where one basis point is equal to 1/100 of 1%. Therefore, the 48 basis rise in the yield of the bond pushes the price of the bond down in an inverse mathematical relationship. The price of the bond is now lower than when the investor purchased it, and if the investor now sells it, the price received will be $980, not $1000.

The relationship is a mathematical one in terms of how one computes yield based on price, the coupon rate, and the stated maturity. If the investor in our example sells it before the stated maturity of 5 years, the price received will be less that what was paid for it. If, on the other hand, the yield is less than when the investor originally bought it, then the investor will receive a higher price than it was originally bought for. Furthermore, if the investor holds the bond to its stated maturity of 5 years, he or she would receive interest payments twice each year plus the original face value of the bond when it matures.

My definition of yield is that changes in yields over a period of time will create changes in interest rates. Just as the price of a bond is influenced by many factors, so are yields, although they react oppositely. A decline in price means a rise in the yield. The essential question is what factors are making the prices and therefore the yields move up or down. When we discuss the effect of a particular factor on yields, we mean, for example, that if the consumer price index has continued to rise over several months, yields on U.S. Treasury bonds will also rise. Or mortgage rates, which react to the movement of these yields, will begin to rise. When we learn how to track interest rates on a daily, weekly, monthly, and quarterly basis, we will use the term *yields* in the same way as the financial markets do. For example, the 2-year Treasury note could have five different yields during a particular week because of the influence of several important inflation and economic factors. Each day we will enter that yield on a weekly interest rate chart.

Now let us take a closer look at the relationship between yields and interest rates. Yields reflect the daily fluctuations of interest rates in the financial markets as they react to economic, inflationary, monetary, fiscal, political, and global factors. They change throughout the day as different factors reported worldwide bombard the current interest rates of bonds and push their yields in one direction or another. Once yields begin to move in a particular direction over a sustained period of time, interest rates will change. If yields begin to rise because a variety of indicators over a period of months show that the U.S. economy is continuing to grow, then interest rates will adjust upward because sustained economic growth often means inflation. The rise of inflation that normally occurs as the economy grows means that the prices of goods and services rise. The increase in inflation ultimately forces interest rates upward. If yields continue to decline, mortgage rates will adjust downward, thus encouraging the purchase of new homes. If yields continue to climb, thereby forcing interest rates to adjust upward, the U.S. economy will at some time begin to slow down because the cost of business, or the interest rates used to borrow money, will be too high. Then the Federal Reserve Board, which is responsible for controlling inflation and sustaining the growth of the U.S. economy, may decide to push short-term interest rates lower as a clear sign that it wants to spur the U.S. economy while also keeping inflation down. The daily events that affect yields over a short period of time will directly affect the rise and fall of interest rates over a longer period of time.

The meaning of interest rates is best understood by dividing the subject into three parts: interest, rate, and yield. All three of these different but related words are too often substituted for one another. There are many interpretations of the definitions of the three little words—interest, rate, and yield. These definitions help in understanding my interpretation of interest rates.

Defining Interest

A paraphrase of one of the definitions of *interest* in *Webster's Ninth New Collegiate Dictionary* is a particular focus on something.* To find out how especially important interest rates can be, just talk to individual investors, retirees receiving fixed-interest payments from bonds, loan officers, stock and bond traders, portfolio managers, economists, chief investment officers, and strategists of all kinds, persuasions, and passions for whom profit and return are the roots of success or the loss of a client, depending on how one looks at it. Some examples include a growing business seeking a loan to expand or build a new plant, a couple with a new baby looking to obtain a loan for a new house, a family needing a new coat of exterior paint on their house, a budding author who wants to take out a loan to refurbish his basement into a writing room, and parents appalled at the cost of education at a private higher educational institution who now have to take out an educational loan for their college-bound child. All these people have a deep and abiding special interest in taking out a loan to accomplish a need. The cost of that loan to the borrower is the current interest rate.

Another definition of interest is the cost of borrowing money expressed as a percent of the borrowed amount.† Individuals and businesses have to pay a price to borrow money; that is, there is a charge to obtain a loan. Every time a loan is taken out to achieve some determined objective or special interest to the borrower, a cost for using that money is paid to borrow that money. The money above the principal or amount loaned is defined as interest.

Defining Rate

Rate represents a particular value, and a *rate of interest* is the specific interest attached to a specific loan needed for different purposes—personal,

---

Webster's Ninth New Collegiate Dictionary, Merriam-Webster, Springfield, MA, 1984, p. 630.

†Ibid.

business, or investment.* You take out a loan with a rate of 10%. You purchase a mortgage at a rate of 12%. You buy a municipal bond with a rate of 6%. You take out a student loan to attend graduate school at a rate of 8%. You borrow funds to expand a plant at a rate of 14%. This rate is the actual cost of using the money borrowed. When you buy a municipal bond, you are actually loaning money to a municipality so that it can build or repair an essential facility such as a school, a sewer, a waste treatment plant, an expansion to an airport, roads and streets, or a prison. The municipality must pay you interest for allowing it to use that money to build that essential facility. The loan is ultimately paid back to the purchaser of the bond. Along the way, a specific rate of interest is paid to the individual who loaned the borrower the money to build the facility. The same holds true for purchasing a corporate bond issued by IBM, which needs funds to build a new plant. Or the purchasing of a U.S. Treasury note, the proceeds of which will cover a portion of the U.S. government's huge budget deficit. Unlike states and their municipalities, the federal government has no capital construction plan. Monies are derived from general operating funds to construct federal projects such as highways, court houses, and Internal Revenue Service collection centers. The cost of using money on behalf of an individual or business is the specific rate of interest.

Defining Yield

Finally, what is the definition of a yield? A *yield* produces revenue or a return from an expenditure or an investment.† We say that yields move up a basis point or down a basis point. When an important factor is reported to the public, yields may move up 5 basis points or down 10 basis points. A *basis point* means $\frac{1}{100}$ of 1%. The difference between a yield of 9.00% and a yield of 8.50% is 50 basis points. Look at a basis point this way. Since the bond market feels that rising inflation increases the cost of doing business, yields will rise because of the risk that continued inflation will push prices further upward. Assume that the current return on a municipal bond yields 6.50%. If the consumer price index, a key inflation factor, rises sharply, yields will rise, say 5 basis points to 6.55% or 5 basis points above the 6.50% level. Remember that as yields rise, prices fall. So a bond investment will be worth less. Viewing it in another way, if yields continue to rise, at some point mortgage rates will adjust accordingly and rise as well.

*Ibid., pp. 976, 977.
†Ibid., p. 1368.

That rise in yields will spell trouble for the U.S. economy, as home buyers find it more difficult to afford the higher mortgage rates.

In other words, the sustained upward movement of yields will eventually cause an increase in specific interest rates such as mortgage rates for home purchases, the coupon or interest rate on a new U.S. Treasury or municipal security, or the interest rate on a consumer loan to remodel a kitchen.

The relationship among bond price, yield, and rate is an important one. Yield and price always react in opposite directions. If a bond yield rises, then the price of the bond declines. Or if the yield declines, the price of the bond rises. But the interest or coupon rate on that bond remains constant so long as the bond is held.

If the maturity of a bond is 10 years and one holds it to the end of that maturity, then no matter how high or low yields and prices fluctuate, the holder will still obtain the same income based on the interest rate of that bond. The principal never changes either. Suppose, for example, that you buy a 6.00% bond that matures in 10 years in the amount of $1000 to yield 6.20% for a price of $985.30. When you buy it, the U.S. economy is growing at a rapid pace. Strong growth in the U.S. economy means a potential for rising inflation, so the bond is cheaper. One year later the U.S. economy has slowed down enough to bring interest rates down. Now you can sell that bond at a yield of 5.80% for a price of $1015.02. In other words, you will still receive the same income, but the price at which you buy the bond and the price when you decide to sell it may be dramatically different if you sell it before the bond reaches maturity in 10 years. Otherwise, if you hold the bond to maturity, you will receive income based on the 6.00% interest or coupon rate plus the original principal amount you loaned the municipality.

As the yields on a municipal bond change, the market for municipal bonds will also change. If yields have been rising, the interest rate or coupon rate of a group of municipal bonds being sold at a particular time will rise.

Definition of Interest Rates: Putting It All Together

Interest rates rise and fall depending on what is happening in the world or as the financial markets react to market conditions. As members of the human race, we are ingrained with both insatiable curiosity and enormous worry about what goes on around us, even if we do not admit it. Despite what some analysts believe, the financial markets are nothing more than reactions to curiosity and reactions to worry, whether real or perceived. Since interest rates react to events, they are a reaction to that insatiable curiosity and to that worry.

The forces that cause interest rates to move are reactions to domestic and world events. Yields react on a daily basis and tend to move instantly in reaction to what is happening in the world, whether it is actually happening or not. Many times the perception is more important than the reality. Yields, as a reflection of these reactions and perceptions, are the motivating force that ultimately pushes interest rates up or down. Clearly, there are many mathematical ways to calculate yields for a variety of different financial instruments, which involve coupon rate, the current yield, the stated maturity, and the price.

In my view, the way to understand interest rates is to combine the definition of interest with that of rate. Interest is both curiosity and worry about a psychological reaction to events that are happening or that may happen in the world. The rate is the magnitude of that psychological interest. Therefore interest rates are no more than a psychological reaction to what is happening in the world. World events include what is happening to global economies, inflation rates, political commentary, and much more. This is of course not all easy to comprehend, but understanding the reaction of these factors to interest rates is the concept. Yield is the daily reaction of all that curiosity and worry as reflected in financial instruments as proxies, particularly bonds and stocks, mortgage rates, and bank loan rates. As yields continue to rise or fall, ultimately interest rates will adjust and move upward or downward in reaction to the movement of yields. Therefore, interest rates represent the psychological consensus of what interest rates will be in the future based on the accumulation of the daily movement of yields. Thus, the psychological reaction to various factors, including economic, inflation, monetary policy, fiscal, global, and political factors, will move both yields on a daily basis and interest rates on a long-term basis.

3
Finding Interest Rate Information Quickly

Finding interest rate information quickly is much easier than you may think. This chapter discusses where to find the important articles, columns, and general interest rate information. (The specific data we will use for the weekly interest rate chart will be discussed in a later chapter.) This chapter also begins the process of determining interest rate information. The process I have devised will allow the reader to keep abreast of the many changes in factors and information that occur over time. Most important, as this new information is reported, the process will allow the user to incorporate it into the weekly interest rate chart.

The basic sources of information consist of four newspapers: *The New York Times*, *The Wall Street Journal*, *Investor's Business Daily* (formerly called *Investor's Daily*), and *Barron's*. Many other newspapers and magazines may be used as supplements to these publications. For example, because I live in the New York metropolitan region, one of my key sources is *The New York Times*. However, if the reader lives in another major city, such as Los Angeles, Chicago, Baltimore, Dallas, Charlotte, or Tampa, the local newspaper will probably contain a good deal of the information that you will need. The use of the other national newspapers we will be describing will provide more full coverage.

The New York Times is published 7 days a week, *The Wall Street Journal* and *Investor's Business Daily* from Monday to Friday, and *Barron's* once a week. The data we will gather from these newspapers is important in five ways. (1) This information is applicable to understanding the movement of interest rates. (2) It is readily accessible at your local newspaper stand or by home or office delivery. (3) The information is easy to find once you know where to locate it. (4) Understanding this information can be achieved with a little instructive assistance. (5) Finally, if there are serious time constraints during a given day, the reader can for the most part use just one of the newspapers. The value of using all the publications is that, taken together, they will provide a variety of different sources and views on interest rate trends.

Each reader may feel that one newspaper provides better information than another or that the illustrations of one show the story better than another. Although I recommend using at least two different newspapers so that a variety of views are obtained, *The Wall Street Journal* should be considered one of the publications to be read on a daily basis because it contains a chart that lists the yields on both German and Japanese government bonds. Each of the newspapers contains basic data concerning the key interest rates we will track and data on the factors that influence interest rates. The reason for using more than one newspaper is that each contains various viewpoints and descriptions about a specific factor or about interest rate trends. Also, each newspaper often contains information and charts that the others do not. While we noted the inclusion of daily yields on foreign government bonds in *The Wall Street Journal*, *Barron's* is the only newspaper that provides a chart showing both short- and long-term global rates. The key point is that the combination of these four publications will provide a wide variety of views on the subject of interest rates in addition to data common to all the newspapers. As the need for more information grows, one newspaper may expand its coverage while the others lag behind.

In Chap. 11 we will discuss how to set up several interest rate charts. There we will learn how to locate the specific information necessary to track interest rate movements. We will refer to this information throughout the book. This information will be the key to gaining an understanding of how interest rates move. It will be the instruction book for executing the process by which we can see why interest rates move. But first we must understand the basic information provided by the four newspapers.

We live in an information-loaded society in which we are constantly bombarded by massive doses of data from visual and print media, and computer networks. The result may create confusion and frustration when one attempts to sift through the enormous quantities of data. As we attempt to digest the information concerning interest rates, we will learn a process for obtaining the proper interest rate information. We will also learn how to obtain maximum benefit from the time spent so that the important information can be gathered and entered in the interest rate charts without spending a lot of time in a time-starved day.

Factors that influence interest rates change as the world changes. What factors are important today may not be important tomorrow. Factors that are unknown today may become the significant factors of tomorrow. The process I have developed will allow for the changes that will undoubtedly occur in future years. This process has been developed over a period of years and can be adapted to reflect new changes that will occur as the world becomes smaller.

In this chapter we will discuss the key newspapers that contain the information we need to make informed decisions about interest rates. What we will cover is key information that will allow the reader to follow the movement of interest rates. The use of the specific statistics we will use in keeping up-to-date interest rate charts for an actual week, month, and quarter will be covered in Chaps. 11 and 12.

The Wall Street Journal

In *The Wall Street Journal*, interest rate information is found on the first page of Section C, "Money & Investing." A column here describes in brief what occurred in both the bond and stock markets. For Monday this column is entitled "Monday's Markets," for Tuesday, "Tuesday's Markets," and so on. This column refers the reader to the most important general source of interest rate information, entitled "Credit Markets."

The "Credit Markets" column can be found toward the back of Section C (check *The Wall Street Journal*'s index for the specific page). This column gives an overview of the prior day's indicators and how they affected the bond market in terms of changes in yields. Then the column subdivides into several sections covering Treasury securities, corporate bonds, municipal bonds, and mortgage securities. Sometimes market activities concerning asset-backed securities and foreign bonds are discussed briefly under their respective headings. Each day's column includes a different set of charts to illustrate various interest rates. One chart published every day, called the "Treasury Yield Curve," includes yields of 3-month Treasury bills to 30-year Treasury bonds (see Fig. 3-1). The curves shown display the yield curves as of the previous day ("yesterday"), 1 week ago, and 4 weeks ago. Just keeping these small charts on individual sheets of paper can provide quick insights into the changes in the yield curve over three different periods of time. Another standard chart published every day is "Yield Comparisons," which shows yields of various types of bonds from Trea-

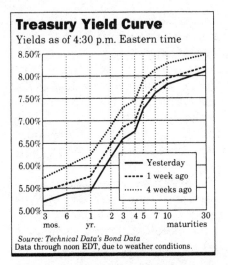

Treasury Yield Curve
Yields as of 4:30 p.m. Eastern time

Source: Technical Data's Bond Data
Data through noon EDT, due to weather conditions.

Figure 3-1. (*From The Wall Street Journal, August 20, 1991, p. C18. Reprinted by permission of The Wall Street Journal, © 1991 Dow Jones & Company, Inc. All rights reserved worldwide.*)

suries to corporates to municipals as of yesterday and the day before, and the high and low during the preceding 52-week period.

During the week the "Credit Markets" column includes a variety of charts. The days on which they appear sometimes differ. On Monday, the "Credit Markets" column publishes a chart of "Bond Yields," which includes AA-rated utilities, long-term Treasuries, and municipals. On Thursday, a chart entitled "Short-Term Interest Rates" depicts the Federal funds rate, 3-month commercial paper, and 3-month Treasury bills (see Fig. 3-2). On Friday, a chart entitled "Municipal Bond Index" shows the interest rates of the Bond Buyer Index (BBI) for 20 actively traded general-obligation or tax-backed municipal bonds (BBI 20) and for 25 actively traded revenue bonds (BBI 25).

On Monday, *The Wall Street Journal* includes several other useful columns. On the front page of Section A, in the second column from the right, is "The Outlook" column. Periodically, this column discusses a specific factor, a particular aspect of economic policy, or financial activities that influence interest rates, and it often includes an excellent chart. The perspective it provides is important to a comprehensive understanding of interest rate trends. On the second page of Section A, "Tracking the Economy" describes economic, inflationary, and monetary factors that will be published during the week. The discussion in this column includes projections of what the numbers might be and varying opinions of the possible ramifications of these numbers concerning interest rates. In addition, this column

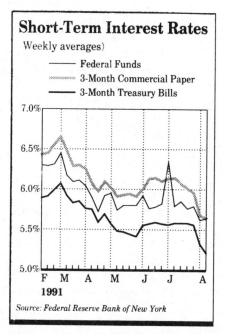

Short-Term Interest Rates

Weekly averages)

——— Federal Funds

············ 3-Month Commercial Paper

——— 3-Month Treasury Bills

Source: Federal Reserve Bank of New York

Figure 3-2. (From *The Wall Street Journal*, August 22, 1991, p. C19. Reprinted by permission of *The Wall Street Journal*, © 1991 Dow Jones & Company, Inc. All rights reserved worldwide.)

includes an important chart which is divided into two parts. First is a part called "Statistics to Be Released This Week." It lists the economic, monetary, and inflation numbers that will be released in the coming week, including the money supply, the unemployment rate, the Purchasing Managers' index, and new jobless claims, and the day on which they will be reported. The second part, called "Statistics Released Last Week," contains the economic or financial statistics reported the prior week. This chart contains information similar to that of *The New York Times* calendar and our other newspapers. You can use this and the other calendars in preparing the weekly interest rate chart.

During the week, when a particular economic or inflation number is reported, *The Wall Street Journal* includes a chart on the front page. The chart illustrates the movement of that number over several years. That number is discussed in a column entitled "Economy," which appears every day on the second page of Section A, except when no indicator is reported.

On the front page of Section C is a page-long chart entitled "Markets Diary." It includes charts and numbers of key financial indicators, many of which include interest rates or factors that influence interest rates. These include "Stocks," "Bonds," "Interest," "U.S. Dollar," and "Commodities."

Also in Section C, preceding the "Credit Markets" column, is a chart that includes the yields of the prior day on many types of bonds. The chart is called "Bond Market Data Bank." It has eight sections, including "Corporate Bonds," "Tax-Exempt Bonds," and "International Government Bonds." The "International Government Bonds" section is important to our understanding of foreign interest rates. It gives five pieces of information about government bonds of Japan, Germany, the United Kingdom, and Canada: coupon interest rate, maturity, price, change in price from the previous day, and yield equivalent to the U.S. semiannual compounded yield-to-maturity. Since the 10-year government bonds of both Japan and Germany are an integral part of our interest rate charts, a more detailed discussion of this chart will take place in Chap. 11.

Two other columns that provide useful information on interest rates are "Commodities" and "Foreign Exchange." Check *The Wall Street Journal* index for the specific page. The "Commodities" column often talks about oil and its effect on world economies and interest rates. The "Foreign Exchange" column discusses the previous day's effects of particular economic or inflation factors on the U.S. dollar as it relates to other currencies.

The New York Times

A key section of *The New York Times* appears Monday through Saturday and is entitled "Business Day." This section includes all the relevant daily information Monday through Friday. From Monday through Friday, "Business Day" is found in Section D. The Saturday edition of *The New York Times* is published in two sections, the second of which contains the "Business Day" information pertaining to Friday. The Sunday edition of *The New York Times* includes a separate business section, which reviews what has been happening during the week.

On the front page of "Business Day," on the left-hand side, is a column entitled "Business Digest." This includes four statistics at the top, including the previous day's Dow, the value of the yen in dollars, the price of West Texas Intermediate Crude oil, and the current yield of the 30-year U.S. Treasury bond. There are several summaries, including "The Economy," "International," and "Markets," under these statistics. Under the last summary is a quick view of interest rates.

The key article for us is the column entitled "Credit Markets." This column reviews the previous day's happenings in the credit or bond markets by discussing the relevant domestic and foreign economic, fiscal, political, inflationary, and monetary factors that moved interest rates. Most of the time this column provides a few interest rates, particularly of the 2-year, 10-year, and 30-year U.S. Treasury securities. The 30-year Treasury bond is often called the "bellwether" bond or the "long bond." The article often notes why yields have changed in the municipal and foreign bond markets as well. Within the "Credit Markets" column from Tuesday through Saturday is a chart entitled "Key Rates." This chart shows nine types of interest rates for the previous day, the day before that, and 1 year ago. The most important pieces of information in this chart are the federal funds rate, the daily 3-month Treasury bill discount yield, and the daily yield of the 30-year Treasury bond.

Each day in the "Credit Markets" column, there are different charts to help you visualize what is currently happening to interest rates. All this information provides additional understanding on the movement of interest rates over time. Using these charts to obtain data for the weekly interest rate chart will be discussed in Chap. 11.

Monday

Each Monday, a chart entitled "Economic Calendar" highlights the important economic and inflation factors that will be published by the relevant U.S. government agency or private research center during the week. It is found in Section D in the "Credit Markets" column. Also on Monday, another chart in the "Credit Markets" column, entitled "Current Interest Rates," shows two types of interest rates: long-term rates and short-term rates. Below the charts are listed a series of other interest rates, including the actual rates depicted in the charts above. Monday's column on the credit markets discusses current views of interest rates, summarizes the past week's activities, and describes forthcoming events. The Monday column attempts to give perspective to what is happening to interest rates. Comments by financial market participants including traders, research analysts, and portfolio managers as well as academics are part of this review. They reflect current views, though they often disagree about the direction of interest rates.

Another important chart appears each Monday on the second page of the business section and is entitled "World Economies." This chart highlights specific factors of the six major trading partners of the United States, including the United States, Japan, Germany, Great Britain, Canada, and Mexico. The factors included are industrial production, real gross domestic product (GDP), current account, unemployment rate, consumer inflation, 10-year government bond yields, and exchange rates. Since other economies affect the U.S. economy, the chart is important in keeping track of the changes in these economies as well as their inflation and currency rates because foreign factors often influence the movement of U.S. interest rates.

Tuesday

Each Tuesday a chart shows the latest results of the weekly U.S. Treasury auction for 3-month Treasury bills. This chart shows the average rates over approximately a 5-month period plus the average rates on the previous day's auction, a month ago, and a year ago.

Wednesday

On each Wednesday, within the "Credit Markets" column is a chart entitled "Treasury Yield Curve." It shows Treasury yields from the 3-month Treasury bill to the 30-year Treasury bond reflecting current and month-ago changes.

Thursday

On Thursday, a chart entitled "Freddie Mac Yields" shows the average weekly yields on Federal Home Loan Mortgage Corporation 30-year and 15-year participation certificates over a 4-month period plus the weekly figures for the current month. Since the housing industry plays an important role in the U.S. economy and is heavily influenced by the rise and fall of interest rates, this chart shows a key interest rate that directly affects the construction of housing units.

Friday

On Friday, a chart shows the weekly information on the Federal Reserve Bank. Since fluctuations in the money supply are a key signal to the Federal Reserve Board in its relationships with the banks and their lending capabilities for home, business, and personal loans, this chart is important to look at. The significant part of the chart is the M2 money supply, which consists of deposits in checking accounts plus money market funds. *The New York Times* chart lists the M2 money supply numbers as of 3 months, 6 months, and 12 months ago. Another chart illustrates tax-exempt interest rates. The tax-exempt interest rate chart shows the composite yield of two municipal bond indices we have already discussed—the BBI 20 and BBI 25—over a 4-month period plus the weekly numbers for the weeks within the current month.

Saturday

On Saturday, a chart entitled "Tracking the Markets" includes several charts. The key charts to view are "Interest Rates" and "Currencies." Both show movements over 5 months plus the weeks within the current month. Using this chart, one can actually see in pictorial form the effects of these factors on what is called the yield curve or maturities from 3 months to the 30-year bond.

Sunday

The New York Times Sunday edition has a separate section entitled "Business," or Section 3, which summarizes the week's activities in all aspects of the business world. Several articles provide a review of the daily information gathered by the reader, thus creating an opportunity to look for trends that have moved interest rates over the past several weeks. The first section is called "Market Watch," and is found on the front page of the "Business" section. Often, this section will highlight an important factor such as the U.S. unemployment rate or the consumer price index or even why interest rates are rising or falling. This section also includes one or more charts and a brief discussion about that indicator's effect on interest rates.

On the second page is the "Business Diary." This reviews the past week's events under subheads such as "The Economy," "International," and "Companies." This column represents a potpourri of the important political, economic, and inflationary events of the past week. Then, at the bottom of the page, the "Data Bank" includes relevant results of specific economic, inflationary, and financial events that happened during the past week. Right next to that chart is one entitled "This Week's Numbers" and "This Week's Developments." The first includes the specific day that important economic and inflationary indicators will be reported the forthcoming week and gives both the figure reported the last period and the consensus forecast. The second chart states the current week's domestic and foreign developments that may or may not affect the business world. These events might include such information as the day that the gross domestic product for Germany will be reported or the day the Federal Reserve Board Chairman will testify before a Senate committee. The Monday "Credit Market" column also includes a calendar of the important events to be reported by U.S. agencies.

In the middle of the Sunday "Business" section is a group of statistics, some of which are helpful in defining interest rates. They include charts of "Top Savings Rates" and "Consumer Interest Rates." Both charts provide an overview of changes in specific types of interest rates, such as certificate of deposit rates, mortgages and bank loan rates, and savings rates. Also located in the middle of the Sunday "Business" Section, on the right-hand side, is a chart entitled "Currency." This chart includes the weekly average of major currencies and gold prices including the Japanese yen, the German mark, the Canadian dollar, and the British pound. It gives figures from the past week, the prior week, and a year ago. On the left-hand side of that page is a series of stock market charts and statistics. However, in the upper part of that group of numbers and charts is a chart called "Interest Rates," which shows the 30-year Treasury bond, municipal bond, and 3-month Treasury bill rates. The numbers are based on a trend over 6 months or more. Within these two pages the reader can often find articles related to interest rates written either by a *Times* reporter or by someone in business, government, or academe.

Often in the Sunday *Times,* one will find a variety of articles that discuss interest rates. Important information can be obtained that gives interpretations of various factors that influence interest rates.

Special Columns

Several other columns of prime importance appear in the daily "Business Day" section of *The New York Times*. These columns provide information on the currency and the commodity markets. Check the index to locate the exact page. One can pick up important information that relates directly to interest rates from "Currency Markets" and "Futures/Options." Both are published Tuesday through Saturday. These articles often discuss the effect of U.S. economic factors, monetary numbers, inflationary factors and global factors on interest rates. One can link this information both to the "Credit Markets" column and to other articles that discuss the reporting of both domestic and foreign economic, financial, inflationary, monetary, and political factors. In the "Currency Markets" column there is a chart entitled "Foreign Exchange" that lists selected currency values of major countries throughout the world against the dollar. The two key figures we will review are the exchange rate on the German mark and the Japanese yen the day before and the previous day.

The other column, "Futures/Options," sometimes discusses the effects of gold or oil prices on interest rates. Within the column is a chart entitled "Cash Prices" that depicts the cash prices of several types of commodities. Under the subheading of "Petroleum" one can find West Texas Intermediate Crude oil prices of the day before and the previous day. These numbers will be discussed in greater detail in Chaps. 5 and 11.

Several other columns and illustrations are of importance in evaluating the movement of interest rates and can be found on the second page of Section D. One column is called "Economic Scene" and appears several times during the week. This column often discusses a variety of economic, monetary, inflationary, and global factors that influence the movement of interest rates. It provides perspective that will help the reader interpret the information on the weekly interest rate chart. Illustrations accompany the auction of U.S. Treasury bills, notes, and bonds. They show the particular interest rates over a period of time. The result is a good visual source of information on the direction of interest rates. Treasury bills are auctioned each week, while the others are issued once a month to every quarter. For example, an auction is held each quarter of the calendar year of 3-, 10-, and 30-year Treasury securities. On the day after the auction takes place, a chart depicting that auction will show the results over a period of time ranging from several months to several years. Since these charts are small, I often keep these auction results on a single sheet of paper and attach them to one of the interest rate charts or put them in an interest rate notebook so that I can see visually what has been happening over time.

Reported Indicators of the Week

Each economic or inflation factor such as the industrial production number or the consumer price index is published by its relevant U.S. government agency and reported in *The New York Times*. The description of that factor occurs either on the front page of *The New York Times* or within "Business Day." Most important, a chart shows that factor over a period of months and in some cases over a period of years. For example, the publication of the U.S. unemployment rate is normally of worldwide significance and appears on the front page of *The New York Times*. As we will discuss later, this factor almost always moves interest rates. Other times, the description and the analysis of a particular factor occurs in the "Business" section. Depending on the reader's time, one can collect these charts for a visual scrapbook of U.S. and foreign economic activity and inflation in conjunction with the interest rate charts.

Investor's Business Daily

Investor's Business Daily is another newspaper that provides information helpful in investigating interest rates. On the first page is a column called "Business News Digest" that summarizes the significant economic, inflationary, and financial factors that influence all the markets. Illustrations also depict these significant factors. In some cases, a chart will cover the movement of the particular factor over 1 year and in other cases 5 years plus through the month of the current year. These charts relate to the article also located on the first page under the title of "Our Economy." This article describes a particular indicator that was reported the day before, such as housing starts, industrial production, or the consumer price index.

Check the index to find the column called "Credit Markets." As in the other publications, this column gives an overview of the prior day's events as they relate to interest rates and the bond market. To the right of the article is a group of charts that track interest rates, including "Selected Interest Rates" and "U.S. Treasury Yield Curve" (see Fig. 3-3). Often other columns are helpful, including one on currency entitled "Foreign Exchange." Other articles on the U.S. economy and on interest rates also appear throughout the week.

Barron's

Barron's includes a wealth of information on interest rates. Since it is published weekly, *Barron's* is an excellent source for summaries of activities during the past week. Reading the appropriate sections can provide a check of what the reader has gleaned from the other daily publications.

Look in the index for the section entitled "Review and Preview—An Investor's Almanac." In this section there are two subsections, "Last Week" and "This Week." The "Last Week" subsection includes a potpourri of business information from the past week. It also includes key economic and inflation indicators that were reported in the prior week. A column of short news clips appears on the right side of the page. This often includes a chart and a brief description of key indicators that affect interest rates, such as initial claims for unemployment insurance, durable goods orders, or housing starts and permits. The "This Week" column provides a brief calendar of factors that influence interest rates that will be published during the coming week. It gives both the consensus estimate plus the figure of the prior month or period.

The most important contribution that *Barron's* makes is the section entitled "Capital Markets." The picture of the interest rate symbol to the right of the title provides easy identification. This section's most important article is called "Current Yield." This piece summarizes the economic, political, monetary, fiscal, and inflation statistics that occurred during the week that directly affect the movement of interest rates. The column highlights the significant factors that moved interest rates during the week and explains them in greater detail.

"Current Yield" includes several important and descriptive charts. The first is entitled "U.S. Treasury Yield Curve" and depicts the yield curve ending the Friday before compared with 1 month ago and 1 year ago. This chart can be found on the opening page of "Current Yields" or on the following page. At the bottom of the page are four more charts: "Global Short Rates," "Global Long Rates," "U.S. Short Rates," and "U.S. Long Rates" (see Fig. 3-4). The first two charts are the only illustrations of global rates in chart form published each week by any of the newspapers we are dis-

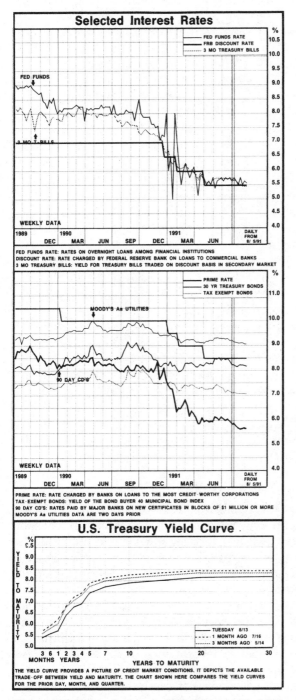

Figure 3-3. (*From Investor's Daily, August 14, 1991, p. 29.*)

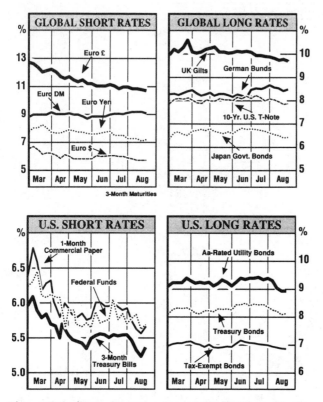

Figure 3-4. (*From Barron's, August 26, 1991, p. 44. Reprinted by permission of Barron's, © 1991 Dow Jones & Company, Inc. All rights reserved worldwide.*)

cussing. The other newspapers publish yield curve charts of particular foreign government bonds, but only intermittently. The chart of global short rates reflects Eurodollars yields in four denominations including British pounds, U.S. dollars, German marks, and Japanese yen. The chart of global long rates reflects the four currencies in terms of 10-year maturities, the longest maturities of these governments.

The last two charts reflect various U.S. interest rates of different capital market instruments. The U.S. short rates chart shows 1-month commercial paper, the federal funds rate, and the 3-month Treasury bill. In the U.S. long rates chart, the three types of instruments illustrated include Aa-rated utility bonds, Treasury bonds, and tax-exempt bonds.

All four charts illustrate the movement of interest rates over a 5-month span plus the weeks in the current month. These charts and the "Current

Yield" article are key sources of interest rate information that provide a weekly perspective not only on what happened to interest rates during the prior week but also on what has happened over the past few months.

The next set of sections we will discuss can be found in *Barron's* "Index to Statistics." This index consists of sections called "The Markets," "The Indicators," "The Indexes," and "Barron's Statistics." In the general index, the reader can find money markets, the Commodity Research Bureau (CRB) index, Treasury yields, gold prices, and other useful data. Toward the back of this business journal are several other statistical pages not specifically listed in "This Week's Statistics." They include "Market Laboratory/Economic Indicators" and "Market Laboratory/Bonds." Data on money supply, money rates, and the U.S. dollar, including a chart that tracks the dollar over several months, can be found in these pages as well as listed individually in "This Week's Statistics."

Other sources of information in *Barron's* include a Treasury yield chart showing all outstanding Treasury bills, notes, and bonds. We will refer to similar Treasury charts throughout our analysis. Oil and gold are often important influences on interest rates, and information on these commodities can sometimes be found in the section entitled "Commodities Corner." The reader should concentrate on the "Current Yield" and the accompanying interest rate charts as the prime source of information on interest rates in *Barron's*. Periodically, *Barron's* publishes major articles on subjects that concern interest rates, such as gold, the U.S. economy, and oil, and on interest rates themselves.

Summary

Each publication provides specific insights into the factors that move interest rates and the interpretations of actively involved individuals who need to understand the movement of interest rates. A daily reading plus the reading of the weekly *Barron's* is vital to keeping in touch with the nuances of what factors influence interest rates. The illustrations and charts provide the visual link to the text of the many types of articles we have discussed. Selectively reading one without reading the others will cause the reader to lose a certain perspective. Reading time of these publications is reasonable considering the importance of the information given and what can be tracked. The most important general information articles in the four publications appear under the heading "Credit Markets." The synthesis of information they provide can help one focus quickly on the factors that move interest rates.

The charts and articles on the U.S. economy serve as the basis for developing interest rate charts. The different perspectives offered by the many economists, traders, portfolio managers, research analysts, business executives, financial reporters, and academics quoted provide a variety of opinions to aid the analysis of the reader.

Over the past several years, each of the four publications has improved and expanded its coverage of the U.S. economy and interest rates. More charts now accompany the text. Wider coverage of foreign factors such as global interest rates broadens the base of interest rate information. By following these publications regularly, the reader will be able to keep up with the changes in factors and events that will influence the movement of interest rates in the future. Initially, reading the publications and selecting information to enter on the interest rate chart will take some time, but as the pieces of the process begin to fit together, the time required will become shorter. The result will be a quick and easy way to understand interest rate trends.

4
Interest Rates and Economic Indicators

Overview

The various economic indicators that we will discuss derive primarily from various federal agencies, including the U.S. Departments of Commerce and Labor, the Bureau of the Census, and the Federal Reserve Board. Several private business associations also publish important indices. Many of these indicators are published daily, weekly, monthly, quarterly, or, in one instance, about every 6 weeks in U.S. journals, newspapers, and magazines. Many also appear regularly in European and Asian publications. Analysts use these indicators to determine trends in the U.S. economy, the level of inflation, and the effect of these indicators on the movement of interest rates. These numbers are constantly subjected to revision and specific offsetting factors, which often complicate the process of understanding the U.S. economy.

The type of data published changes only infrequently. It may take years for federal agencies to change the specific types of data used to compile a statistic because of the costs of evaluating new statistics and testing their reliability. Again, this creates difficulty in interpreting these figures. The severe reductions in the budgets of many federal agencies during the 1980s made updating far more difficult. But these indicators are the only numbers that are available to analysts in all types of businesses and government. These published numbers are extremely important, because they affect institutional and personal investment, business and governmental decisions. Each publication that reports an individual indicator often includes an illustration of its behavior over the past several months, a detailed discussion, and a chart listing the components of the indicator.

Each indicator reflects certain problems that may make comparisons of different months' numbers difficult. Understanding these problems—such as weather, overemphasis on one or more components of an indicator, and seasonal factors—is important to gaining clear insight into the total indicator. We will discuss these problems for each factor.

One extremely important rule is that *one month's number does not mean a trend.* Each of these indicators has to be viewed over a period of at least several months. If housing starts are trending downward, if factory orders are declining, if the unemployment rate is climbing, if the National Association of Purchasing Management index is falling, and if retail sales are slumping over more than 3 months after special factors have been excluded, then one can assume that a trend is developing. As one watches interest rates react to these numbers during a particular month, the movement will reflect the psychology of the financial markets at that time and may not indicate a trend. After several months of following these economic factors, however, a trend may well develop and interest rates will respond accordingly. If the U.S. economy sours over time, rates will decline to reflect a lessening of inflation. Of course, the opposite may just as easily happen if these indicators show the reverse: Housing starts climbing, factory orders rising, employment increasing, the Purchasing Managers' index ascending, and retail sales climbing all mean that the U.S. economy is growing. Therefore, interest rates will begin to rise because a growing and then expanding economy means that the price of goods and services will increase as demand increases. As prices increase, inflation will increase, and rising inflation brings with it rising interest rates.

The effect of each of these indicators on interest rates can be enormous, particularly if the investment markets believe that it is pointing to a specific direction of the U.S. economy. These indicators are the elements that create business cycles. These cycles reflect strong economic growth, a slowdown in the economy, recession, and recovery. Interest rates reflect the effect of these factors on the different stages of the business cycle.

Interpretation of these indicators is replete with pitfalls of how to decipher them in relation to the movement of interest rates. An indicator may be reported during a particular month which shows that the U.S. economy is moving in one direction, but by the next month the same indicator may show that the U.S. economy is moving in another direction. Again, remember that *one month does not make a trend.* Several months of indicators must be evaluated in order to formulate a trend. Data collection difficulties, special situations, psychological responses instead of realistic responses, misunderstood factors, unknown factors, domestic political influences, and the growing international political and economic relationships among the U.S., Western European, Eastern European, Asian,

Mexican, and Canadian economies are some of the problems that cause interpretation difficulties. Many individual investors and professional analysts try to ascertain why these factors move interest rates one way or another. Bond and equity portfolio managers, research analysts, company treasurers, bankers, individual investors, nonprofit institutions, and local and national government officials all the way up to the President of the United States worry about how the sum of these indicators influences interest rates. Interest rates affect everyone in one way or in another, and these indicators help the reader to determine the effect of rising or falling interest rates on businesses and personal investment decisions. Let us examine the economic indicators.

How We Will Evaluate the Economic Indicators

We will discuss the various components of each economic indicator, point out the problems that occur when these figures are published, and show what components are the most important to understand. Charts are published regularly in the four newspapers we discussed in Chap. 3. We will include several of these charts in our discussion in this chapter, to show what they look like and to help illustrate some of our points.

The information we gather from these indicators will form part of the basic data for the weekly interest rate chart. These are not all the possible economic indicators available to the public. Those that I have selected represent basic indicators that can have the most effect on the movement of interest rates. Economic indicators must be weighed in the context of inflation, monetary, political, and global indicators. The order of the discussion that follows is based primarily on those indicators that represent officially published monthly reports by the various public agencies and private business organizations with the exception of the new unemployment claims figure, which is published weekly. Some indicators are published only quarterly or every 6 weeks. These indicators will be discussed in the latter part of this chapter.

In our discussion of these and other indicators, we will often refer to durable and nondurable goods. Following are some goods in each of these two categories. There are other goods in both groups, but the ones listed here will provide a good idea of what each group covers.

Durable Goods

Lumber and wood	Fabricated metals
Furniture	Nonelectrical machinery
Stone–clay–glass	Electrical–electronic equipment
Primary metals	Transportation equipment

Nondurable Goods

Food products	Printing–publishing
Textiles	Chemicals
Apparel	Leather
Paper	Rubber–plastics

National Association of Purchasing Management Index

The National Association of Purchasing Management (NAPM) index is published monthly. Because the NAPM report on business activity is the first major economic indicator published each month, it is the first indicator of the performance of the U.S. manufacturing economy the previous month. Furthermore, it precedes the unemployment and employment numbers reported several days later as the second major economic indicator. These changes measure the percent change in each month. The NAPM index is a survey of 300 purchasing executives from 21 manufacturing industries in all 50 states. It consists of the following five elements (their weights within the index are shown in parentheses):

1. New orders (30%)

2. Production levels (25%)

3. Employment (20%)

4. Supplier delivery times (15%)

5. Inventories (10%)

A rise in new orders would mean that the economy is picking up, and that other factors, such as industrial production, will also rise. If supplier deliveries slow down, then companies will have more product than they can ship. This, in turn, will indicate greater strength in the economy. Purchasing managers report actual purchases of supplies at their respective companies and indicate the reasons for these purchases based on their perception of the direction of the U.S. economy. Sales of these supplies are interest rate sensitive. Therefore, the higher the interest rate, the higher the cost of purchasing these goods and the more unwilling managers become to pay the higher prices. These concerns reflect thoughts about the rise or fall in the U.S. economy. The respondents state whether the purchasing changes in a given manufacturing sector are better, the same, or worse than the prior month. Some industries reported include paper goods, textiles, laboratory equipment, machinery, electronics, and petroleum. When aggregated together, they form an index.

The NAPM index is based on two important readings. (1) If the index is above 44.5%, the manufacturing sector of the U.S. economy is expanding, and (2) if the index is below 44.5%, it is contracting. (See Fig. 4-1.)

Once the NAPM index is reported, it suggests the possible movement of other economic indicators concerning manufacturing activity that will be forthcoming during the rest of a particular month. For example, if the NAPM index shows a rise in new orders, then production should increase. As that happens, increases will show up in the industrial production figures, which in turn will boost the capacity utilization or operating rate of the factories that produce these goods. Manufacturing employment will begin to rise, and new orders for durable and nondurable goods will begin to rise. If the economy is in recession and these indicators start to rise, economists would interpret this as a sign of economic recovery. Interest rates would then begin to rise because rising economic indicators imply the potential for rising inflation. A rise in inflation means that the cost of goods and services will increase, which means that interest rates will rise.

Three facts should be noted in evaluating the NAPM index. First, the index is a manufacturing index that represents approximately 18% or more of the U.S. economy. Second, the index is weighted toward indus-

Figure 4-1. *(From Investor's Daily, July 2, 1991, p. 1.)*

tries that are particularly weak during an economic slowdown or recession, such as automobiles and housing. Yet these industries involve so many other secondary industries that the effect of a downturn or upturn of autos and housing does have a substantial effect on whether the U.S. economy grows or slows down. Lastly, the areas surveyed for the index are sometimes subject to severe and prolonged weather conditions that might affect the overall figure for a given month. Nevertheless, because the NAPM index is the first U.S. economic indicator to be reported in any month, it becomes important as a possible trend setter for manufacturing activity. If the index rises for two consecutive months—say, moving up from 43% to 46%—this would be a strong signal that the U.S. economy may be recovering. Seconds after the third monthly increase in a row is announced, interest rates will rise because a recovering economy means inflation. And inflation means higher interest rates.

Construction Spending

Construction spending is published monthly by the U.S. Commerce Department and reported in the first week of the month. Its components consist of nonresidential building, such as industrial plants, warehouses, offices, and shopping centers; residential building, including both single- and multifamily homes; and national and local government construction of public works such as highways, schools, correction centers, and ports. Government building represents about 25% of all construction. The need for new infrastructure is in the trillions, so this part of the index carries considerable significance. Among the different types of projects are the repair, expansion, or new construction of sewers, bridges, jails, highways, primary and secondary schools and higher-education colleges in state systems, resource recovery plants, and housing for low- and moderate-income persons. Construction spending usually lags behind new housing starts by several months. As a result, if construction spending rises for more than 3 months, this indicator would mean a possible rising trend in other economic indicators. A multitude of companies produce the construction materials and home furnishings that are reflected in other economic indicators reported later in the month, such as housing starts and building permits.

There are several problems with construction spending as an indicator. Weather, including hurricanes, earthquakes, freezes, and excessively hot weather, often affects construction. Weather problems in a region will distort the final figure. High interest rates thwart consumers from buying and builders from obtaining loans. During certain times of the year, consumer demand may evaporate, thus slowing down the building process. The

U.S. government's bail-out of the savings and loan industry continues to have a negative effect on the availability of construction financing, heightened by the 1990/1991 U.S. economic recession.

U.S. Unemployment Rate and Employment Numbers

The U.S. unemployment rate is the number of persons unemployed measured as a percentage of the total labor force. The job numbers and the unemployment rate are published monthly by the U.S. Labor Department's Bureau of Labor Statistics (see Fig. 4-2). The unemployment rate is considered a lagging indicator. As companies begin to meet demand, they will often use up inventories and rely on overtime to increase production. Once businesses determine that demand will be sustained, they will begin to hire more workers, and then the unemployment rate will come down. If the unemployment rate begins to fall, it indicates that the economy is recovering. On the other hand, the employment number is considered a coincident indicator in that it reflects the number of jobs currently available in the economy. The charts accompanying the articles on job figures all illustrate the unemployment rate. Depending on the mood of the markets,

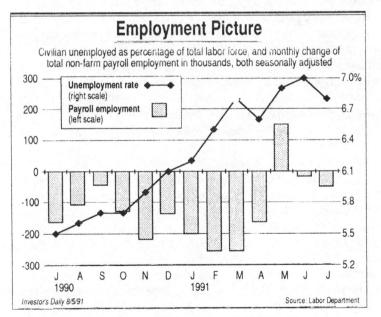

Figure 4-2. *(From Investor's Daily, August 5, 1991, p. 1.)*

based on the multitude of interpretations, interest rates can be sensitive to either the unemployment rate or the employment numbers or both.

The employment or job figures represent nonfarm workers employed in the United States. The components of the employment figures are manufacturing and service-sector jobs. These components further break down into sectors including construction, real estate, retail trade, financial markets, transportation, health service, public utilities, and governmental jobs. When reading articles on the employment numbers, make sure that military employment is separated from nonmilitary employment for a truer picture, since the salaries of military personnel are paid by the taxpayer.

Also reported along with both the unemployment and employment numbers are several other indicators in the form of indices that reflect inflation as a result of the increase or decrease in the number of jobs. In many instances, the movement of interest rates is tied to these inflation numbers. These indices include average weekly hours worked in the private sector, factory hours worked, factory overtime hours worked, average hourly earnings, and length of the average work week.

The length of the average work week is considered a measure of economic turning points. In addition, it links to other factors. If the factory work week rises, it will mean a possible rise in industrial production and the capacity utilization indicators. When the economy begins to grow, companies extend the hours of the current work force before they begin to add more jobs. Average hourly earnings is a good indicator of inflation. If this indicator increases over several months, it implies that the economy is strengthening. As the economy strengthens, the financial markets may determine that inflation will begin to rise if the economy keeps expanding. That can be enough of a concern to push interest rates upward. And if the perception that inflation will rise becomes nascent reality, interest rates will rise sharply. All of these components determine the possible direction of interest rates because they indicate increased or decreased demand for worker activity.

Two types of surveys are used to determine employment figures. The *household survey* counts each person employed in one job, using a sample of 60,000 household members 16 years or older. The household survey determines the unemployment rate. The *payroll survey*, on the other hand, counts the number of jobs that an individual has, using a mail survey sample of 330,000 nonagricultural businesses. The payroll survey is considered by many analysts to be more reliable because the household survey is subject to volatility and consists of a much smaller sample.

Several factors can distort these individual monthly employment figures, particularly the payroll figures. That is why tracking this indicator over several months is important. Sometimes sampling errors skew the numbers and make them difficult to interpret. Extreme weather conditions in heavily populated regions may prevent employees from traveling to their jobs. The beginning and the end of the secondary and college years, when students return from their summer jobs to school, distorts the unemployment numbers. Strikes in various industries such as airlines and the public sector can distort monthly figures.

Sometimes analysts differentiate between part-time and full-time jobs or self-employed workers. These special conditions, such as the inclusion or exclusion of part-time holiday workers in retail stores during the Christmas or Easter seasons, will influence the total employment number. During a recession, when many workers are out of work, there is usually a rise in self-employment. As the economy turns around, many of these self-employed workers rejoin the corporate work force. Employment figures often reflect the job hunting of college students looking for summer work in spring and leaving at the end of summer. These types of special conditions can inhibit interpretation of the employment numbers. Sometimes the articles that discuss the monthly employment numbers will note these problems and mention them so that they do not cloud the reader's analysis.

Revisions often occur during the publication of the next month's number. Since the payroll survey is a questionnaire, the Bureau of Labor Statistics does not receive all the forms back in time to include them in the payroll survey. The result is revision to that figure at the time the next month's figures are reported. For example, when a particular employment figure is reported, it may also include a report of a significant revision of the prior month's employment figures. These revisions can sometimes change the perception of what is actually happening in the economy. Sometimes, the financial markets will focus on the revision rather than the current figure and adjust interest rates accordingly.

The New York Times always includes an important chart that lists the unemployment rates of major states such as California, New York, Pennsylvania, New Jersey, and several others. Understanding state and regional economies can help create a more accurate picture of what is happening to the U.S. economy as a whole. Rising unemployment due to layoffs reduces state sales, personal income, and corporate tax receipts. The compilation of tax receipts is normally performed on a quarterly basis. For our purposes, this information can provide better insight into the employment numbers. Periodically, the publications we are using describe what is happening to specific regions, states, and cities. These articles represent what is actually happening at the local level, which will ultimately filter up to the national level as the figures are compiled.

During 1990 and 1991, several sectors of the U.S. economy began to lay off far more of their workers than they had during previous difficult economic times in the preceding decades. A particularly hard-hit sector was the service sector, such as banking. These layoffs, as well as the restructuring of American businesses, represented major structural changes resulting from intense global competition, in which producing more at far less cost appears to be the only way to survive, and changes in the international geopolitical environment, such as the dissolution of communism in Eastern Europe and the establishment of a Western European common market. In addition, the computerization of worldwide business and financial markets is also affecting the job picture. Fewer people are needed in both the service and manufacturing industries as computers perform tasks previously accomplished by workers. Just look at the changes in the automotive sector, which now uses robots to perform a multitude of tasks once accomplished by people. The newest sector to have severe layoffs is state, county, and local governments. Tens of thousands of governmental jobs are being lost, and this is contributing to dramatic changes in how these entities will provide needed social, health, fire, and police services. These structural changes will become an important part of how analysts view employment numbers as these changes become integrated into the workings of the U.S. and foreign economies.

The employment numbers are among the most closely watched figures of the entire panoply of economic indicators tracking interest rate movements. The financial markets wait in tense anticipation for the number to be reported on the first Friday of the month. There are two reasons why so much emphasis is placed on this statistic: (1) The employment number is the earliest indicator published that represents overall U.S. economic activity during the preceding month; and (2) the jobs figure is a coincident indicator indicating what is happening in the U.S. economy at the current time. In many ways, it suggests the trend of the other indicators that follow in succeeding weeks. Interest rates react quickly to this indicator. For example, if a particular month's employment report shows a substantial loss of jobs, the Federal Reserve Board may lower its discount rate by half a percent—say, from 6.50% to 6.00%—because that particular month's employment report represents the fourth month in a row that substantial job losses have been reported. If job losses continue for several more months, the Federal Reserve Board may again lower interest rates to pull the United States out of a recession and stimulate growth by reducing the cost of credit so that banks can lend funds to businesses and individuals at lower rates and people can purchase homes at lower mortgage rates.

New Unemployment Claims

Initial claims for state unemployment insurance are published weekly by the U.S. Department of Labor (see Fig. 4-3). They are the earliest indicator of trends concerning the direction of the U.S. economy a few months

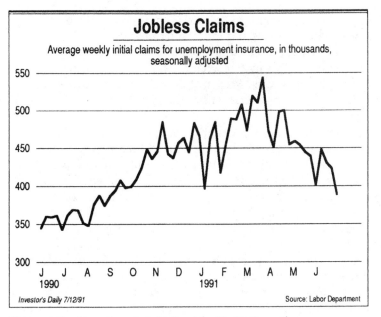

Jobless Claims

Average weekly initial claims for unemployment insurance, in thousands, seasonally adjusted

Investor's Daily 7/12/91   Source: Labor Department

Figure 4-3. (*From Investor's Daily, July 12, 1991, p. 1.*)

hence. This indicator is shown both by the number of claims that have been filed in that week and by the difference between the current week's number and that of the preceding week. For instance, in a given month a claims number could be up 14,000 over the past week, showing a new weekly claims figure of 455,000 people applying for unemployment insurance. The weekly claims are reflected in the monthly unemployment rate and employment numbers reported in the following months.

New jobless claims are reported as the average weekly initial claims for state unemployment insurance benefits, adjusted for seasonal variation. From time to time, *Investor's Business Daily* or *The Wall Street Journal* publishes an excellent chart showing claims over a period of years. Initial claims represent a leading indicator of future changes in the unemployment rate. Many analysts place considerable weight on this number, particularly as it moves from week to week, because analysts can then smooth out some of the variations in the weekly number. Rising claims over a period of weeks means that the unemployment rate will rise and employment numbers will fall. If the economy is in recession, a decline in claims over a period of time may indicate that it is finally on the bumpy road to recovery.

There are several problems with the unemployment claims indicator. The changes on a week-to-week basis often display volatility. But over several weeks and months, the indicator will definitely show a trend in the

U.S. economy as to how many individuals are applying for unemployment insurance. Many analysts and the leading financial publications use a 4-week moving average because it reflects a trend and smoothes out aberrations in the figure. No matter what method is used to show unemployment claims, interest rates react to this indicator. However, unemployment claims must be viewed as one of many indicators of the state of the economy.

Year-end figures are somewhat distorted because of the usual turnover in employees. This includes the leaving of part-time workers from the labor force after major shopping holidays. For example, a seasonal adjustment to initial claims is made during the Easter season, when more part-time workers are hired to meet normal holiday-buying demand. Also, the inclusion of a holiday can distort a weekly figure. For example, Memorial Day, Labor Day, and Veterans Day reduce the number of new claims for the week in which they fall.

Oftentimes, the Department of Labor cannot adjust adequately for recurring shifts in claims around calendar quarters. Some states tie jobless payments to earnings in the preceding quarter, so that some people defer applications until the new quarter begins, when their base for calculations may be higher. The end result is that economists tend to average initial claims over long periods.

Nevertheless, the unemployment claims figures are an important indicator of what is happening and what may happen in the U.S. economy. Interest rates will reflect how high or low these numbers are from week to week. Monthly figures can be tracked using the weekly interest rate chart. By entering the average weekly figures into the monthly interest rate chart, one can easily see how claims are rising or falling over this period. The initial claims indicator relates to the other indicators we are evaluating, such as monthly employment, durable goods orders, factory orders and the index of leading economic indicators.

Index of Economic Indicators

The Index of Economic Indicators is published monthly by the U.S. Department of Commerce (see Fig. 4-4). The index is designed to predict the direction of economic activity in 6 to 9 months. Three indices are actually reported. The first is the Index of Leading Economic Indicators, which attempts to track economic activity 6 to 9 months in advance. The second is the Coincident Economic Indicators Index, which tracks current economic activity. The third is the Lagging Economic Indicators Index, which shows previous economic trends. All three indices are published late in the

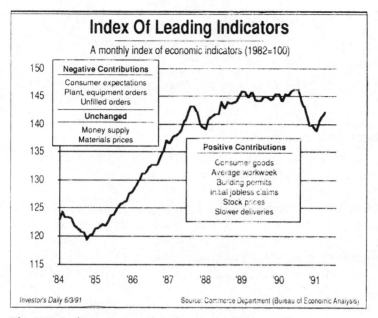

Figure 4-4. *(From Investor's Daily, June 3, 1991, p. 1.)*

month, after other individual economic indicators have been reported. Each index is measured as a percent change from one month to the next. Some analysts consider that if the first index—the Index of Leading Economic Indicators—falls for 3 months in a row, this is a harbinger of economic contraction. If it rises for the same period of time, it means the beginnings of an economic recovery. A sustained rise in this index over many months indicates an expanding economy.

The Index of Leading Economic Indicators consists of those indicators that reflect the direction of the economy within the next 6 to 9 months. There are 11 leading economic indicators:

1. Average work week of production workers in manufacturing

2. Average weekly claims for state unemployment insurance

3. New factory orders for consumer goods and materials, adjusted for inflation

4. Vendor performance or the pace of delivery times of goods (slower deliveries means the economy is picking up)

5. Contracts and orders for new plants and equipment, adjusted for inflation

6. New building permits issued

7. Changes in durable goods orders backlog or unfilled orders

8. Change in materials prices

9. Index of stock prices as measured by the Standard & Poor's 500 stock index

10. Money supply (M2), composed of money in checking accounts and certificates of deposits

11. Index of consumer expectations as measured by the University of Michigan's Institute for Social Research

These factors make up the final index of leading indicators based on a percent change. *The New York Times* includes this list in the article that describes the main Index of Leading Economic Indicators. Some analysts feel that consumer expectations, stock prices, and money supply reflect the psychological components of the index, with the remainder considered as fundamental components.

The Coincident Economic Indicators Index shows current economic activity. This index includes the following components: industrial production, personal income excluding transfer payments to social security recipients and others, manufacturing and retail sales.

The third index, the Lagging Economic Indicators Index, tends to move only after the economy has changed direction. This index includes capital spending, average duration of unemployment, labor cost per unit of output, commercial and industrial loans outstanding, ratio of consumer installment debt to personal income, and the average prime rate charged by banks. Some analysts feel that the ratio of coincident to lagging indicators signals turning points in advance of the leading indicators. If the ratio rises, it represents a favorable sign of economic strength. Almost all the publications will make note of the coincident to lagging ratio.

There are a few problems that must be understood in order to use this economic indicator. Many components fluctuate from month to month. Much of the data is collected from regional bureaus located throughout the nation. Sometimes that data cannot be collected in a timely manner. In other instances, specific regional problems unsettle the total number. The results are often revisions of the previous month's figure. Sometimes interest rates react not to the current number but to the revision of the prior month's number. The reaction of interest rates depends on so many other factors, such as monetary, inflation, global, and political factors, that assessing these factors is important in determining what are the most dominant in moving interest rates. Finally, the indices of economic indicators are a compilation of statistics that aid in understanding the direction of the

U.S. economy. A rise in the Index of Leading Economic Indicators, for example, means that the U.S. economy is growing. When that happens, the potential for inflation is rising. The financial markets react by pushing up interest rates out of fear of rising inflation.

Durable Goods Orders

The durable goods orders indicator is published monthly by the Bureau of Economic Analysis of the U.S. Department of Commerce, and is adjusted for regular seasonal fluctuations. It is measured as a monthly percentage change. This indicator is defined as "big-ticket" or expensive goods orders to factories of items expected to last more than 3 years, including automobiles, bulldozers, aircraft parts, desks, ships, refrigerators, washing machines, and computer equipment. Durable goods orders reflect the future trend of manufacturing activity. The charts in *The Wall Street Journal* and *The New York Times* show the changes in billions of dollars. *Investor's Business Daily* depicts the figures as a year-over-year rate of change.

The durable goods orders indicator consists of the following components:

1. Nonmilitary and military capital goods orders
2. Transportation orders, including cars, ships, tanks, and aircraft
3. Primary metals orders
4. Orders for nonelectrical machinery, including computers
5. Orders for electronic and other electrical equipment
6. Unfilled orders
7. Inventories

Durable goods orders are considered to be sensitive to interest rates, because consumers and businesses usually borrow to pay for these goods. If businesses are concerned about negative effects of rising interest rates on the costs of paying for the production of these goods, they would ordinarily start canceling orders.

Another example of the effect of a component of durable goods orders on interest rates is orders for primary metals. Lack of these orders affects the production of automobiles and construction materials. Both the automobile and construction sectors are major components of U.S. economic activity. Stronger or sustained orders in these two sectors means that economic growth is stronger. The financial markets interpret these heightened numbers as signs of either continued or recovering economic growth with accompanying inflation. The reaction to the potential for inflation will push up interest rates.

Unfilled orders define growth or decline in manufacturing activity. If these orders continue to fall, it is a sign that the economy may be weakening as it relates to the manufacturing sector. If the financial markets believe that to be the case, then interest rates will begin to fall over time. Remember that yields will fall until such time as interest rates reflect the decline in the yields. The production and subsequent shipments of major home appliances to wholesalers usually increase at the same time as the housing construction industry begins to pick up. These shipments are a sign of economic recovery or sustained economic growth which is reflected in an ultimate rise in interest rates.

Nonmilitary capital goods orders are a key component to watch, because they reflect the intentions of businesses to expand and modernize production facilities by purchasing new equipment. The articles in the financial publications often point out this particular component. Many analysts consider this component a good measure of future business production plans. Furthermore, to obtain a more clear picture of what is happening in the U.S. economy, one should exclude both defense and transportation items, because they tend to fluctuate each month and distort the underlying number. For example, military hardware takes years to develop, and then it goes into production. But the production of a particular type of military aircraft happens infrequently enough that if it is reported in one month's figures, it will distort it. This holds true for commercial aircraft orders as well. In a particular month, a single large order may throw off the total durable goods orders number for that month.

The durable goods orders index is published early in the month. It thus becomes in turn one of the components of the overall factory orders figure, which is published at the end of the month. Durable goods orders is linked to many other economic indicators, including a rise or fall in initial claims, manufacturing employment, and new housing starts and building permits. For example, if durable goods orders begin to decrease because demand is slowing down, ultimately jobs may be lost, which would be reflected in both the unemployment claims report and the unemployment and jobs reports.

There are several problems in understanding this indicator. Durable goods orders is a volatile indicator, and is often subject to major revision the following month as more data becomes available or when data is fully collected. For example, if the durable goods orders rises in one month, it may be revised downward the next month. Tracking over several months will smooth out these fluctuations so that a trend can be seen.

Spending patterns for both military equipment and commercial aircraft are erratic. Orders for both military and commercial aircraft always fluctuate. In some months there are enormous orders, while in other months there may be none at all. The cyclical nature of business conditions often can be misleading. If business managers feel that prices are too high, they may wait until larger discounts are offered by the manufacturer. Many managers take advantage of these prices, but often it distorts the durable goods orders figure. A major change is the enormous investment in computerization of inventories to improve efficiency in producing orders. This is an important change in business. It keeps inventories at levels that allow for business to manage its product sales in line with consumer demand through computerization efforts between both the seller and the manufacturer. While durable goods orders indicate U.S. economic movements, the use of inventory control moderates the volatility of the nondefense component. The backlog of unfilled orders is a helpful component in tracking the total durable goods orders number. Although the nature of manufacturing production continues to change, it must always be viewed in conjunction with the growth and importance of the service sector.

Durable goods orders make up three parts of the Index of Leading Economic Indicators: orders for consumer goods, plant and equipment orders, and durable goods backlog.

If automobile sales begin to rise, one can often expect that durable orders will pick up in the following month. This would be a sign that recovery from recession is beginning. This sign of economic recovery pushes interest rates up, because it implies the possibility of inflation as demand increases and prices rise. The financial markets become uncomfortable with any future possibility of inflation, and therefore interest rates rise.

A host of other factors are linked to the future of durable goods, including retail sales, building permits, the manufacturing component of the monthly employment figure, industrial production, and capacity utilization.

Factory Orders

Factory orders or orders for factory goods is published monthly by the U.S. Department of Commerce (see Fig. 4-5). These orders are an important economic barometer of manufacturers' plans for production of both nondurable and durable goods. It is a broader indicator than the durable goods orders number reported several weeks earlier. According to the U.S. Bureau of Labor Statistics, factories make up about 23% of the nation's gross domestic product. This indicator of factory orders is therefore a key indicator.

New orders for factory goods relates directly to the durable goods orders indicator. The major distinction is that the durable goods orders indi-

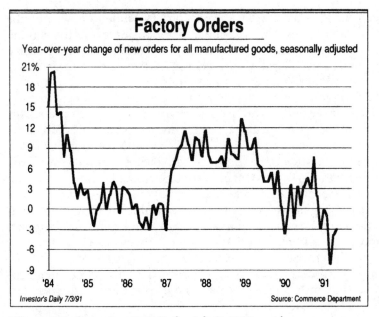

Figure 4-5. (*From Investor's Daily, July 3, 1991, p. 1.*)

cator is reported before the factory orders indicator, which is reported at the end of the month. That means that the durable goods indicator gives a trend of the manufacturing sector earlier in the month.

Factory orders are composed of five major components:

1. All industries, divided into durable goods and nondurable goods orders. Durable goods orders include nonelectrical machinery, electrical machinery, automobile equipment, aircraft missiles and parts, and primary metals. Nondurable goods orders include food, textiles, chemicals, paper, and printing.
2. Capital goods industries, including nonmilitary and military orders.
3. Total shipments.
4. Manufacturers' inventories.
5. Backlogs of unfilled orders.

The backlog of unfilled orders is considered by many analysts to be a good predictor of the direction of the economy. The Federal Reserve Board pays particular attention to this component as an indicator of what direction the U.S. economy may be moving. There are also several market sectors:

1. Automobile equipment
2. Consumer goods
3. Machinery and equipment
4. Business supplies
5. Construction materials and supplies
6. Information technology industrial equipment
7. Health-care products
8. Military and nonmilitary equipment
9. Home goods
10. Apparel
11. Petroleum and coal products
12. Rubber and plastics

There are several problems with this indicator. The indicator is considered volatile, and therefore subject to month-to-month changes. Sometimes a particular monthly number reflects a large order that will overweight a particular component and thus affect the total number. These orders could include military or domestic airplanes and computers. For example, if a substantial order for commercial aircraft is withdrawn by one of the U.S. airlines, it does not necessarily mean that the economy is worsening. The backlogs of other commercial aircraft may well be enormous, and therefore with only so much capacity, it will take years to fill all of them. Thus a fall-off of orders in the production of commercial aircraft has to be viewed in the context of backlogs as well as possible changes in the airline companies. But if there is a any substantial rise or decline in orders of a major manufacturer of aircraft such as Boeing, it will distort the factory orders number of a particular month.

Most analysts exclude the volatile sectors of transportation, including both automobiles and military equipment, from the durable goods component. If the automobile industry is anticipating a strike, it will pile up inventories. If several plants close in one month, the factory orders indicator will be distorted. This action will distort not only factory orders but also the other indicator of durable goods orders. Others feel that a choppy pattern of factory orders could mean uncertainty in the manufacturing sector.

Orders for nonmilitary capital goods—excluding aircraft, which is quite volatile—is a closely watched component of factory orders as an indicator of industry plans to expand and modernize production facilities. Sometimes orders can be substantial at the end of the year because of the potential for price increases in the next year. Factory orders, like many other indicators, are also subject to major revisions for past months as more data is collected or new orders come in after the collection period.

Interest rates react to factory orders because this indicator confirms other indicators such as durable goods orders, manufacturing employment, and housing construction. For example, a decrease in factory orders may forecast an industrial slump with attending layoffs. A decrease in factory orders over several months will put pressure on interest rates to fall, because inflation is expected to fall as orders decline. A rise in factory orders, among other signs, would imply the beginning of economic recovery, again indicating the potential for a rise in inflation, which will push up interest rates. If factory orders continue to rise, reflecting an expanding economy, interest rates will increase, sometimes sharply, a clear sign of a further rise in inflation.

Housing Construction

The housing construction indicator is divided into housing starts and applications for housing permits. It is published monthly by the U.S. Department of Commerce. Housing starts are divided into two categories: single-family and multifamily. The report contains data on four regions: the Northeast, the Midwest, the South, and the West. The housing sector consists of a multitude of other sectors that make up the entire housing industry. Single-family residences require lumber, concrete, electrical fixtures, carpets, kitchen equipment, and paint. Apartment complexes may require brick and mortar, elevators, security systems, steel, and aluminum, as well as all the components used in single-family residences. The construction workers in this sector form a component of the employment and unemployment numbers as well as initial claims for unemployment state insurance.

When housing starts fall over several months, it has an enormous ripple effect throughout the U.S. economy. On the other hand, when housing starts begin to climb, it is one of the earliest signs of an economic recovery. The housing industry includes many other sectors that participate in the building of homes and apartments: home furnishings, construction materials, appliances, building equipment, construction and mortgage financings, and many others. Taken together, these sectors generate large numbers of jobs, supplies, services, and furnishings. The lowering of interest rates is a key for this indicator. So long as interest rates (mortgage rates) are high and builders or developers have difficulty obtaining credit, both consumers and builders will be cut off. The result is that the building industry slumps. When that happens, construction jobs decline until the building industry picks up. Once interest rates begin to decline during a recovery, provided that lending institutions lend to both consumers and developers, the building industry will begin to revive.

Housing permits are obtained through local building departments and are a good indicator of future housing construction activity. Many analysts attach considerable importance to this part of the housing construction cycle. Sometimes interest rates move more on housing permits than on housing starts.

There are several problems to consider in evaluating this indicator. Weather can create major monthly distortions. For example, winter months in the Northeast and Mid-Atlantic regions limit housing starts. On the other hand, warm weather in these same regions can spur housing starts, particularly when the economy is growing. Most important, high interest rates are a serious deterrent to housing starts or permits, no matter what the weather may be. Because the direction of interest rates directly affects the mortgage rate a consumer will have to pay to purchase a home, the higher that mortgage rates rise, the more difficult it is for many buyers to be able to make the payments to purchase a new house. Even if one can afford new housing based on the price alone, high mortgage rates are clearly a deterrent to many consumers because they increase the overall payment.

Of great importance is that *one month does not indicate a trend*. Normally it takes about 3 months to establish a trend regarding housing starts. Furthermore, while building permits reflect the potential for future construction, developers do not have to build until they feel that consumers are willing to buy. As housing starts change over several months, the rise or fall of other economic indicators—industrial production, employment in the construction industry, factory orders, and ultimately new home sales—will be linked to this indicator.

Some analysts feel that the pent-up demand for housing that was met in the 1980s by substantial housing construction may limit the number of new units in the 1990s. Demographic changes for the future indicate that the number of people who own homes is declining for all but those who are middle-aged and older. The demographic trends indicate that a smaller number of families and individuals will be in a position to purchase new homes in coming years. This trend is new, according to recent governmental studies.

In a study published by the U.S. Census Bureau, it was reported that 57 percent of Americans cannot afford to purchase median-priced homes with a 30-year conventional mortgage. The study points to a substantial growth in consumer debt as one of the significant reasons why many families will not be able to purchase housing. During the 1980s, the ratio of debt to 1-year's disposable income rose from 65.4% to a whopping 83.5%.

The result was to reduce substantially the amount of income available to pay the debt service on homes because of the continuing payments on other debts. The figures are astounding: Thirty-nine percent of married couples could not afford a median-priced home, compared to 75% of all single people and 87% of single women with children.* In addition, state and local taxes, including personal income, sales, and corporate taxes, continue to rise to pay for health-care, public safety, and welfare expenditures that are rising faster than the ability to raise revenues, particularly during times of economic slowdown. Should these taxes continue to rise, this will further reduce disposable income and will add to the financial burden of those looking for first-time homes. The ability to purchase new homes in the median-priced range may well be a difficult process in the next decade. Even though housing construction will rise during times when economic growth is positive, the rate of growth in building new homes may be slowed because of these key factors. Furthermore, the related industries that make up the housing sector may also suffer, including building materials, furniture, and household appliances.

There is an important distinction between the number of single- versus multifamily housing starts and permits. The 1986 Tax Act eliminated many popular real estate tax shelters. This act restricted many developers from obtaining financing for multifamily projects. Furthermore, the effects of the savings and loan crisis forced banks to tighten their credit requirements. Any credit problem restricts the willingness of banks to lend money to developers to build new homes. If banks begin to lend more money and mortgage rates decline, housing starts and applications for building permits will begin to rise. Lastly, federal rules mandating access for handicapped people to apartment houses have caused many multifamily builders to reconsider building.

The effect of housing starts and permits on interest rates reflects the market's perception of what the U.S. economy is doing. Since the numbers are reported by regions, the reader can get a closer view of a particular geographic area. If housing starts in the Northeast are contracting when housing starts in the West are rising, one must look closer at the numbers. They could be affected by weather in one or the other region. Also, the effects of a slowdown in the U.S. economy are first seen in one region, such as the Northeast, and may or may not spread to other regions. During the 1990/1991 recession, the decline in housing starts was widespread from California to Massachusetts. Any pickup in new construction thus may depend on special factors.

---

*"Housing May Be Less Affordable Than Indexes Show as Debt Rises," *Investor's Daily*, July 31, 1991, p. 7.

New Home Sales

New home sales data is published monthly by the U.S. Department of Commerce using information from the U.S. Department of Housing and Urban Development (see Fig. 4-6). The sales figures are seasonally adjusted. The number of home sales represents the third report on the housing construction industry, in addition to housing starts and applications for building permits. A rise or fall in mortgage rates affects the entire housing industry directly, and therefore all other allied industries such as furniture, carpeting, household appliances, building materials, and so forth. In turn, mortgage rates are affected directly by the movement of interest rates. Interest rates react to new home sales because they tend to reinforce housing trends.

High interest rates prevent consumers from purchasing new homes. When consumers decide not to purchase new homes, it is one of the key factors in initiating a slowdown in the U.S. economy. Normally, the housing industry recovers when interest rates become low enough to bring down mortgage rates to a point where home buyers are willing to take out mortgage loans. The rise in new home sales is a positive for the U.S. economy, but after a period of time begins to affect inflation as the price of housing increases or so long as housing is in demand. If inflation does rise,

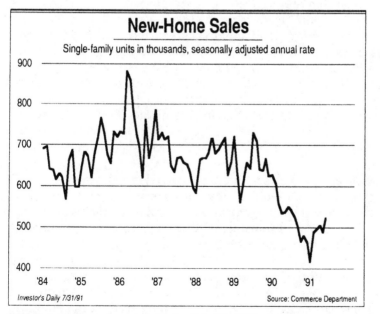

Figure 4-6. (*From Investor's Daily, July 31, 1991, p. 1.*)

a sustained increase in housing may force interest rates higher to keep inflation in check. As interest rates decline, the housing industry picks up.

Other factors linked to new home sales figures include a rise in the employment number, an increase in confidence indices, and a rise in personal
income. Another important point is that housing starts may rise while
new home sales decline in a given month. The reason is that new home
sales do not include custom-built housing for which sales contracts are
signed in advance. A few additional months will smooth out this problem.

Retail Sales

Retail sales, published monthly by the U.S. Commerce Department, are adjusted for seasonal variations but not for inflation. Retail sales for a particular month is based initially on a survey of 3000 retailers, compared with the
12,000 retailers included in the final survey conducted one month later,
which is released as part of this next month's figures. For example, the report on retail sales released in September includes a revision of the August
figures (because by this time 9000 more retailers have been surveyed) plus
the initial survey on September retail sales. Retail sales accounts for about
half of all consumer spending, represents about one-third of the nation's
economy, and comprises about one-fifth of gross domestic product.

The retail sales figure is divided into two components, durable goods
and nondurable goods. The durable goods sector represents 36% of total
retail sales. It includes cars and light trucks, which represent 20% of total
retail sales, as well as furniture and other home furnishings and building
materials and hardware. The nondurable component, which represents
64% of total retail sales, consists of such items as general merchandise,
clothing and accessories, department store sales, gasoline station sales,
restaurants and bars, drugstores, and food store sales. Both new furniture
and new clothing are important indicators in determining consumer
spending patterns, because these items are expensive and not considered
necessities.

There are several problems with this indicator. Weather will affect retail
sales in a given month. If there is a major snow storm in the Northeast or
Mid-Atlantic region, traveling difficulties will limit shopping; conversely,
2 weeks of unusually warm weather in New England and the Middle At-
lantic states in late February will bring consumers out to buy, and retail
sales for the month will shoot up—but only until cold weather returns.
Fashions can also affect these numbers. Since women's clothing sales are
about five times men's clothing sales, a major seasonal fashion that
women do not like can have a serious effect on the retail sales number. A
high consumer debt burden and uncertainty about economic conditions,
particularly during a slowdown in the economy, will affect sales figures.

Retail sales figures are often erratic and tend to jump up and down from month to month. Despite these problems, however, retail sales trends can indicate the direction of the U.S. economy. During economic slowdowns or when recession besets the nation, consumers are more concerned about paying off debt than about buying new clothes. Since consumer spending is about two-thirds of U.S. economic activities, the willingness of consumers to buy is critical to economic growth.

A vitally important aspect of the retail sales indicator as well as all other indicators is that there are always revisions, which can distort the reader's interpretation of that figure. The retail sales monthly number is often revised because the initial monthly figures are based on a small sample of reports. The initial data consists of about 3000 businesses. By the time the next month's data is reported, about 9000 additional businesses have been surveyed. The larger sample will often cause major revisions of the previous month's figures. The numbers also exclude spending on services such as lawyers and doctors, which account for a proportionate amount of consumer outlays. The Commerce Department does not adjust for inflation, so a rise in retail sales may only reflect price increases. Seasonal differences are important, such as the holiday times around Christmas and Easter. During these particular holiday periods, buying is expected to be large. A lack of buying at these times means that consumer confidence is low. Many analysts prefer to compare sales with those of the previous month so that they can remove seasonal differences. When the publications we discuss report these sales figures, they also report the previous month's figures so that the reader can do the comparison. Others feel that year-to-year comparisons are more accurate. Again, these comparisons are often given in the reporting by our publications.

A rise or fall in retail sales can push interest rates up or down. If retail sales continue to climb, interest rates will climb. As demand for new clothing, furniture, home appliances, and other items increases, it creates the potential for inflation. The perception is that if inflation rises, interest rates will reflect that rise. Often during times of economic slowdown, prices are reduced sharply in order to stimulate sales. Once the economy begins to recover, at some point the discounted prices will be raised as the demand for the goods increases. Then interest rates will soon reflect the rise in prices or inflation.

Automobile Sales

Because automobile sales represent 20% of total retail sales, this value is an important component to consider. These numbers are published monthly by the U.S. Department of Commerce, and are seasonally adjusted. The articles in the four publications we are using highlight car and light truck sales. Car sales include those of ten car manufacturers: General Motors, Ford, Chrysler, Honda, Toyota, Nissan, Mazda, Mitsubishi, Subaru, and Isuzu. Of the ten, seven are Japanese companies that build cars in plants located in the United States. Each of our publications divides the automobile sales figures in slightly different ways. For example, *The Wall Street Journal* breaks up the data between total cars including domestic and imported; total trucks including domestic and imported; total domestic vehicles; and total vehicles. Light truck sales figures are compiled from General Motors, Ford, Chrysler, Nissan, and Isuzu.

There are several issues to consider with regard to automobile sales. Often, incentives such as cash rebates are offered to consumers. These financing deals can inflate the auto sales figures enough to distort a monthly number. There is controversy about determining whether sales with or without incentives is a more accurate number. Although foreign competition is a factor, it often reflects the U.S. consumer's view of car value, safety, and maintenance. Weather again can play havoc with these numbers. Severe weather may prevent the consumer from traveling around to compare car values. Large sales to rental fleets can also create distorted monthly figures.

High interest rates on bank auto loans can put a damper on consumer desire to purchase a car. During economic slowdowns or recessions, banks also tighten credit, which will lessen the willingness of consumers to purchase autos at the higher car loan rates. As interest rates decline and consumer confidence picks up along with employment and personal income, banks become more willing to reduce car loan rates enough to encourage the purchase of new cars.

Industrial Production

The industrial production figure is published monthly by the Federal Reserve Board, and is seasonally adjusted starting from a base of 100 beginning in 1987. This statistic measures the production of the nation's factories, about 25% of the nation's total business activity. Because the employment report is published earlier in the month and includes how many people are working and the average number of hours they worked, the industrial production indicator is considered by economists to be fairly accurate in assessing the nation's production capacity. The industrial production figure is obtained by multiplying the number of production workers with jobs by the length of the manufacturing work week. Industrial production is a coincident indicator of business activity because it tends to rise and fall at the same time as the U.S. economy. The industrial production indicator is most sensitive to changes in the business cycle.

During recessions, it is one of the most closely watched indicators. As industrial production begins to pick up, other factors begin to influence this indicator. For example, as manufacturing employment begins to increase, durable goods orders rise, and other statistics that relate to manufacturing production move upward. As these figures push upward, interest rates become unsettled and begin to rise because growth in the economy means the potential for price increases or inflation.

The publications that report the industrial production figure break it down into four parts:

1. Total production, consisting of consumer goods, business equipment, and defense and space
2. Manufacturing production only, consisting of durable goods and non-durable goods
3. Mining
4. Utilities

Among other sectors that fall within the total number are construction supplies, military hardware, primary metals, chemicals, and transportation equipment. During specific parts of the business cycle, production of certain items takes on more significance. For example, during a recession, a certain sign for recovery is the production of lumber. If that component rises, it is a signal that the housing market may begin to rise. The same can be said for automobile production. The result for interest rates is that they will begin to rise if these indicators become a trend indicating economic recovery. Since recovery means potential for an increase in inflation, interest rates begin to increase.

Several factors can distort the monthly industrial production figure. Strikes in a major sector of the U.S. economy, such as automobile or airplane manufacture, significantly reduce production levels. Holidays shorten the period of data gathering and thus distort a particular monthly figure. Many analysts exclude automobiles from the industrial production figure to gain a more accurate picture of what is being produced.

Weather can be a nuisance. Inclement weather such as snow storms prevent workers from reaching the factory, which slows down production for a given month. An example might be that if unusually warm weather occurs in early March, the production of air conditioners would be accelerated. The surge in the supply of air conditioners would affect the May industrial production number. Some factories close for a specific period during the hot summer months. In some cases, large orders of high-priced equipment can distort the number, such as a large order for aircraft from a foreign nation or a significant order for mainframe computers. Production figures are based in part on employment data gathered by the U.S. Department of Labor. This data is inflated by faulty seasonal adjustments.

The industrial production number is linked to many other manufacturing indicators, such as factory orders, the National Association of Purchasing Management index, durable goods orders, and manufacturing employment data. Interest rates are affected by a combination of these numbers. In some cases, when these indicators are linked together, they confirm other numbers, force reconsideration of prior numbers, or question current figures. *One month does not make a trend.* If there is a question, then it is appropriate to wait until new figures are reported in the following month. These twists and turns affect one's interpretation of interest rates.

Capacity Utilization

Capacity utilization figures are published monthly and simultaneously with industrial production figures. Both are compiled and reported by the Federal Reserve Board. The capacity utilization figure measures output and changes in productivity levels. It compares the production rate with capacity levels. The result is an operating rate. The Federal Reserve Board divides its calculations of industrial production in a given month by its estimate of the capacity of U.S. production facilities from many different sources. The components of capacity utilization are based on specific operating rates that make up the total:

1. Manufacturing
2. Durable goods
3. Nondurable goods
4. Mining and oil
5. Utilities and motor vehicles

Some analysts consider capacity utilization not only as an economic indicator but also as an inflation indicator because it is an operating rate. Analysts consider an operating rate of 85% a sign that inflation will accelerate in coming months. That is, after reaching an operating rate of 85%, production begins to bottleneck, delivery backlogs, and shortages occur, pushing prices upward all along the line. A high factory operating rate and a tight labor market will exert inflationary pressure on the U.S. economy. If the total operating rate becomes too high, overworked factories may have trouble meeting demand. This problem may lead to higher prices or inflation. The higher the inflation, the higher interest rates will go. The more overworked people there are in factories, the more equipment becomes susceptible to breakdown, both human and physical.

If the demand for more production continues when skilled labor is scarce, it forces plants to pay higher wages to workers with fewer skills. The closer U.S. industry moves toward full operating capacity, the greater difficulty it has producing enough to meet demand. That attempt to meet rising demand often leads to shortages and price increases. As the 85% number is reached over several months, interest rates tend to rise because it means the potential for increased inflation.

Several issues affect the capacity utilization figure. Some analysts believe that the computerization of U.S. industrial production has restructured the way products are made and inventories controlled. Industry has become more efficient: It can increase output much more before hitting production snarls. In other words, computerization has led to far greater speed and efficiency in processing orders, shipping products from the factory to the customer, and controlling inventories at the warehouse by keeping products moving off the shelves as fast as can be accomplished. The basis of this approach comes from the Japanese "just-in-time" delivery method now central to many U.S. factories. It has rearranged factory setups and inventory controls to keep production lines operating steadily. Sectors such as machinery, household appliances, and motor vehicles have been successful in using this process of production efficiency. No doubt many more will follow. Some factories can operate at 90% capacity without running into bottlenecks and without lengthening delivery times. Even with this more efficient production, the capacity utilization figure is still a measure of the U.S. economy. Interest rates will react to these figures as a sign of a rise or fall of the U.S. economy. As capacity increases with the concomitant rise in inflation, interest rates will also rise. As capacity declines as the U.S. economy declines and prices of goods moderate, interest rates will decline as a sign of reduced possibility of inflation.

Inventories-to-Sales Ratio

The inventories-to-business-sales ratio is an important measure of economic confidence. It is published monthly by the U.S. Commerce Department. The ratio means that it would take a specific number of months to deplete the backlog of goods held on shelves at that specific monthly sales pace. For example, if the ratio is 1.54, it would take 1.54 months to clear the shelves of inventory. A high inventory-to-sales ratio means that businesses are overstocked and will postpone ordering and producing goods. Should this occur, the U.S. economy would slow down. Then interest rates would begin to come down, and inflationary pressures will ease.

The composition of business inventories as reported in the various publications consists of manufacturers, retailers, and wholesalers. Then total business sales is followed by the inventory-to-sales ratio. For example, if inventories rise excessively in relation to sales, this could cause production reductions and job layoffs as businesses try to sell off the backlogs. Or if inventories decline, industrial production will rise as companies begin to replenish their supplies.

With the aid of computerization, managers measure demand in relation to inventories. If a company becomes too optimistic about future sales, inventories may still build up. The bloated inventories dissolve the optimism, prompting nervous executives to either reduce or cancel orders. The reduction in orders means the possibility of layoffs at factories. As the ratio of inventories to sales declines, it represents a healthy financial picture for businesses because it shows that sales are increasing faster than inventories. A rising ratio implies that inventories are at an uncomfortable level, since they are being covered by lower and lower sales.

There are a few problems in understanding this ratio. If shelves are more sparsely stocked, it could be because of strong demand or a deliberate cutting back by manufacturers and merchants who foresee poor demand. As interest rates rise, the cost of financing will increase, also affecting the ratio. Forecasts of price trends could cause businesses either to step up restocking if inflation is rising or to hold off if they expect prices to fall. If inflation remains at low levels, companies can keep inventories more in line with current needs or demand and not worry about future price increases. This means that if the cost of the goods that a company needs over time will remain relatively the same because inflation is low, they will not have to restock later at higher prices. Thus the inventories-to-sales ratio must be understood in terms of inflation. The rise or fall of interest rates is a signal to those making these decisions about stocking up or reducing inventories. As the global economy continues to expand, more and more parts and materials are being imported from foreign trading partners. That increases foreign production as well as keeping prices competitively low. This growing change can affect the inventories-to-sales ratio, again by keeping inventories in line with current demand.

Revisions to the prior month's figures showing either a smaller rise than initially reported or a larger rise than expected can directly affect how interest rates move. A higher inventory-to-sales ratio means economic growth, which in turn means that demand is rising steadily with accompanying price increases or inflation. The prospect of a rise in inflation means that interest rates will rise. It is important to link the inventory-to-sales ratio to other manufacturing figures such as industrial production, capacity utilization, the NAPM index, durable goods orders, and manufacturing employment.

Consumer Confidence Indices

Consumer confidence indices indicate the willingness of the consumer to spend. They reflect how people feel about business conditions in the United States. More specifically, these indices are a sensitive measure of a nation's vulnerability to an economic slowdown or recession as well as an economic recovery or sustained economic growth, because they measure consumer spending which represents nearly two-thirds of U.S. gross domestic product. Consumer confidence is a key component of economic activity. The desire to buy automobiles and to purchase new homes is measured by these indices.

There are two indices concerned with how business conditions affect consumer confidence. The first is called the *consumer confidence index* (Fig. 4-7) and is compiled by the Conference Board, a nonprofit group consisting of senior-level business executives. This index consists of a survey of 5000 households using 1985 as a base year of 100. It is composed of three indices: the first measures current conditions and is weighted at 40%, the second measures expectations over the next six months and is weighted at 60%, and the third is the weighted average of the first two. Specific concerns include jobs and salaries, as well as buying plans for automobiles, major appliances, and new homes.

The second index is the *index of consumer sentiment*, published by the University of Michigan's Institute for Social Research. It measures consumers' opinions about both the current and the future outlook for the economy as it affects their personal financial decisions. The survey results are based on 500 monthly telephone interviews of households across the nation. It uses 1966 as a base year of 100, although the index began in 1946.

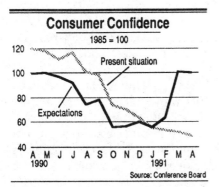

Figure 4-7. (*From Investor's Daily, May 1, 1991, p. 1.*)

Therefore, it falls or rises in percentage points. Questions are asked about how people feel about job prospects, wages, and the economy in general, both currently and for the next 6 months. The U.S. Commerce Department includes this index in the monthly Index of Leading Economic Indicators because it is designed to forecast the direction of the U.S. economy in the next 6 to 9 months.

Both indices can have a strong effect on interest rates.* When added to other indicators that already have been reported, these indices add support to various economic conditions for the foreseeable future. Depending on the psychology of the financial markets when these indices are reported, they can move interest rates. As consumer confidence begins to increase, they may spend more. If that happens, prices will rise to accommodate the demand and interest rates will rise accordingly. Or if consumer confidence begins to wane and demand lessens, industrial production will decrease, layoffs will occur, orders for new durable and nondurable goods will decline, and interest rates will begin to decline as these indicators show a slowdown in the U.S. economy.

One other confidence index is used by economists to measure consumer confidence in relation to business activity. The Conference Board conducts a survey of help-wanted classified advertising volume in 51 major newspapers in the nation. That survey is called the *help-wanted index* (see Fig. 4-8). Economists feel that it is a good measure of peaks in the economic cycle because businesses will increase worker hours before seeking new workers. Periodically, both *Investor's Business Daily* and *The Wall Street Journal* include a chart on the front page indicating the month-to-month changes in help-wanted ads.

Gross Domestic Product

The *gross domestic product* (GDP) is published quarterly by the U.S. Department of Commerce. The GDP is defined as an inflation-adjusted measure of the nation's total output of goods and services produced by labor and property located within the borders of the United States. It does not report on business activity by U.S. residents in other countries. The GDP excludes the output of a worker who resides in the United States but has a job in Canada. It also does not count profits from a foreign factory producing goods in the United States. In addition, profits from a U.S. company earned abroad as well as interest receipts from other countries are not counted in the GDP. The GDP is the common standard used by other major industrial countries to measure their economic performance. It is a

---

*Because the Conference Board's index is reported on a fixed date and is available to the public, it is more widely known.

Help Wanted Listings

A monthly index of classified advertising volume in 51 major newspapers (1967 = 100)

Investor's Daily 8/2/91　　　　　　　　　　　　　　　　Source: Conference Board

Figure 4-8. *(From Investor's Daily, August 2, 1991, p. 1.)*

measure of demand in the U.S. economy reflected in final sales. The number represents the annual growth rate in a particular quarter, seasonally adjusted. For example, one might say that the gross domestic product grew at an annual growth rate of 0.4%.

An important component is corporation profits, reported along with the GDP figure. It is considered more of a coincident rather than a forecaster of economic activity. The profits derived from current production are considered useful in measuring the effects on the economy. There are five parts to the profits figures:

1. Profits before taxes
2. Profits after taxes
3. Profits from current production
4. Domestic profits of nonfinancial corporations
5. The foreign component of profits

GDP includes the activities of private businesses, nonprofit institutions, and local governments. The GDP number represents two-thirds of U.S. economic activity. Because it is also a quarterly number for the previous quarter, it is often discussed in the media as a trend or confirmation of the individual monthly U.S. economic indicators that preceded it, such as housing starts, retail sales, industrial production, capacity utilization, and factory orders.

Interest rates often react to the reporting of the GDP because it reflects the publication of more specific economic indicators that have been promulgated over the past quarter. For example, interest rates will fall if prior indicators are linked together to show a trend. For example, when unemployment rates rise, manufacturing jobs decrease, factory orders decline, and capacity utilization and industrial production figures fall, price pressures or inflation is reduced enough to push interest rates down.

There are three estimates of the GDP figure, each published in succeeding months. The first estimate is the *advance*, the second estimate or first revision is the *preliminary*, and the third estimate or second revision is the *final*. The two revisions occur because some data takes longer to collect. A particular reaction to any of the revisions to the GDP figure often depends on what other economic and inflationary factors have been reported to the public. The articles in the key publications will also provide prior estimates.

Gross domestic product or GDP as reported is defined as gross domestic product less inventory change, which equals final sales. There are six major components of final sales:

1. Personal consumption expenditures. This consists of three subcomponents: durable goods such as automobiles, nondurable goods such as paper goods, and services such as dry cleaning. This is the largest component, at more than 64% of total final sales.

2. Business investment. The subcomponents are structures such as manufacturing plants and durable equipment including machinery.

3. Housing investment.

4. Inventory change.

5. Net exports or exports of goods and services minus imports.

6. Government purchases. This component is the second largest, at nearly 20% of the total. Government purchases includes federal purchases of national defense and nonmilitary goods and state and local purchases of goods.

Two other important figures, published as part of gross domestic product, are also closely watched by decision makers. They are called the GDP inflation indices. The first is the *implicit price deflator*. It measures not only the price changes of a "market basket" of goods and services but also changes in the composition of that basket. The second is the *fixed-weight deflator*, which measures price changes by keeping the same composition of the market basket of goods. The fixed-weight index is considered by many economists the more accurate price gauge. Unlike the implicit price deflator, it is not affected by changes in the composition of national output. However, both inflation indices are monitored by analysts because of controversy as to which of the two is more accurate in reflecting inflationary pressures.

The major problem with GDP is that revisions can change the outlook for interest rates as each revision is published. Because it is a quarterly figure, monthly figures published during the months of the next quarter might suggest a different interest rate trend. GDP does put into perspective what has happened over time. Many times the GDP reinforces the monthly figures that were previously published during that quarter. Sometimes, the inflation factors are skewed because of one-time events. A rise in these figures could, for example, reflect a postal rate increase or a federal pay rise.

Federal Reserve Board
"Beige" or "Tan" Book

The Federal Reserve Board compiles anecdotal reports from businesses throughout the 12 regional bank districts of the Federal Reserve System. Only recently has the survey been recognized as an important economic indicator and an interest rate mover. The survey can be purchased from any of the regional Federal Reserve Board offices. It is reported in summary detail in all of our financial publications. These 12 reports are called the "Survey of Current Economic Conditions." The survey is usually referred to as the "Beige" or sometimes the "Tan" book. It is issued about 2 weeks ahead of the regular Federal Open Market Committee meetings, which are held about every 6 weeks. The survey is an important summary of regional economic conditions in concise form. The survey includes an excellent but short summary of current economic and business conditions within the U.S. economy, and then brief analyses of each of the 12 districts. The districts are Boston, New York, Philadelphia, Cleveland, Richmond, Atlanta, Chicago, St. Louis, Minneapolis, Kansas City, Dallas, and San Francisco.

Summary

Interest rates reflect the conditions of the U.S. economy. They are a key indicator on which businesses, government officials, and individuals make financial and political decisions. While the interpretations of these numbers may differ, everyone is looking at the same interest rate indicators and making judgments as to how to act.

There are many economic indicators that are reported weekly, monthly, quarterly, and at 6-week intervals. Each indicator confirms or denies other economic indicators that are published and discussed in the various publications. All invariably affect the movement of interest rates. These indicators should be viewed as connected links, one factor linking to another. Employment figures link to industrial production to factory orders to the index of leading economic indicators, and so forth. Each of these figures is watched closely not only by the financial markets, investors, and businesspeople, but also by the White House, Congress, and industrial nations worldwide.

The condition of the U.S. economy is clearly reflected in the movement of interest rates. Our interest rate charts will become the process by which one can see how interest rates react to a reported indicator or series of indicators. Compiling weekly, monthly, and quarterly interest rate charts will provide a view of the U.S. economy. This view or changes to the U.S. economy influence the movement of interest rates. As the U.S. economy declines, inflationary pressures also decline. When that happens, interest rates decline. If the U.S. economy is growing and the growth is sustained, inflationary pressures pick up. When that happens, interest rates rise. These up and down cycles are always reflected in the movement of interest rates. Careful use of the weekly, monthly, and quarterly interest rate charts will clearly aid in understanding the movement of interest rates and their trends.

The reader should also be aware of the problems that affect most of the economic indicators. The key to interpreting these figures is that *one month does not make a trend,* but several months will indicate a trend. Monthly revisions are a common problem to all indicators. That is the reason why reviewing several months' worth of a specific indicator is necessary to confirm a trend relative to the growth or slowdown of the U.S. economy. When an indicator is reported, be sure to look for any aberrant conditions that may have distorted that monthly figure. Often the quarterly numbers, such as the gross domestic product, can aid in providing a longer overview of what has been happening. But again, even these numbers are subject to important revisions. Keeping the interest rate charts up to date will allow adjustment for these revisions and therefore a more clear view of the trend in the U.S. economy as it affects the trend of interest rates.

Remember that some economic figures are quarterly and are reported several months later. They must be viewed in the context to the latest indicators. Use the illustrations to obtain a visual scan of the U.S. economy. Watch for articles in the various publications on specific U.S. regions, the most populous states, and the larger cities. The articles about these areas are what the national numbers are reflecting. Each of the publications we have discussed describes the indicators in a slightly different way and illustrates them in different-looking charts. The main point is that all of them attempt to evaluate the indicator. The reader has to make judgments as to the view that is most important in determining why interest rates move in one direction as opposed to another.

5
Interest Rates and Inflation Factors

The most fearful time for any sailor is when black clouds begin to gather in the skies, signaling a storm on the high seas. To those involved in the businesses that are dependent on interest rates, a rise in inflation is no less a signal than black clouds to a sailor. As inflation rises, so do interest rates. Why? Because demand is increasing faster than supply, therefore prices begin to rise. An example is when salaries for certain skilled positions rise because the demand for the specific knowledge far exceeds the supply of those who have it. The result is that the cost of filling these positions rises. Another example is when a severe frost in Florida diminishes the supply of oranges. The result is that the price of oranges rises. In other words, the costs of conducting business, whether selling products or finding the right person for the job, depend on both the supply of those products or services and the demand for them. If the demand for a particular product is greater than its supply, we pay more because that product is scarce. As we pay more, the price rises. When prices rise, interest rates rise. And conversely, when prices fall, interest rates fall.

Several significant factors reflect inflation. Each of these factors is eagerly awaited by Wall Street and business decision makers in the U.S. and world business and financial markets. Each reflects a different part of the inflation picture. Each inflation factor is tied directly into other economic factors, such as capacity utilization, retail sales, or industrial production. If rising inflation begins to affect the cost of purchasing a car because it costs more to make the car, the consumer will pay more. When the consumer decides to pay the price, the interest rate the consumer pays will rise as the price of the car increases. The consumer will be willing to pay a higher price only up to a point. At that point, the consumer will decide that not only is the car sticker price too high but more important, the cost or interest rate on the auto loan is now high enough for the consumer to reconsider purchasing a new car. Once consumers decide not to buy cars, auto manufacturers slow down their production. Later, when the car loan interest rate has declined far enough, consumers will again consider purchasing a new car. The rise and fall of the car loan interest rate represents the cost of inflation. The relationship between supply and demand is an extraordinary balancing act predicated on consumer psychology.

Other factors affect the inflation characteristics of supply and demand. These same factors are the instruments of a rise or a fall in interest rates. The growth of the U.S. economy can force inflation upward. Supply shocks, such as the sharp rise in oil prices when the Middle East political situation heats up, can push inflation up and thereby interest rates. The effect of the need for capital in countries such as Germany to rebuild the infrastructure of what was formerly East Germany can force inflation up. A major drought in the Midwest or in California that parches the land and destroys crops pushes the cost of wheat, fruits, vegetables, and other agricultural products upward because of diminished supply. A severe frost in Florida limits the supply of particular crops and forces up prices, which causes inflation to rise, which pushes up interest rates. If the Federal Reserve Board—the watchdog of economic growth and inflation—determines that the economy is growing so strongly that it is creating too much inflation, it will push short-term interest rates higher to quell inflation before it hurts the U.S. economy. We will discuss several key inflation factors that move interest rates upward or downward.

The Producer Price Index

The *producer price index* (PPI), published monthly by the U.S. Department of Labor, is based on an index beginning in 1982 with a base of 100. It shows the percent change from one month to the next on a seasonally adjusted basis. The PPI estimates the prices received by domestic producers of goods at various levels of processing. It measures the prices that factories charge to wholesalers, retailers, and distributors for goods moving off the assembly line. The PPI is an excellent gauge of the cost of goods before they reach consumers. The PPI tends to anticipate prices at the retail level. Generally, changes in prices at the producer level affect consumers after various lags ranging upwards of 6 months. This change is reflected in the consumer price index, which we will discuss later in this chapter.

There are three levels along the production line. Each level has its own index. All three must be viewed together to understand the cost of producing a finished product. The three levels or indices are crude, intermediate, and finished.

The Crude Goods Index. Crude goods are goods entering the production chain for the first time. They include grains, cattle and hogs, raw cotton, crude oil, foodstuffs, soybeans, fluid milk, fresh vegetables and fish, hay, corn, turkeys, fresh fruits, cane sugar, and chickens, among other goods.

The Intermediate Goods Index. Intermediate goods are partly finished, requiring further processing, or are completed goods that are parts of other products. These goods consist of plywood and softwood lumber, fertilizer, machine belts, processed yarns, paperboard, pulp, printing ink, leather, synthetic fibers, finished fabrics, industrial chemicals, lead, zinc, copper, aluminum mill shapes, precious metals, steel, paint materials, paper, synthetic rubber, nonferrous metals including wire and cable, Portland cement, cadmium, inedible fats and oils, medicinal and botanical chemicals, and airplane engines and parts.

The Finished Goods Index. Of the three indices, the finished goods index is the one highlighted in the news media, and therefore the one that receives the most attention. However, the other two indices are equally important in understanding the effects of producer prices on interest rates. The items in the finished goods index measure the prices of goods before they leave the factory, refinery, or farm for sale to retailers. They consist of consumer goods and capital equipment as well as meat, eggs, fresh and dried vegetables, dairy products, processed fruits and vegetables, soft drinks, roasted coffee and processed turkeys, processed chickens and milled rice, tobacco products, cars, pharmaceuticals, soaps and detergents, apparel, home electronics, household items, heating oil, toys, and pasta.

An example of this three-level production process is wheat. Wheat is a crude good used to produce flour, an intermediate good which is used to produce a loaf of bread, a finished good. Another example is wool sheared from sheep, a crude good which is used to produce a bolt of cloth, an intermediate good which is used to make a suit or dress, a finished good.

When the PPI is published in the newspapers and other news media (see Fig. 5-1), a chart shows the finished goods change between one month and another, the finished goods change minus food and energy, and both the intermediate and crude goods changes. Many articles on the PPI focus on the core or underlying rate, which excludes the price movement of food and energy. These two groups of commodities are often subject to major fluctuations, so they can skew a particular month's number. Whether the core index or the total finished goods price index is more im-

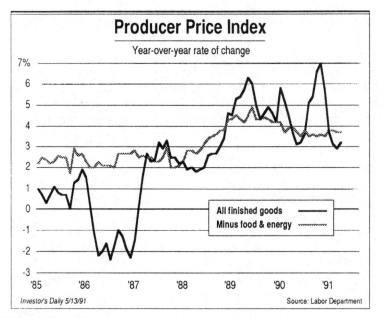

Figure 5-1. *(From Investor's Daily, May 13, 1991, p. 1.)*

portant is a matter of long-standing debate. Because of that volatility, many analysts feel that the core rate is more accurate than the total finished goods price index.

What are some of the problems and issues affecting the PPI? The PPI is linked to many other indicators. The causes of price increases or decreases depend on the growth or slowdown of the U.S. economy, the competitiveness of U.S. goods versus foreign goods, energy prices, and shortages of supplies. The PPI excludes imported goods, because these goods are more expensive to produce in the United States. The effect depends on the strength or weakness of the U.S. dollar. A stronger dollar pushes up the prices of U.S. goods, making foreign goods cheaper in our domestic market. Many times the stiff competition between foreign and domestic goods keeps the rise in domestic producer prices from being passed on to the consumer in order to maintain market share. However, the same can be said for foreign competitors. The index does not include the price for services such as doctors, lawyers, accountants, and banking fees. If these prices rise dramatically, they will not be reflected in the PPI, thus understating the rate of inflation at the producer price level. Weather is a critical factor in skewing prices. Droughts or freezes in major producing regions such as Florida, Kansas, or California can push up prices of agricultural goods as supply is diminished. Shocks of major proportions can affect one or more months' numbers, such as a dramatic price rise in oil. Seasonal events, including a one-time annual rise in tobacco prices, affect the PPI of that month.

A trend toward lower producer prices reflects a decline in the rate of inflation because consumer demand for products is weakening because of, say, a sustained rise in unemployment. This causes factory orders to decrease, which forces prices downwards. A major slump in the manufacturing of automobiles and housing will be reflected in lower producer prices, which will be indicated by the PPI over the months. Then interest rates will move lower to reflect the lower prices at the producer level. However, a shortage of supplies of specific commodities and skilled workers adds to producer price inflationary pressures. When the January PPI is published, it often shows the effects of beginning-of-the-year price increases. A final issue is the revisions that are often made to a previous month's number. Again, the adage is vitally important: *One month does not an indicator make.* The analyst must look at several months' values to determine a trend in the PPI. Interest rates, however, react to the monthly number, so it is appropriate to consider several months to detect a trend.

The price competitiveness between domestic and foreign goods sometimes determines what the consumer will pay. Even so, if producer prices are rising as indicated by the monthly PPI numbers, then retail prices can be expected to rise as shown by the consumer price index. The rise and fall of interest rates depends on the movement of inflation figures such as the PPI. The higher the PPI moves, the higher interest rates move. Many times, the market anticipates that if the PPI is rising, so will the consumer price index—and up go interest rates. These two figures are directly linked together.

The Consumer Price Index

The *consumer price index* (CPI), published monthly by the U.S. Department of Labor, is reported several days after the PPI. It measures the rise or fall in prices that consumers pay for a "market basket" of goods. This market basket is designed to represent the average expenditures of a particular segment of the population at a certain time. An important use of the CPI is that it determines the cost-of-living adjustment for people receiving social security and other federal benefits. Salary adjustments and social security payments are pegged to the consumer price index.

The CPI is divided into two main areas: 55% represents services and 45% commodities. Since the PPI does not include services, the CPI becomes a key indicator of this segment of the U.S. economy, which accounts for two-thirds of economic activity. Viewed another way, the CPI consists of seven major components. The largest is housing prices, at 42% of the total CPI index, followed by transportation at 19%, including new vehicles, used vehicles, motor fuel, and public transportation. Then comes food and beverages, accounting for 18% of the total and including food eaten at home and away from home, as well as alcoholic beverages. Other components include apparel at 7%, medical care at 5%, entertainment at 4% (including movies, sporting events, and other live performances), and miscellaneous items at 5% (including college tuition costs as well as day-care and nursery fees).

Because the rise or fall of the PPI influences the prices that consumers pay, many of the problems that affect the PPI affect the CPI. Weather such as droughts and cold spells, particularly in agricultural producing regions of the nation, affects the CPI in the ultimate price the consumer pays for these products in finished form. The cost of energy includes the cost of gasoline and oil-based goods. Oil prices tend to rise during vacation periods, especially during the summer months. Insects can devastate crops, particularly vegetables such as tomatoes and corn. Other items that contribute to price movement are the costs of college tuition, the soaring costs of medical care, the higher prices for imported goods when the dollar is lower (which makes U.S. goods cheaper), and the jump in prices in spring and summer lines of clothing. Other types of price increases that can affect the CPI from time to time include postage stamp costs, hotel rates, and airline tickets. Revisions play a key role, as often more data is supplied during the weeks after the first CPI number is reported. Many times, the financial markets will focus on the prior month's revision as much as on the number for the current month.

The CPI is one of the most closely watched numbers regarding inflation as a key to what will happen to interest rates. When the CPI is reported, the news media often focus on the core or underlying rate of consumer inflation. The core rate subtracts food and energy from the overall CPI number. (See Fig. 5-2.) Sometimes even the core rate is subject to a closer look. For example, if federal tax increases are imposed on items such as alcohol and tobacco, it will push the core rate higher, thus skewing the figure. The acutely awaited publication of the CPI often affects other possible actions. If inflation appears to have fallen to an acceptable level and has been sustained over a period of months, the Federal Reserve Board may decide to lower interest rates to move a debilitated economy out of recession and to stimulate its growth. Since the Federal Reserve Board always walks a tightrope between keeping inflation at reasonable levels and sustaining economic growth, the CPI figure becomes extremely important to the board's decision to raise or lower short-term interest rates.

Included with the CPI monthly figure is another associated index called the *urban wage earners index*. It covers urban wage earners and clerical

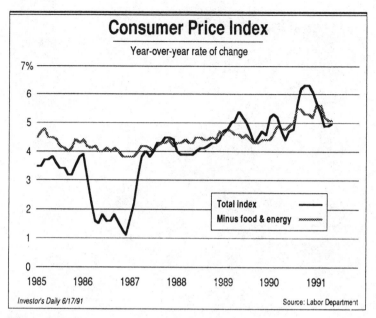

Figure 5-2. (*From Investor's Daily, June 17, 1991, p. 1.*)

workers. This index is used by the federal government and private businesses negotiating salaries or union contracts to determine wage increases. If this index continues to rise, it means that inflation is rising,
which will be a factor in pushing up interest rates.

Personal Income and Consumer Spending

Personal income and consumer spending are published together on a
monthly basis by the U.S. Department of Commerce (see Fig. 5-3). They
are not adjusted for inflation, but the newspapers that report these figures
do include the numbers adjusted for inflation. *Personal income* consists of
wages and salaries, factory payrolls, and transfer payments through social
security. The rate of growth of personal income can dictate the strength of
consumer spending. For example, a slow rate of growth in personal income slows down consumer spending. Therefore economic activity slows
down, which would be reported in the industrial production, capacity utilization, and durable goods orders figures. If economic activity slows
down, then inflation will begin to moderate because demand will decrease. The decline in inflation that results from these actions will ulti-

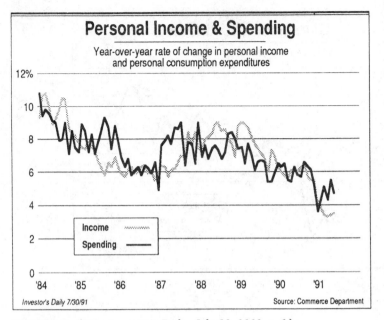

Figure 5-3. (*From Investor's Daily, July 30, 1991, p. 1.*)

mately reduce interest rates. A major thrust to the constant rise of both personal income and consumer spending is the substantial increase in working women in the labor market. It has created a far larger group of two-wage-earner families.

Consumer spending is important in that it accounts for two-thirds of total consumption in the nation's economic activity. It includes personal outlays for all types of consumer spending except interest payments on debt. Most articles on consumer spending report spending for both durable goods, which are expensive and last more than 3 years, and nondurable goods. Consumers become reluctant to spend if interest rates are too high, because the credit required to pay for large purchases such as automobiles, refrigerators, and homes becomes too costly. When consumers decide not to spend for a host of reasons, including a slumping economy when one's job may be at stake, then interest rates will begin to decline in the hopes that lower borrowing costs will induce consumer spending.

The *personal savings rate* is included in the report on personal income and consumer spending and is the ratio of savings to after-tax income. The savings rate is considered a good measure of consumer caution. The more money consumers park in banks in the form of money market funds, certificates of deposit, or discretionary savings accounts, the more concerned consumers are about the effects of a weakening economy, particularly about layoffs. An important aspect of the savings rate is that the higher the savings rate, the less dependent the United States is on foreign capital. This means that more funds are available for domestic purposes such as rebuilding roads, repairing bridges, and constructing new schools. Furthermore, the increased savings create opportunities for business investment and less dependence on the federal government to raise interest rates to draw in foreign funds to help pay for the U.S. budget deficit.

There are several problems and issues concerning personal income and consumer spending. Labor strikes, which suspend workers' pay, can skew a monthly figure. Reducing the growth of personal income thwarts spending. Weather can be a key problem in any given month, preventing people from getting to work during periods of severely inclement weather. Cold fronts in regions of prime agricultural activity can destroy crops or at least reduce harvests significantly. The higher prices that result are then passed on to the consumer as reflected in the CPI. Consistent pay increases and rises in benefits for federal and other local government employees, which represent a statistically significant group, can increase personal income and encourage additional spending. The payment of taxes in April normally holds back consumer spending and reduces the number reported for that month. A rise or fall in energy prices can help or hinder the consumer's willingness to spend. For example, the price one pays to heat a home will affect the amount available for other spending.

A rise in personal income and the willingness of the consumer to spend reflect the rise and fall of interest rates. The higher interest rates rise, the less willing consumers are to spend, because it costs them more to borrow money to purchase goods. A rise in inflation, which forces interest rates upward, thwarts consumer spending.

Consumer Borrowing or Credit

The *consumer borrowing* indicator is published monthly by the Federal Reserve and is seasonally adjusted. It is reported to the public just after personal income and consumer spending. It consists of various types of installment credit owed by consumers, mostly on a monthly payment basis. Some examples of this type of debt are car loans and revolving credit, primarily from retail and bank card debt. Mortgages and home equity loans are not included in this indicator, because they are secured by real estate.

The consumer borrowing indicator reacts to the level of interest rates. If interest rates are too high, consumers will use less credit and therefore spend less. These conditions add to the possibility of a slowdown in economic activity. If unemployment rises because high interest rates slow down the U.S. economy, consumer spending will slacken. Many analysts believe that signs of a decrease in consumer borrowing indicate the beginnings of an economic slowdown. As consumer borrowing declines, so does consumer spending. If consumer spending slows, then both auto and retail sales figures will show declines.

The Commodity Research Bureau

The *Commodity Research Bureau (CRB) futures index* measures the hourly movement of commodity futures prices. The day-to-day movement of this index of 21 equally weighted commodities that includes grains, metals, oil, and fiber prices is followed as an indicator of inflation. That is why the Federal Reserve Board watches the CRB futures index closely. Since the Fed influences short-term interest rates directly, the trend in this index is an important factor in determining what action it may attempt to keep inflation moderate.

The CRB index is composed of four sectors: The largest is agricultural commodities, which amounts to about 62% of the total index and includes cattle, cocoa, coffee, corn, hogs, oats, orange juice, pork bellies, soybean meal, soybean oil, soybeans, sugar, and wheat. Industrial commodities follow at 14% and include copper, cotton, and lumber. Precious metals amount to about 14% and include gold, platinum, and silver. Lastly, petroleum commodities, which account for 10% of the total, include crude oil and heating oil.

The CRB index tends to be overlooked except when a trend begins to develop. For example, if the index continues to rise for several weeks, the markets interpret the increase as a sign of potential inflation with the concomitant result that interest rates begin to rise. When the PPI and the CPI begin to show that the inflation rate is steady at a reasonable level, the CRB index might well confirm what the other two indices are showing. Or conversely, if the CRB has been rising over a period of weeks, the effect will show up in both the PPI and CPI figures.

The Employment Cost Index

The *employment cost index* is published quarterly by the U.S. Department of Labor Statistics, and is seasonally adjusted. (See Fig. 5-4.) The publication of this index reflects the prior quarter. Normally, it is reported about 1½ months later. This indicator of inflation measures private industry com-

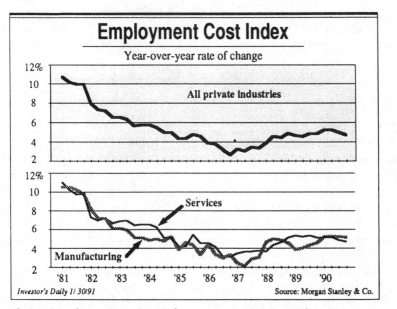

Figure 5-4. (*From Investor's Daily, January 30, 1991, p. 1.*)

pensation, including hourly workers' wages, salaries, and fringe benefits. Some analysts consider this index one of the single best barometers of inflationary pressures because of the accumulation of 3 months of data.

There are several problems with the employment cost index. A sharp rise in the costs of medical and dental insurance skews the index. For example, medical costs have risen about 15% annually for the past few years. The effect is felt not only by the companies that pay a share of it for their employees but also by state and local governments that have to reimburse monies used to help both the elderly and the indigent through federal and state aid programs. This dramatic rise is pitted against the rise in salaries and wages, and the cost of doing business. When the U.S. economy has been growing for a considerable time, skilled labor—machinists, secretaries, tool-and-die makers—begins to be difficult to find. When the shortage becomes prolonged, it pushes up the wages of these workers enough to cause concerns about inflation.

The employment cost index, when viewed along with several months of the PPI, CPI, consumer borrowing index, and the CRB index, can act as confirmation of the direction of inflation. The effect of these indices will directly affect the movement of interest rates. These inflation indicators constantly push and pull interest rates. A rise in inflation pushes interest up and may ultimately force the Federal Reserve Board to consider taking action. On the other hand, low inflation is a boon to economic growth by allowing interest rates to decline. A key ingredient in a resurgent economy coming out of recession is lower interest rates brought about by a decrease in inflation.

Gold

Gold is a controversial indicator that is often considered a hedge against inflation. Although today futures and options provide another way to hedge against inflation, gold is still important enough to be considered a factor in the movement of interest rates. As gold moves up or down over time, analysts will relate it to concerns about inflation.

Four key factors influence the movement of gold. The most important is the overall influence of inflation. Fear of inflation pushes the price of gold upward. As more people become concerned about a rise in inflation which in turn also pushes interest rates upward, individuals begin to purchase gold as a hedge against this rise in inflation. The opposite action occurs when both inflation and interest rates are at acceptable levels; then gold prices decline as individuals invest in other types of assets with the potential for higher returns, such as stocks and bonds.

The second factor relates to the strength or weakness of the U.S. dollar. As a general rule, the price of gold tends to move in a direction opposite to the value of the dollar: the lower the dollar, the higher the price of gold. A rise in the U.S. dollar may imply that the U.S. economy is strong while inflation is quiescent and that interest rates are stable at lower levels.

The third factor is the psychological tensions created by international concerns about inflation. Perhaps a rise of inflation in Germany caused by strong economic growth will force its central bank to raise interest rates to quell inflation and slow down its economy. Because Germany influences the rest of Western Europe, any rise or fall in its interest rates will affect the rise and fall of gold prices. A rise in German interest rates could stimulate the purchase of gold as a hedge against rising world inflation.

The fourth factor is that gold is a limited commodity. If one country hordes it or produces less of it, the price will rise. For example, South Africa mines 40% of the world's gold. If it experiences a reduction in its gold output, this will be reflected in a rise in gold prices.

Other factors can also influence the price of gold. Major shocks to the financial sector, such as the collapse of a major financial institution or bank that causes panic in worldwide financial communities, will push the price of gold upward. Another factor might be a large purchase of gold by a major industrial nation because its stock market has collapsed. Another possible reaction to gold concerns Middle Eastern nations. The failure of oil prices to keep pace with the rising cost of a major Arab country's economic development programs can prompt its monetary authority to sell gold from time to time. Another example is that, in recent years, Japan and other Far East countries such as Taiwan and South Korea have bought huge amounts of gold as a means of reducing the soaring volume of dollars created by their favorable trade balance with the United States and the European countries.

Gold still reflects rising inflation because as prices rise, gold can be a hedge against it. One important result would be an increase in interest rates. However, it is often difficult to gain a clear picture of exactly what is moving gold prices on a daily or week-to-week basis. Nevertheless, the movement of the price of gold over time may well influence the movement of interest rates. I have included this factor as one of the factors in the weekly interest rate chart.

Oil

Oil is traded in various domestic and foreign markets. The results are published in many newspapers. The investor should follow the movement of West Texas Intermediate Crude Oil future prices. The specific price information is crude oil for delivery in the month ahead, traded on the New York Mercantile Exchange. The rise and fall of oil prices directly affect the rise and fall in inflation, which in turn affects the rise and fall of interest rates.

The importance of oil is enormous. During 1990, the U.S. imported about 51% of its oil, compared to 45% in 1979 and 35% during the Arab embargo in the early 1970s. During 1990, the United States imported an average of 8.3 million barrels a day, more than half of it purchased from the Organization of Petroleum Exporting Countries (OPEC). In 1985, imports amounted to 5.1 million barrels a day, with OPEC contributing about one-third of that total. Oil accounts for about 43% of U.S. energy use. In other words, by the fourth quarter of 1991 the United States consumed 17.2 million barrels a day (MBD) compared to Europe at 13.4 MBD and Japan at 5.5 MBD.* One can easily understand the importance of the Gulf states to oil because Iraq, Kuwait, and Saudi Arabia have about 45% of all oil resources and account for almost 20% of all present productive capacity. About 24% of all oil imported into the United States comes from these three countries.†

What effect does oil have on inflation? There are many examples. One

---

*"Quarterly Oil Monitor: Third Quarter 1991," *County NatWest/Washington Analysis*, p. 7.

†Allanna Sullivan, "Energy Options: It Wouldn't Be Easy But U.S. Could Ease Reliance on Arab Oil," *The Wall Street Journal*, August 17, 1990, p. A4.

economist determined that every $6.25 increase in the price of a barrel of oil will add a full percentage point to the consumer price index.* To put it another way, an $8 permanent increase in the price of oil in a given year would reduce economic growth by 0.2% to 0.3%.†

There is no doubt about the importance of oil in today's economic and financial world and, more important, the role it plays in the movement of interest rates. Some changes have lessened the effect, but not enough to eliminate it as an important inflation factor. Furthermore, one never knows when a sharp rise in oil prices could occur, which would raise interest rates because the cost of energy would increase, causing inflation to increase. There has been considerable diversification by European countries into other forms of energy, such as hydroelectric and nuclear power. The United States has also benefited from such diversification, but the enormous demand for oil is still there. The willingness of other OPEC countries to make up any oil losses during the 1991 Gulf war mitigated the rise in the price of oil. In other words, the willingness for coordinated action by many Middle Eastern nations to keep oil prices reasonably stable is much greater today than in prior decades. These countries have learned what can happen to their financial and real estate investments in the United States and Western Europe when oil prices are either too high or too low. Too high oil prices negatively affect Western economies. Too low oil prices reduce the value of their investments. Therefore, the balancing act to obtain an economic level of oil pricing is important to the level of interest rates.

Another important factor concerning the use of oil is that, during the severe oil crisis of the 1970s, many companies redesigned their plants to make energy use more efficient. Diversification by utilities into coal and nuclear power has lessened the effect of oil somewhat. But environmental concerns about coal and the continued movement to stop building new nuclear plants still keep oil a key energy source.

Nevertheless, the strong effect of oil price movements on the U.S. economy and interest rates is still an important inflation factor. For example, U.S. household debt hovered between 45% and 50% from 1964 to 1980.

---

*Donald Ratajczak, Director of the Economic Forecasting Center at Georgia State University, quoted by Pamela Sebastian, in "Economy: Analysts Ponder Chances of Recession, Look to Consumer Spending, Oil Crisis," *The Wall Street Journal*, August 13, 1990, p. A2. Reprinted by permission of *The Wall Street Journal*, © 1990 Dow Jones & Company, Inc. All rights reserved worldwide.

†Allen Sinai, chief economist of The Boston Company, quoted by Joel Kurtzman, in "Dancing Past the Recession: Oil Prices. Flat Growth. The Deficit. Things Are a Mess. But Wait, There's a Way Out," *The New York Times*, August 12, 1990, Sunday Business Section, p. 6.

Then it jumped to 65% by 1990. Any significant rise in the price of oil would force consumers to spend less on other merchandise. In turn, the U.S. economy would suffer. While interest rates would rise on the inflation effect of the rise in the price of oil, over time, if the U.S. economy slowed down, it would lower interest rates. From an international perspective, Japan, which is almost totally dependent on imported oil, would find itself in the same predicament, with a loss of purchasing power. Japan's ability to purchase U.S. products would diminish, thus hurting the U.S. economy. The same can be said for Europe, but to a lesser extent, even though Eastern Europe is highly dependent on oil.

Summary

Inflation is a key indicator in moving interest rates up or down. The many inflation factors we have discussed vary in their effects on interest rates, but they all do affect the movement of interest rates. Some factors dominate in a given period of time. Sometimes it is the steady rise in several factors indicating growing inflation that pushes interest rates upward. Probably more important than any other factor is the psychological fear of inflation, whether it is actually rising or not, which causes interest rates to gyrate frantically. The threat of that darkening cloud, whether real or not, can cause even the most experienced sailor to steer toward calmer waters.

6

Interest Rates and Monetary Factors

The Federal Reserve Board (the Fed) has significant influence on interest rates worldwide. It sets monetary policy with the twin goals of ensuring that there is enough money and credit available to sustain economic growth while at the same time attempting to keep inflation under control. Therefore, the chair of the Fed becomes the nation's key economic policy decision maker. What financial columnist Robert D. Hershey, Jr., has to say about the people who analyze the Fed is aptly true:

> Even in the most placid of times, what goes on at the Federal Reserve's stately Constitution Avenue [Washington, DC] headquarters is the subject of intense, if often arcane, debate. The Fed and the markets in which it moves are scrutinized by what must be the world's highest paid fraternity of professional students who . . . examine every action—often every opaque word—and then set about arguing the meaning and the merits.*

"Fed watchers," as they are often called, live, breathe, and interpret every comment or report that the Fed makes or is supposed to have made. Or, as *The Wall Street Journal* put it: "Interpreting the Fed's policy intentions is more of an art than a science, and the subject often deteriorates into a tangled semantics debate."†

---

*Robert D. Hershey, Jr., "A Tough Time for Fed Watchers," *The New York Times*, March 9, 1986, p. 4. Copyright © 1986 by The New York Times Company. Reprinted by permission.

†Tom Herman, "Interest Rates Surge on Talk of Policy Shift in Credit Markets," *The Wall Street Journal*, December 8, 1987, p. A3. Reprinted by permission of *The Wall Street Journal*, © 1987 Dow Jones & Company, Inc. All rights reserved worldwide.

What Is the Federal Reserve Board?

What is this powerful U.S. government agency? The Federal Reserve System was created by Congress in 1913 to encourage economic growth without creating inflation. The Federal Reserve System is managed by the board of governors of the Federal Reserve System. The board consists of seven members, who meet in its headquarters in the nation's capitol. The members of the Fed are appointed by the President of the United States with the advice and consent of the U.S. Senate to serve 14-year terms. The terms are staggered, with one term expiring every 2 years. The President designates one member of the board as chair and another as vice chair for terms of 4 years. Not more than one member of the board may be selected from any one of the 12 Federal Reserve Districts established under the Federal Reserve System. The President of the United States is directed by law to select members of the board from among representatives of the financial, agricultural, industrial, and commercial communities as well as from various geographic regions of the nation.

The prime responsibility of the Fed is to establish monetary policy for the United States. The goal of monetary policy as set by the Fed is to encourage economic growth without increasing inflation by controlling the money supply. Under the board of governors, the committee that determines monetary policy is called the Federal Open Market Committee (FOMC) and is composed of seven members of the board of governors plus the 12 presidents of the regional Federal Reserve Banks. However, only the governors and five of the bank presidents can vote. All 17 members of the FOMC participate in the process of determining Fed monetary policy.

The FOMC analyzes the data submitted by the Fed's staff, establishes monetary policy, sets money supply targets within the framework of its view of the economy and inflation, and then suggests means to implement its policies from among the Fed's operating tools. The New York Federal Reserve Bank is a permanent member of FOMC because it carries out the directives concerning money transactions of the FOMC through its Open Market Desk, from which it adjusts the supply of reserves in order to fix their price. The result is that the New York Fed is the most powerful of the 12 regional banks. The other presidents of the Federal Reserve Banks serve on a rotating basis for 1 year and come from the following geographic groups: The first group consists of Boston, Philadelphia, and Richmond; the second group of Cleveland and Chicago; the third group of Atlanta, St. Louis, and Dallas; and the last group of Minneapolis, Kansas City, and San Francisco. In addition, there are also 25 branches of these 12 regional banks to serve particular geographic areas within the jurisdiction of these regional banks: Buffalo, Cincinnati, Pittsburgh, Baltimore, Charlotte, Birmingham, Jacksonville, Miami, Nashville, New Orleans, Detroit, Little Rock, Louisville, Memphis, Helena, Denver, Oklahoma City, Omaha, El Paso, Houston, San Antonio, Los Angeles, Portland, Salt Lake City, and Seattle.

What Is Money?

A question that is often asked is just what is money in today's world? One can define *money* as an acceptable means of exchange, a standard of value, or a way to save or store purchasing power for future use. *Money supply* or the *money stock* can be defined as the total amount of money circulating around the banking system in one form or another. The money supply numbers are collected and reported late on Thursday, then published in the next day's financial newspapers. There are three major types of money supplies. The first type of money supply or stock is called M1, or the funds most readily available to spend. It consists of currency and checking accounts along with savings accounts such as passbook savings, small certificates of deposit, bank money-market funds, and nonbank travelers checks.

The second type, called M2, consists of M1 plus savings deposits in small-denomination time deposits, plus money-market mutual funds less than $100,000. Currently, the M2 money supply indicator is closely watched by the Fed policy makers. It is therefore also watched by everybody else.

The last type, called M3, consists of M2 plus large-denomination time deposits at all depository institutions of $100,000 or more, shares in money-market mutual funds restricted to institutional investors, and large-denomination term repurchase agreements. Repurchase agreements are made when the Fed decides to make a repurchase agreement with a U.S. dealer or foreign central bank. It buys a security for immediate delivery with an agreement to sell the security back at the same price by a specific date, usually within 15 days, and receives interest at a specific rate. This technical arrangement—a common undertaking on a day-to-day basis—allows the Fed to inject reserves into the banking system on a temporary basis to meet a temporary need and to withdraw these reserves as soon as that need has passed.

The opposite action is a matched sale–purchase agreement. When the Fed makes a matched sale–purchase agreement, it sells a security outright for immediate delivery to a U.S. dealer or foreign central bank. They strike an agreement for the Fed to buy the security back on a specific date, usually within 7 days, at the same price. A matched-sale agreement is the reverse of a repurchase agreement. It allows the Fed to withdraw reserves on a temporary basis. The money is technically moved in and out of the banking system by these maneuvers. The purpose is to control the money supply in order to stimulate U.S. economic growth without increasing inflation.

The Fed currently believes that the M1 figure is too volatile and that the M2 is more stable, and therefore a more reliable indicator of the amount of money flowing through the banking system. Whether the Fed decides to add or subtract money from the banking system can be gleaned by following the path of the M2 indicator. The M2 money supply is the most closely watched of the three major types of money supplies. Money supply numbers are manipulated to fall within a specified target range. For example, M2 might have a target range of between 2.5% growth and 5.5% growth. If the M2 growth rate declines below 2.5% at a time when the economy needs stimulation, the Fed will have to lower interest rates to encourage more money supply to circulate within the system and therefore provide the banking reserves necessary to make loans and other types of investments. Another example is that slow growth of M2 could deter the increase in mortgage and installment credit that would stimulate sluggish housing construction activity and encourage more car sales. The M2 number is important in understanding why the Fed lowers or raises short-term interest rates. The reader can watch the various economic and inflation indicators we have discussed in previous chapters or the same indicators that the Fed is watching to see if there might be any change in Fed monetary policy. Furthermore, if M2 is exhibiting slow growth by being at the low end of the target, these indicators would limit the supply of credit available to the real estate market, which in turn makes it more difficult to purchase new homes. The result would be an attempt by the Fed to decrease short-term interest rates by increasing the supply of money, thereby making it easier to afford credit in the form of lower mortgage rates and home equity loans as well as commercial loans.

In order to control the money supply, the FOMC establishes *reserve requirements,* the percentage of total deposits that institutions must maintain within the Federal Reserve System in the form of vault cash or as deposits. Also, the chief executive of the Fed and therefore the FOMC is required by law to deliver testimony to the House Banking Committee's Subcommittee on Domestic Monetary Policy and the Senate Banking Committee twice a year on the state of the economy and the course of monetary policy. For example, the chair would suggest that the Fed felt that economic growth as measured by gross domestic product would grow at an annual rate within a certain range, the inflation rate as measured by the consumer price index would rise within a certain range, and the unemployment rate would decline also within a certain range. As part of that report, the Fed states the money supply targets. For example, the M2 growth target might be in a range of 2½% to 6½% for the remainder of the current year and within a similar range for the forthcoming year. When the chair of the Fed again reports to Congress 6 months later, these targets might change as a reflection of the then state of the U.S. economy and the rate of inflation. The FOMC meets about eight times during the year at its headquarters in Washington, DC. The basis for meetings of the FOMC is the "Tan" or "Beige" Book, which we discussed in Chap. 4. The Beige Book, which is published before the meeting, consists of a summary analysis of the U.S. economy and then more detailed descriptions of the economies within the jurisdiction of the 12 regional banks. Using this information as a base, the FOMC decides what actions to take. If the FOMC decides to take action to thwart inflation or stimulate the economy either by adjusting interest rates or through the control of the money supply, the decision can be implemented immediately. Money supply transactions are executed at the New York Federal Reserve Bank, and particular interest rate adjustments are made in Washington, DC. In order not to cause undue harm to the financial markets, the written statement of what the Fed decides to do is not released to the public until the next board meeting, approximately 6 to 8 weeks later.

The FOMC develops a consensus regarding the appropriate course of action depending on their views of the U.S. economy and inflation. That consensus is incorporated into a directive to the Federal Reserve Bank of New York, which is the bank selected to execute the money transactions to either encourage the flow of money, restrict it, or maintain a neutral policy pending a review of forthcoming economic and inflation data. The flow of money that affects use of bank credit is a prime mover of the U.S. economy and is responsive to inflationary pressures. The Fed directive sets forth the FOMC's long-run targets of key monetary and credit aggregates. It also establishes short-term operating guides for rates of growth in the money supply aggregates and an associated range of tolerable changes in money-market conditions. Any policy carried out by the FOMC emphasizes the supplying of bank reserves at a rate consistent with its economic and inflation objectives. These policies affect depository institutions, which are required to maintain bank reserves in certain proportions against various types of their deposits such as savings and time deposits. The "open-market operations" executed by the Federal Reserve Bank of New York directly affect the level of reserves in the U.S. banking system. An increase or decrease in reserves has the direct effect of raising or lowering short-term interest rates.

These open-market operations are executed in the form of purchases of U.S. securities, which add reserves to the banking system in order to stimulate the economy if inflation is at a reasonable level, or sales of U.S. securities to withdraw reserves from the banking system in order to reduce inflation and slow down an economy which may be growing too rapidly. Increasing reserves means that more money is available to depository institutions to make new loans to businesses and consumers. The increase in the money supply results in lower interest rates. Decreasing reserves means that there is less money available for depository institutions to make loans. The lack of money supply pushes interest rates upward. All of the manipulations by the Fed may be well and good, but if the consumer, whether an individual or a business, decides not to borrow, increasing the money supply will not help. Let's take a closer look at how the Fed controls the money supply.

Controlling the Money Supply

The Fed controls the supply of money, and thereby the flow of credit. By controlling that supply, it hopes to promote economic growth while at the same time keeping inflation at a moderate level. The Fed tries to walk a very thin line, attempting a balancing act by keeping money circulating to encourage economic growth and employment while at the same time keeping the economy from growing so fast that it will cause inflation to increase. Should inflation rise as the economy surges forward, interest rates will increase. If interest rates rise too high, the economy will begin to slow down as the cost of credit becomes too burdensome to businesses and consumers alike. At some point during a business cycle, the Fed will determine that the economy is overheating or growing too fast. Then the Fed will begin to push interest rates higher to cool down the economy, even if it means that the economy will experience a temporary slowdown. At another point in the business cycle, when the economy is in recession, the Fed will determine that it needs stimulation. That is when the Fed begins to push interest rates down. In order to push interest rates up or down, the Fed can use a number of tools that cause the ebb and flow of the money supply.

How does the Fed execute monetary transactions to encourage economic growth or slow it down? If the economy is contracting or in recession, the Fed can introduce cash into the banking system. The new cash will allow banks to loan funds so that businesses can expand and consumers can purchase goods. On the other hand, if the economy is growing too fast and stimulating inflation, the Fed can diminish the supply of money to restrain businesses and consumers and slow down the economy.

To introduce cash into the banking system or build up its reserves, the Fed buys U.S. government securities on the open market or by paying cash to banks in exchange for government securities. The Fed is thus injecting cash into the marketplace. Banks are then able to lend that cash to businesses and consumers, creating even more money in the form of increased loans. As the supply of money expands, more funds become available to the public and interest rates begin to decline because money is more plentiful.

Too much money can create problems of excessive demand for a limited amount of goods. When that happens, prices increase, which creates inflation. As inflation rises, so do interest rates. Then the Fed has to reduce inflation by slowing down the U.S. economy, which together will reduce the rise in interest rates. The Fed attacks the two problems by draining money out of the banking system or reducing its reserves. It accomplishes this important task by selling U.S. securities to government dealers who buy or sell these securities and thus takes money from the system. The cash received by the Fed is deposited in the Fed's reserves, where it is largely unavailable for loans. When this action occurs, it means that less cash is available for loans by banks to businesses and consumers. Then the banks must raise the price of scarce money by increasing interest rates.

The Federal Funds Rate

One of the most important indicators of Fed policy is the *federal funds rate.* This is the interest rate that commercial banks charge each other when one lends excess reserve funds to another overnight. The federal funds rate moves up or down all day long, and is reported the next day in the financial newspapers (see Fig. 6-1). Once the Fed determines this rate—say, 5.25%—then the federal funds rate number will oscillate around this target rate until the next move is executed. The federal funds rate is determined by the Federal Reserve Board. It represents the fundamental cost of credit. Or to put it another way, the cost of that credit is interest rates. The federal funds rate is an expression of Federal Reserve policy in an immediate way. If the Federal Reserve Board decides to lower short-term interest rates, it can accomplish this by manipulating the money supply and allowing banks to obtain more money to lend through the use of the federal funds rate among banking institutions. The federal funds rate is lowered because the Fed supplies more reserves or money to the banks in order to allow them to make more loans. If the Fed lowers the federal funds rate, it is referred to as *easing.* If the Fed raises the federal funds rate, it is called *tightening.*

Here is how it works. Banks must hold a specific amount of reserves as mandated by the Federal Reserve Board. Depending on daily transactions, some banks have excess reserves while others have deficiencies of re-

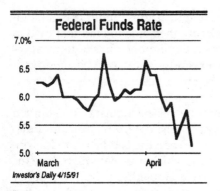

Figure 6-1. (*From Investor's Daily, April 15, 1991, p. 1.*)

serves. A bank with a deficiency in reserves that needs more money to meet demand for loans borrows from a bank with an excess at a specific overnight rate. The interest charged for this transaction is the federal funds rate. As we discussed above, the Fed influences the total supply of reserves outstanding by buying or selling securities for its own account. By executing this particular transaction, the Fed can control the level of the federal funds rate.

The federal funds rate is tied directly to the movement of short-term interest rates. The shortest is the 90-day Treasury bill rate or 3-month T-bill rate as it is often called. Any change in the federal funds rate directly affects the movement of the 3-month Treasury bill because it is the key short interest rate that is auctioned weekly by the U.S. Department of the Treasury and has the most liquidity in financial markets worldwide. In other words, the 3-month Treasury bill is the shortest issue by which the bond market can react to what the Fed may be doing or what is anticipated that the Fed will or will not do to effect monetary policy. The others are the 6-month and 1-year Treasury bill interest rates. The movement of the Treasury bill rates affects many other interest rates directly. The movement of the federal funds rate is a key signal of Fed monetary policy. Since the Fed does not report in writing what happened in its meetings until the next meeting, which is normally 6 weeks later, the only way one knows that policy may or may not be in the process of execution is by watching the movement of the federal funds rate.

The Fed will decide to cut back on the growth of bank reserves because it has determined that inflation is rising too fast as a result of a sharply growing economy. This action tightens the supply of reserves available to the banking system relative to its demand for them. That in turn drives up the federal funds rate, because excess reserves are scarce and therefore it will cost more to borrow them. The increase in the federal funds rate drives up other short-term rates, beginning with the 3-month Treasury bill. The rise in the federal funds rate is an indicator that reflects the Fed's judgment that inflation is too high despite a growing economy. One must view any movement of the federal funds rate over a period of time. By examining the various economic and inflation factors over several months, one can often understand why the federal funds rate moves upward or downward.

There are several difficulties in understanding the federal funds rate. Seasonal pressures at the end of the year push rates higher because there is a desire by banks to show a higher level of excess reserves on their balance sheets. This also reflects the need of consumers to withdraw funds for holiday shopping or to pay year-end bills. Sometimes there is an inordinate amount of "rolling over" of loans, which can skew the federal funds rate. Periodically there are large bank withdrawals by individuals from deposits made by the United States for social security payments, which will increase as our elderly population increases. Approximately every 2 weeks, ending usually on a Wednesday, there is a maintenance period. Within that time frame, banks hold reserve balances with the Fed to meet the reserve requirement established by the Fed as well as to manage the clearing of money transactions among banks. At the end of this period, the federal funds rate can change sharply because banks may have to borrow reserves to square their books from other banks through the federal funds market. In case of emergencies, the banks can borrow directly from the Fed. In any case, the action takes place only on that day.

Another important issue is that the Fed can control short-term rates but not long-term rates. The bond market sets long-term rates based on its expectations of what the conditions of the U.S. economy and inflation are going to be. Clearly, the movement of short-term interest rates affects the movement of long-term rates, but they are more affected by economic, inflation, and political factors, domestic as well as international—factors that are beyond the control of the Fed. Too often the federal funds rate will move one way as an indication of Fed monetary policy, but long-term rates may well move in another direction. For example, if the Fed pushes short-term interest rates downward, the bond market may decide that it is too soon to do so or that their view of the condition of the U.S. economy and inflation is different from that of the Fed. The bond market may even decide that there is too close a relationship between the Fed and the White House. There are many factors to consider when evaluating the movement of long-term interest rates. Some include the scarcity of intermediate and long Treasury notes and bonds and the movement of foreign interest rates, which often move in different directions than U.S. interest rates because of differences in the conditions of foreign economies and their rates of inflation.

By tracking the federal funds rate on a daily basis and following the comments of the Federal Reserve chair—particularly when testifying before Congress—as well as statements issued by the vice chair or other members of the Federal Reserve Board, the reader can begin to understand the Fed's determination of monetary policy. Twice a year, the Fed chair makes important speeches to both houses of Congress. In these speeches the Fed chair articulates monetary policy concerning the economy and inflation and establishes the range within which the money supply growth rate figures should move.

Depending on what direction the Fed believes the U.S. economy is heading and its relationship to other world economies and the level of inflation, the Fed will execute monetary policy, primarily by maneuvering the federal funds rate through its control of bank reserves. Because the movement of the federal funds rate can be seen quickly by the financial markets, it affects the rise or fall of short-term rates directly. The difficulty is in trying to figure out whether the Fed has indicated a monetary policy change or whether it is just a technical aberration in the financial marketplace. The financial markets will not actually know the Fed's decision until the minutes of the FOMC are released before the next meeting of the Fed. If the Fed decides to lower the federal funds rate or ease several times over a relatively short period of time, the financial markets may decide that too much easing will create inflation, and therefore push interest rates upward.

The constant effort to second-guess the Federal Reserve Board as the federal funds rate moves up and down on a daily or weekly basis can cause false alarms in the financial markets. By analyzing the many factors we have discussed and the others to follow in later chapters, one can often obtain a good sense of the two areas on which the Fed must determine monetary policy decisions—the condition of the U.S. economy and the level of inflation.

The Discount Rate

The *discount rate* is the Federal Reserve Board's key lending interest rate as well as an important public sign that the Federal Reserve Board is signaling a major change in its monetary policy (see Fig. 6-2). If the Federal Reserve Board decides to stimulate the economy, it may lower the federal funds rate several times before it lowers the discount rate. The rise or fall of the discount rate may occur several months after the federal funds rate has dropped. The change in the discount rate is made after the federal

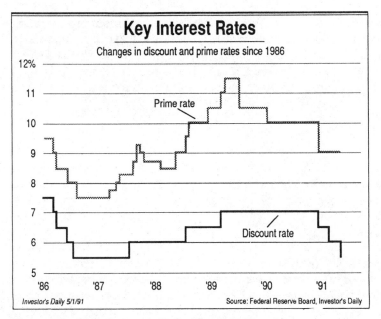

Key Interest Rates

Changes in discount and prime rates since 1986

Prime rate

Discount rate

Investor's Daily 5/1/91   Source: Federal Reserve Board, Investor's Daily

Figure 6-2. (*From Investor's Daily, May 1, 1991, p. 1.*)

funds rate has already been moving in a certain direction. Most times, the Fed prefers to keep the discount rate lower than the federal funds rate. In other words, if the federal funds rate has been adjusted enough times that it is below the current discount rate, then the Fed will cut the discount rate to bring it in line with the federal funds rate. When it does lower the discount rate, it is giving a clear sign to the financial markets that past actions concerning the movement of the federal funds rate were a reflection of monetary policy to stimulate the economy. Once that rate change is made, many other types of interest rates also begin to change, including mortgage rates, credit card rates, and car loan rates.

The *discount rate* is defined as the rate of interest the Federal Reserve Board charges depository institutions when they borrow from a Federal Reserve Board District Bank's discount window. In other words, it is the interest rate the Federal Reserve Board charges on loans it makes to banks or depository institutions as compared to the federal funds rate, which is the interest rate charged between banks. Sometimes, when the banking system as a whole is deficient in its reserve requirements, it can borrow some reserves from the Federal Reserve System at a specified rate called the discount rate. That window is called the *discount window*. Depository institutions try not to borrow from the discount window because it might indicate reserve problems to the Fed. The key distinction between the two interest rates is that the decision to raise or lower the discount rate is made only by the Federal Reserve board of governors at its headquarters in Washington, DC, and is a reflection of prior movement of the federal funds rate. The more important federal funds rate is set by the Federal Open Market Committee, which includes not only the governors but also five of the 12 regional Federal Reserve Board presidents.

The Prime Rate

The *prime rate* is a third type of interest rate (see Fig. 6-2). It is defined as the rate that major banks charge their most important customers. The prime rate is of concern primarily to small and medium-size businesses that have loans pegged to the prime rate. It also affects consumers who have home equity loans, credit card, or other installment loans pegged to the prime rate. The prime rate is adjusted after both the federal funds rate and often the discount rate have been adjusted. The prime rate is considered less important than the federal funds rate, because any change in this rate usually occurs after the discount rate has been cut or raised.

The Federal Reserve Board's Power

Some analysts argue that the Fed has lost some of its influence. It is important to address this issue briefly. One important reason relates to the rapidly growing globalization of financial markets. The movement of foreign interest rates, particularly the prime economic and financial powers of Japan and Germany, could lessen the influence of the Fed's actions on foreign interest rates. The need to fund our U.S. budget deficit through auctioning U.S. Treasury securities, particularly to foreign investors, can affect long-term U.S. interest rates despite actions taken by the Fed to control short-term interest rates. The difficulties in coordinating world interest rates, particularly among the largest industrial powers, is often cause for differences of opinion concerning the level of a particular country's interest rates. As an example, if the United States wants Germany to lower its interest rates to encourage exports to that country, the German monetary authorities may make it quite clear that they will not lower their interest rates because of their own concern for inflation. The result could mean that the United States, through the Fed, may have to lower its interest rates to encourage more loans for purchasing U.S. goods.

The financial markets influence long-term rates based on expectations about inflation and the condition of the U.S. economy. While the Fed may have lost some power because of the growth of the international financial markets and the economic strength of Japan and Germany, it can cause serious problems in the U.S. economy and to the inflation rate. If the Fed makes the wrong judgments about the condition of the U.S. economy and pushes up interest rates when they should be kept at current levels, it is possible that the Fed could push the U.S. economy into recession. If, on the other hand, in order to stimulate the U.S. economy out of recession, it pushes interest rates down too far, too fast, it could cause inflation to rise, which would thwart the attempt of the U.S. economy to recover. The differences of opinion regarding how to coordinate interest rates is full of controversy. But most important, no matter what the disagreement is in international circles, the Federal Reserve Board is a major player.

Conclusion

The key Federal Reserve Board indicator the reader should follow in order to understand the movement of interest rates, particularly short-term interest rates, is the federal funds rate, because it is an indicator of the Federal Reserve Board's policy moves. It is the most visually active policy indicator among the Federal Reserve Board's tools to encourage economic growth or moderate inflation, because it changes daily. Any action taken by the Federal Reserve Board can be easily seen after several days by watching the movement of the federal funds rate. If the Federal Reserve Board decides to slow down the economy and reduce inflation, it will increase the federal funds rate by decreasing the money supply and thereby the reserves within the banking system. As we have pointed out, there is always enormous guesswork as to when or if the Federal Reserve Board will lower the federal funds rate. Since the reader is watching the same indicators as the Fed, both economic and inflation, it is entirely possible to see the movement of the federal funds rate. In Chap. 11 we will discuss precisely where to find the federal funds rate within the four financial publications we use to track the indicators that determine interest rates.

7

Interest Rates and Fiscal Factors

The Federal Budget Deficit

The federal budget deficit is an important factor in the movement of interest rates. The size of the deficit represents a long line of zeros. In 1980 the deficit was $74 billion. By 1986 it had risen to $221 billion, then began to fall to as low as $149 billion in 1987, only to increase again to $175 billion in 1990 and $269 billion in 1991. Estimates for fiscal year 1992 hover around $400 billion, a record high. Add all these numbers up and one has an accumulated federal deficit through 1991 of $2 trillion. The financial markets believe, for the most part, that unless the deficit is reduced, the U.S. Treasury will have to continue borrowing to fund the deficit. The borrowing of funds will cause interest rates to rise because the United States is dependent on major investors from both domestic and foreign institutions and companies to purchase U.S. securities that fund the deficit.

The U.S. Treasury auctions Treasury bills, notes, and bonds throughout the year. The most important auction is the quarterly issuance of 3-, 10-, and 30-year notes and bonds. The amount of Treasuries available for purchase is determined by the U.S. Treasury. For the 3-, 10-, and 30-year Treasuries, the amount per auction can be as high as $30 billion or more. Because of these large amounts of Treasuries to be auctioned, the bond market becomes extremely nervous as to whether there will be enough buyers. The result is that yields tend to rise as the date of the auction approaches. The question is how high yields will have to rise in order to induce investors, both foreign and domestic, to purchase the Treasury securities. If these auctions are successful in that all or most of the securities are sold, interest rates will generally decline. However, if the auction goes poorly in that major investors in governmental securities show reluctance to purchase the issues, then yields will rise until they are high enough to coax investors to purchase them. So long as the U.S. budget deficit remains, Treasury securities will have to be sold, with the result that these large amounts of deficit funding will cause consternation in the financial markets. Should the deficit become even larger, thereby leading to even larger amounts of Treasuries to be auctioned, then interest rates will remain high or rise even higher. Many analysts believe that the need to purchase U.S. Treasuries will curb investment spending and over a number of years lead to less capital formation to expand businesses and lower economic growth in the United States as well as in other parts of the world.

The enormous cost of servicing the national deficit or federal debt reduces the overall standard of living, as less money is available for other public economic and social needs. The massive monies absolutely needed to build new highways, schools, and resource recovery plants; repair existing highways, roads, and bridges as well as schools; and expand seaports and airports are essential for long-term economic growth. The less capital is available to build this infrastructure, the less able the United States will be to compete with other countries. If one cannot transport goods and products from one city or state to another along highways that are in excellent condition, or if U.S. ports are not expanded or improved to enable them to continue exporting U.S. goods to foreign countries and receiving foreign goods, then U.S. economic growth will be restricted over time. Because of the deficit, the federal government does not have the funds to spend on these essential projects. As more debt is taken on by the federal government, the deficit continues to widen. This puts pressure on interest rates to rise in order to induce investors to purchase U.S. securities, which in turn increases the debt service that the U.S. government must pay to debt holders. The significance of the rise in U.S. interest rates is that it is symptomatic of an effort by the U.S. government to compete with the interest rates on the bonds of foreign countries. In other words, investors may prefer the higher rates of German bonds to those of U.S. bonds. One of the issues affecting interest rates is the need to rebuild the infrastructure of Eastern Europe compared to the need to fund the U.S. budget deficit at a time when capital is short. This creates competitive pressures—which country will be able to obtain the greatest percentage of the capital it needs through investors' purchases of its interest-rate-bearing securities?

There is considerable controversy over whether the U.S. budget deficit actually affects interest rates. One argument states that there is no apparent statistical correlation between interest rates and the U.S. budget deficit. Those who argue along this line believe that statistical evidence does not reveal any observed support that U.S. budget deficits are associated in some way with high real interest rates (remember, to determine real rate of interest, one subtracts the rate of inflation as expressed by the consumer price index from the then-current yield). For example, if a U.S. Treasury 30-year bond has a current yield or coupon interest rate of 9.00%, the 9.00% is called the nominal rate of interest or the current yield plus inflation. If one subtracts the current U.S. rate of inflation—say, 4.5%—from the 9.00% yield, then the remaining number is 4.5% or the real rate of interest.

Another argument in support of the lack of relevance of interest rates to the U.S. budget deficit says that the deficit is not important when viewed as a percentage of the U.S. gross national product.

Still others, including Nobel Laureate Milton Friedman, argue that it is not the U.S. budget that is the problem, but excessive governmental spending and overly high taxes. Cut them both, he says, and the deficit will shrink. Friedman also argues that the markets have become tenacious in believing that a continued U.S. budget deficit will reduce our standard of living because it will stunt U.S. economic growth.

Whatever the arguments against the lack of correlation between high interest rates and the U.S. budget deficit, the financial markets clearly believe that interest rates react to it. Each and every year, the financial markets thrive on the political machinations of arriving at a budget agreement. Interest rates or yields react to each event in the development of a U.S. budget.

The U.S. Budget

President Bush's Budget Director, Richard Darman, stated in the introduction to the President's budget proposal to Congress in 1990 that "The typeface is small, the text is tedious, and tables are seemingly endless. The sheer size of the budget makes it seem like a monster. It contains almost 190,000 accounts. At a rate of one per minute, eight hours per day, it would take over a year to reflect upon these."* Yet the importance of the budget cannot be denied.

The U.S. budget represents the social, economic, and financial priorities of the nation or, as one federal budget message stated, it is "an implicit statement of values and expectations of the future."† Missions include education, military, social welfare, and infrastructure. What missions the na-

---

*"Darman Conducts a Tour of Wonderland: The Federal Budget," *The New York Times,* January 27, 1990, p. 12. Copyright © 1990 by The New York Times Company. Reprinted by permission.

†Ibid.

tion chooses to accomplish, how it decides to accomplish them, and who will pay for them are still critical issues. These missions are political in that they represent the views of the President of the United States. The process of obtaining agreement between the White House and Congress about these missions is invariably reflected in the financial markets by the rise and fall of interest rates. That rise and fall is a response to who will pay for these missions in the future—foreigners or U.S. citizens—and what effect the cost of these missions will have on our cost of living, inflation, and U.S. economic growth.

To provide an idea of how enormous the U.S. budget actually is, let us take a look at a prior budget—the fiscal 1991 budget. The actual price tag for the fiscal 1991 budget outlays was $1.3 trillion. The percentage breakdown was as follows: Military programs already in the works accounted for 20.7%, social security and medicare payments 28.2%, and interest expense 14.7%. So far, 63.6% of the total budget was taken up by mandated expenditures. Next, federal pensions accounted for 12.9%. So far, 76.5% of the budget was already spoken for. The remaining 23.5% was spread among health care, education, transportation, commerce and housing credits, international affairs, the National Aeronautics and Space Administration, science and technology, natural resources, energy, agriculture, and veterans benefits.

The way out is tough going. The cost of health care has risen dramatically, from 6% to 12% of gross domestic product, over the past 25 years. There are increasing claims on mandatory programs. For example, transfer payments to individuals under health and social welfare programs plus social security payments comprised about 25% of the budget during President John Kennedy's time and now represent about 40%. In fact, mandatory programs established by Congress plus net interest expenditures that are paid to the holders of U.S. Treasury securities account for more than 63% of the total budget. Mandatory programs such as social service programs means that the federal government stipulates what dollar share states must pay to fund these programs. As less and less federal money is made available, more and more of the burden of providing the dollars falls on the states. The federal government determines the standards for the programs but not the funds. Therefore the states must pay a far larger share to hire staff and purchase equipment in order to meet federal requirements. The contingent risks of federal credit programs and government-sponsored enterprises gone haywire—such as the savings and loan scandal, which has cost taxpayers several hundreds of millions of dollars over the past few years—are just a few of the major cost problems that increase the U.S. budget beyond providing monies for helping the poor and needy or providing monies for interstate highway systems or federal prisons.

What special events will increase or decrease our budget deficit, aside from constant increases in necessary expenditures such as in health care? These events might include a deeper-than-expected recession that increases transfer benefit payments to increasing numbers of the unemployed; natural disasters such as floods or crop failures, which require federal emergency help; engaging in military acts; major financial disaster; increased foreign aid to other countries facing natural disasters; lack of congressional willpower to reduce spending while still protecting the social net and improving educational opportunities. Who can tell what will happen in an ever-changing world full of uncertainties?

The relationship between the states and the federal government is a constant strain on the costs of providing services. As the federal government tries to reduce its budget deficit, more of the costs of social and health care programs are shifted to the states. The reduction of federal aid plus the skyrocketing costs of health care and social welfare that occurred during the 1980s directly increased the costs of running state, county, and local governments. So long as state and local revenues were rising during economic expansion, the costs of these programs could be met. But once a slowdown in economic growth occurred, and worse, recession hit, revenues dried up at a time when expenditures kept growing at a far faster pace. Again, the sharp rise in medical care, social welfare, and public safety costs, and the enormous cost of building infrastructure to provide the central nervous system for economic growth, require an understanding between the federal government and its states as to who will pay for these rising costs.

What role the United States takes in understanding its place in the arena of world markets and at the same time addressing domestic concerns will no doubt be reflected in how we deal with the U.S. budget. The financial markets still believe that in order to compete in global economies, the U.S. budget deficit must be reduced. That major concern is often reflected in the rise and fall of interest rates during the specific times leading up to the adoption of a final U.S. budget, from the initial presentation of the President's budget to Congress on April 15 to its final adoption on October 15. The result of the final resolution of that particular year's budget can determine the direction of interest rates.

The relationship between the attempt of Congress and the administration to obtain a workable solution to the U.S. budget is closely watched by the Federal Reserve Board. The Federal Reserve Board takes the position that the U.S. budget deficit must be reduced to encourage more savings and therefore more investment potential. The level of interest rates is reflected in the concern of the Federal Reserve Board to see a reduction in the U.S. budget deficit. Interest rates rise during times when there is conflict between Congress and the administration over the various programs and how much to cut. Interests rates fall if a credible budget is ultimately adopted.

The major foreign powers, such as Japan and Germany, have continued to suggest that the United States reduce its budget deficit. When these major industrial countries determine that a budget solution will not reduce the deficit, they often imply that less foreign investment will be forthcoming. In other words, they may not purchase as much in U.S. Treasury securities as they did in prior years. If the U.S. financial markets believe that the threat is real, interest rates will rise. Another issue that raises or lowers interest rates is the publication of the semiannual and annual federal deficit figures. For example, if the deficit for the current fiscal year is nearing all-time highs, interest rates will rise because the issuance of more U.S. Treasury securities will be required to fund the deficit.

When the U.S. budget is finally published, it includes a set of economic and inflation assumptions regarding the growth of the gross domestic product, unemployment, the consumer price index, personal income, and both the 3-month Treasury bill and the 30-year Treasury bond. The financial markets make judgments as to whether these forecasts are realistic or not. Often differences of opinion result between Congress and the administration. The result is that the financial markets reflect their agreement or dissatisfaction with these forecasts by pushing interest rates up or down.

Another great controversy is what to do with "Cold War" money. If military costs are indeed reduced over time, there are a host of major areas in which to spend the money, the least of which is to reduce the budget deficit, which would be an important factor in keeping interest rates from rising. Some of the programs include building housing for low- and moderate-income families; increasing spending on education; repairing roads, bridges, and water and sewer systems; and cleaning up radioactive and toxic wastes.

The Tax Issue

As the federal government tries to reduce the U.S. budget deficit by reducing federal monies that fund the programs they create, the states are put into the position of having to make up the difference. As the states try to do this, they turn to counties, cities, and towns to provide their fair share toward social welfare and health services, including funds for rebuilding and expanding infrastructure. However, as we have pointed out, the costs of many of these services have begun to far outstrip the ability to raise revenues. As long as the economy is growing at a reasonable rate, it will provide increases in personal income receipts, corporate tax receipts, and sales tax receipts. The problems occur when a long-term economic slowdown hits the nation, and even worse, a recession. During these particu-larly difficult times, tax receipts decline as people worrying about their jobs spend less. The result is that states, counties, and local governments are forced to increase tax rates to pay for programs. Often programs are mandated by the federal government but do not provide any federal dol-lars. That is the responsibility of the states. Since other forms of local gov-ernment exist at the behest of the state, the states turn to them to help out.

The result of this increase of local tax rates is to slow down the growth of the U.S. economy, because consumers have less to spend. If they have less to spend, then inflation will be kept at moderate levels, which in turn will keep interest rates from rising.

8

Interest Rates and Global Factors: The Trade Deficit

Global Issues

Five key issues form the environment within which interest rates play a significant role. No longer are U.S. economic, inflation, political, and monetary factors the only important criteria that affect the movement of U.S. interest rates. Economic and monetary factors that relate to Germany and Japan as well as other countries are equally important to the movement of U.S. interest rates. And, more important, the movement of their interest rates affects U.S. interest rates. If one nation attempts to stop inflation by raising interest rates, the effect of that nation's move can move U.S. interest rates upward. The five global issues highlighted below establish the context in which the reader can begin to understand that gaining a perspective on the global interest rate environment is intriguingly important in understanding the movement of U.S. interest rates.

The first issue is international commercial competition. Competition among nations to sell their products and services to major markets worldwide continues today as it has over the centuries. The United States no longer dominates world markets. Major trading partners today include Japan and Germany as well as the newly industrialized economies of the Far East, such as Taiwan, Hong Kong, Singapore, and South Korea. Attempts to segment the world into supranational economic markets include the European Economic Community, the Eastern Europe market, the Asian or Pacific Rim markets, and the Canada-United States-Mexico market. The interplay among these regions, along with the Caribbean and

South America, is in a constant state of political and economic change. The problems of these economies, inflationary environments, monetary activities, and the political machinations of these nations can affect the movement of U.S. interest rates.

The second issue concerns the surging growth of integrated financial communications. Financial market centers continue to expand globally. Not only are the United States, Japan, and England obvious financial centers, but also Germany, Spain, and other countries are being tied together by sophisticated communications networks. In fact, a financial services company need not even be located in these specific financial centers. So long as the company has the computer systems and communication networks, a company could be located almost anywhere.

The third issue stipulates that inflation and growth indicators of foreign economies are equally important as U.S. inflation economic indicators. No longer is U.S. economic policy the only guide to understanding the movement of U.S. interest rates. The changes and gyrations of the German and Japanese economies and financial markets have important influences on U.S. interest rates. Capital flows, exchange rates, inflationary concerns, and trade balances affect the nature of U.S. interest rates.

The fourth issue concerns the variety of parts and materials that make up one product manufactured in one country. Vacuum cleaners, stereo equipment, cars, clothes, and hundreds of other products are not made just from parts originating in the country in which the product is produced. Products are made from parts that come from many different countries. This integration of parts into one product is changing trade patterns and economies worldwide. "Made in the U.S.A." is less common today because of the integration of multinational parts into one product. Japan's expansion of automobile plants in the United States requires not only U.S. parts but also Japanese parts.

Lastly, the need for industrialized countries to meet in order to solve problems concerning the disparity of worldwide interest rates is a constant concern as each of these countries attempts to deal with changes in their economies. These concerns are addressed within the Group of Seven countries made up of the United States, Japan, Great Britain, Canada, Germany, Italy, and France. The decisions of this group will affect U.S. interest rates. As the supranational economic centers evolve, perhaps instead of the Group of Seven, we will have the Supra-Group of Five: the European Economic Community, Asia, U.S.-Canada-Mexico, the Caribbean, and South America.

These global issues are important in understanding that U.S. interest rates react to international events just as readily as they react to domestic events. Factors related to the U.S. economy, including both inflation and the budget deficit, also determine how other industrialized countries will react. How they react to both their own and to outside economic, inflationary, and fiscal problems will often determine the movement of U.S. interest rates. The result of this confluence of integration among the industrialized nations has lead to a U.S. trade deficit. Many times the expansion or narrowing of the U.S. trade deficit will push U.S. interest rates one way or another.

The U.S. Trade Deficit

A trade deficit is actually an imbalance of payments between countries. The balance of payments is a systematic record of one country's receipts from, or payments to, other countries. The balance of payments comprises the current account in addition to both long-term and short-term capital flows (investments with maturities more or less than 1 year). The current account, the broadest measure of U.S. trade, includes both trade in goods and services as well as specific financial transfers. It reflects not only the exporting of goods and services to foreign countries but also the amount of money the United States must raise abroad, mainly by borrowing from foreign investors, to finance its trade with other countries. Ideally, the payments account means that countries have to balance their respective books between each other, similar to balancing a checkbook. The current account balance reflects the investment made in this country by foreign countries. These investments include the purchase of U.S. securities or real estate, and participation or ownership in U.S. companies. The difference between what foreign companies invest and what the U.S. invests is called *net investment*. For many years, foreign countries have invested more in the United States than the United States has invested in foreign countries. That difference represents the net investment. That foreign investment has helped in financing the U.S. trade deficit.

The key components of the current account are goods and services. There are two parts to goods and services. First is the U.S. merchandise trade deficit, composed of tangible items such as foodstuffs, manufactured goods, and raw materials. Second is the service trade deficit, which includes intangibles such as interest on dividends, technology transfer, professional services such as insurance and financial. Trade in services also includes earnings of U.S. companies on overseas investments. A service deficit means that foreigners are earning more on their investments here than American investors are earning in foreign countries. One other way to look at the U.S. trade deficit is to view it as the relationship between U.S. exports to foreign countries and foreign imports to the United States. The more the United States exports and the less it imports, the narrower the U.S. trade deficit becomes. A key component is the cost of oil. If oil rises in price, it can represent a major part of imports.

So long as the U.S. sustains a trade deficit, it will be a detriment to long-term U.S. economic growth. The major risk for obtaining foreign investment in U.S. assets or paying the interest or dividends on these investments is that the United States could be subject to the business slumps of its foreign creditors or a major financial crisis of a foreign banking institution. As the world changes and needs enormous amounts of capital to rebuild the infrastructure of many countries, the United States will be in a constant competitive battle to obtain that capital to fund its own budget deficit. The effect on U.S. interest rates may be considerable. If other foreign countries raise their rates to attract capital, the United States will have to raise its interest rates to compete for the same capital.

There is controversy about both the definition of the U.S. trade deficit and the exact effects of the deficit on the U.S. economy and therefore on interest rates. One argument suggests that the trade deficit could have been avoided if the United States had maintained a high savings rate, as Japan does. If the U.S. savings rate had been higher, the country would not have had to depend on foreign investment in U.S. assets to fund the U.S. budget deficit. If the United States continues to sustain a trade deficit with foreign countries, the dollar will have to fall lower against foreign currencies so that we can export our goods at cheaper prices to foreign markets. However, the lower the dollar falls, the more potential there is for inflation.

Another argument maintains that the United States has to reduce its budget deficit so as not to depend on foreign investments to fund that deficit. Still another argument is based on how one determines the cost of investments in the United States and foreign countries. The U.S. Bureau of Economic Analysis is currently determining investments based on market value rather than costs. If costs are used instead, the numbers change dramatically. The cost of manufacturing a product is far different from what it will be sold for because the market value includes the profit based on the demand for that product. The point is that the value of foreign investments in the United States has increased so much that it is far above that of U.S. investments in foreign countries. The result is that the United States has become a net debtor nation. For example, the Bureau of Economic Analysis is adjusting the value of U.S. gold held in this country. The value is currently based on book value, which has been $42 an ounce. Just by revaluing gold to $400 an ounce, one would add about $90 billion to the value of U.S. holdings. Economists point out that since the United States made investments in foreign countries 30 years ago, the true value of those investments is many times what they are now booked at. Analysts showed that a $1 million investment in Germany in 1961 would be worth about

$2.3 billion in today's dollars because of the depreciation of the dollar. Had inflation averaged about 2% a year for the last 30 years, the investment would total more than $4 billion.* Disagreement with this argument comes from the fact that since the United States still borrows from abroad, it will still create a trade deficit.

Narrowing the U.S. trade deficit is necessary to reinvigorate the long-term growth of the U.S. trade economy. Every time the size of the U.S. trade deficit is reported, the movement of U.S. interest rates is affected. In general, the wider the U.S. trade deficit, the greater is the potential for interest rates to rise. The narrower the U.S. trade deficit, the greater is the potential for interest rates to decline. To put it another way, a wider deficit usually means that the dollar must be lowered by bringing down interest rates.

Origins of the
U.S. Trade Deficit

The most recent U.S. trade deficit developed because of complacency and the general neglect of foreign markets by U.S. producers in the 1960s and 1970s. During those decades, domestic sales were large and growing. Americans had not yet developed a strong desire for foreign goods. Foreign competition was largely ignored. However, the Japanese and Europeans recognized the tremendous growth of the U.S. economy after World War II. Clearly, the potential for an expanding U.S. market encouraged many countries to consider increasing their market share in the United States. The Japanese, the Europeans, and later the newly industrialized countries of the Far East (Taiwan, Singapore, Hong Kong, and South Korea) began to develop products specifically for American consumers. These products, especially those involved in the technological revolution in chips, computers, and electronics, were manufactured at lower costs using a disciplined and less expensive labor force. Aggressive marketing based on the lower costs of their products, technological innovation, and the gadget consciousness of the American public began to create an enormous flow of these goods into U.S. markets, especially from the early 1980s on, when the U.S. economy was surging as a result of consumer demand. The substantial increase of the dollar, which made our products more expensive than foreign products, particularly during the early 1980s, caused a tremendous inflow of these goods. By the mid-1980s, the dollar

---

*Chuck Freadhof, "World Economy: Presto! U.S. Once Again a Creditor Nation," *Investor's Daily*, June 8, 1991, back page.

had risen by 70% and made imports so cheap that 20% of all goods sold in the United States came from abroad. The result was that the United States imported more goods than it exported. And that was the beginning of the U.S. trade deficit. In addition, as the dollar fell, brought on by international policy coordination, the cost of buying U.S. real estate and owning U.S. companies became lower. The result was an enormous amount of foreign participation in the U.S. economy. The more we imported, the wider the trade deficit grew and the less competitive American products became. As Americans spent more and more on these foreign products because they were cheaper and of better quality than U.S. products, they saved less. Because they saved less, fewer funds were available to pay for the U.S. trade deficit. The result was the interest rates rose to compete for foreign money or to induce foreign investors to pay for our U.S. trade deficit.

During the 1980s, the trade deficit was a measure of jobs, wages, and profits that foreign industries had won at the expense of U.S. manufacturers. Foreign companies increased both market share and profits, thus expanding their economies while limiting the growth of the U.S. economy. As the value of the dollar rose from 1980 through early 1985, it pushed up the prices of U.S. exports and reduced the prices of foreign imports. As imports surged, the U.S. merchandise trade deficit rose from $36.4 billion in 1980 to $148.5 billion in 1985 to $152.1 billion in 1987, the peak year of the 1980s.

When the dollar declines, as it did in the middle 1980s, U.S. manufacturers began to reverse the process. Now U.S. goods were becoming more competitive with foreign goods in terms of price. The result was that U.S. manufacturers began to export more than they were importing, and so the U.S. trade deficit began to narrow. U.S. businesses were encouraged to increase their efforts to sell overseas and in some cases to cut their prices to create market share, which led to a growth in demand for their products and an increase in export volume.

The continued widening of the U.S. trade deficit through most of the 1980s contributed to the increased need for the United States to attract foreign capital to finance its current account, which in turn forced the United States even further into debt. That debt continues to be financed by foreign purchases of U.S. securities at rates high enough to ensure that there is foreign participation. The increased debt means that the United States pays substantial amounts of interest to foreign investors, which detracts from more essential domestic expenditures expressed in the U.S. budget. For example, in the 1991 U.S. budget, interest alone represented 15% of total federal expenditures.

Even when the U.S. dollar declined, foreign producers retained their market share, even though many U.S. products were in fact cheaper than foreign goods for long periods of time. One of the prime reasons that the U.S. trade deficit was sustained during the mid-1980s, in addition to the maintaining of market share, was that most raw materials are priced in dollars. In Japan, a 70% decline in the dollar means a 70% decline in the cost of oil, iron ore, chemicals, and feedstocks, which substantially offsets the initial effects of a higher exchange rate. In other words, capital costs in Japan and Germany are far lower than in the United States. Therefore Japan, for example, can shave profit margins to hold the line on prices and still make an acceptable return. When the dollar was expensive, many foreign producers did not pass along the full savings to U.S. customers. These countries thus had a substantial cushion to absorb anticipated price increases as the dollar became cheaper. Ultimately, as the dollar declined over time, the U.S. trade deficit began to narrow. As the dollar became cheaper, American goods became less expensive on a global basis and were able to compete with foreign goods. The Federal Reserve Board had to keep a close watch of the effects of the dollar, not only on the U.S. trade deficit but also on inflation and therefore interest rates.

The relationship between the growth or slowdown of global economies and trade is one of the most important points of focus for financial market participants. For example, David M. Jones, a veteran "Fed watcher" and Chief Economist at Aubrey G. Lamston & Co., noted that "when I started 17 years ago, I'd spend 80 percent of my time worrying about the Fed, worrying about domestic inflation, domestic capacity. Now, I spend 80 percent of my time worrying about the foreign side—or at least how the foreign side affects the domestic side."* Lyle Gramley, the former chief economic forecaster for the Federal Reserve Board and now Chief Economist for the Mortgage Bankers Association, said that at that time "I considered the international division as a kind of nuisance. The direct link from interest rates abroad to interest rates in the U.S. to the outlook for the U.S. economy—I never had to deal with that intellectually before. Whoever thought that developments in West Germany were going to be a very important influence on interest rates in the U.S.? Maybe somebody did. It wasn't me."†

As an example of the dollar amount of the U.S. trade deficit, it peaked at $152.1 billion in 1987 and declined to $101.7 in 1990, primarily because U.S. manufacturers had become much more competitive as the dollar declined.

---

*David Jones, quoted by David Wessel and Constance Mitchell, in "Limited Leverage: Fed Has Lost Much of Its Power to Sway U.S. Interest Rates," *The Wall Street Journal*, March 12, 1990, p. A12. Reprinted by permission of *The Wall Street Journal*, © 1990 Dow Jones & Company, Inc. All rights reserved worldwide.

†Lyle Gramley, quoted in ibid.

Furthermore, not only did prices decline, the quality of the products improved. The trade deficit in the mid-1980s was one of the most important factors influencing interest rates. Today, keeping track of the U.S. trade deficit is still important, but it must be viewed on a more equal basis with other domestic and global factors. The trade deficit will remain important as long as the United States has to finance its current trade deficit and as long as it has to compete with other countries in terms of price and quality of goods and services. As the world economies continue to restructure into supranational economic markets, the effect of a changing U.S. trade deficit may widen or narrow depending on what changes may occur.

A major change that has been taking place relates to the location of plants in other countries to reduce labor costs. When the dollar declined dramatically in the late 1980s, many foreign countries built plants in the United States to take advantage of a large unemployed pool of manufacturing labor and the need to continue supplying products to the U.S. market. Today, many countries are building plants not only in the United States but also in other countries where labor is cheaper. If the Japanese locate some of their electronic equipment plants in Thailand, it will affect the U.S. trade deficit. According to Kevin L. Kearns, writing in *The Wall Street Journal*, the United States imported $7 million of consumer electronics equipment in 1988 from Thailand. By 1990, that figure had grown to $310 million.* The newly industrialized nations of the Far East saw their trade surpluses grow enormously and contribute to the U.S. trade deficit. The cheaper labor costs and disciplined workers produced far less expensive products including computers, stereo equipment, automobiles, vacuum cleaners, and many other products which added to the U.S. deficit. The reduced labor costs from the relocation of production facilities to the newly industrialized countries of the Far East and others is an important consideration in understanding structural changes in the composition of the U.S. trade deficit. At the same time, interest rates will react to these changes as it affects inflation, the value of the dollar, the growth of the U.S. economy, and ultimately our ability to compete with foreign products.

Interest Rates and the U.S. Trade Deficit

Interest rates may react to the trade deficit figures reported each month. For example, when the dollar declines, and the United States is competing more favorably with other countries, the specter of inflation arises as U.S.

---

*Kevin L. Kearns, "Behind Those Shrinking Trade Deficit Numbers," *The Wall Street Journal*, July 25, 1991, p. A9.

products become cheaper. Interest rates may therefore rise due to inflationary pressures. Or, to put in another way, if the dollar were to rise again to a point where it would make American products less competitive and the price of oil rises as well, inflation would rise, our trade deficit would widen, and interest rates would rise. As the U.S. trade deficit increases, it tends to reduce the value of the dollar against foreign currencies, making other countries' products more expensive and ours less expensive or more competitive. Once we become more competitive by increasing the demand for U.S. products because they are better made and less expensive, more jobs will result and the U.S. economy will grow. However, if the U.S. economy grows too fast, thereby producing inflation, then interest rates will rise. Creating competitive markets to expand all economies while at the same time maintaining a moderate level of inflation requires a balancing act. Interest rates rise or fall as the financial markets determine what is important about the figures reported about the U.S. trade deficit.

When the United States is in recession, the trade deficit will narrow so long as the United States imports decline, which normally results in lower interest rates. However, the trade deficit can widen even during a recession if the United States does not export its merchandise because foreign economies may be reacting to slowdowns of their own, thus reducing demand for U.S. goods and services. As the U.S. economy begins to recover, the possibility of the trade deficit widening begins to increase as U.S. demand picks up. As demand begins to increase, the potential for inflation arises, which will eventually push up interest rates. Of equal importance, as exports grow and ultimately increase at a faster rate than imports, the trade deficit will narrow. The United States is the second-leading exporter behind Germany. Therefore the relationship between imports and exports is critical in understanding the U.S. trade deficit. The nuances and changes in the U.S. trade deficit are important to follow, because the recognition of a widening of the U.S. trade deficit by the financial markets will increase pressure on U.S. interest rates to rise. Just as important, as the U.S. trade deficit narrows, it will help decrease interest rates. The delicate balancing act between the growth and slowdown of foreign economies, which affects the demand for U.S. products, is another key component in understanding the U.S. trade deficit and its possible effect on interest rates. Of equal importance is the fickle nature of consumers of any country's products. Sometimes price is important, and sometimes quality is important. These attitudes by consumers of all countries form part of the equation of the U.S. trade deficit. Emphasis on quality plus price competitiveness continues to be the philosophy of U.S. manufacturers. The narrowing and widening of the U.S. trade deficit and its implications for inflation are an important factor in moving interest rates up or down.

As the reader reviews each month's changes in the U.S. trade deficit as reported by the newspapers, it is important to remember once again that one month does not make a trend. More important is to watch for the quarterly figures on the U.S. trade deficit for the beginnings of a trend. The reader should also link the condition of the U.S. economy and interest rates to possible changes in the U.S. trade deficit. As you review the various publications, watch for the percentage of exports versus imports in order to understand the relationship between economic growth and demand in the United States versus the same in foreign countries. This relationship will affect the rise and fall of interest rates, as we have pointed out throughout this chapter.

9

Interest Rates and Global Factors: The Dollar, Foreign Interest Rates, and International Policy Coordination

The relationships among the dollar, foreign interest rates, and policy coordination are important in understanding the movement of U.S. interest rates. First let us look at the dollar. The movement of the U.S. dollar against foreign currencies affects the movement of interest rates. If U.S. interest rates rise, the dollar rises. If the dollar rises, it makes American products more expensive and less competitive against foreign products. If U.S. interest rates fall, the dollar usually falls. The falling dollar creates two possible effects. American products become cheaper, but the potential for inflation also increases. A careful balancing act is required to lower the dollar without increasing inflation, which would push interest rates up.

A Brief History of the Dollar in the 1980s

From 1980 to early 1985, the dollar's value against other key currencies such as the West German mark and the Japanese yen rose substantially because U.S. interest rates were at historic highs. Depending on how one measures the rise, it ranged between 60% and 100%. By the time the rise of the dollar had peaked in February 1985, it had become overvalued in the view of most international economists by at least 40%. The result was to seriously impinge on the competitiveness of U.S. products with those of other nations.

American goods were simply priced out of world markets. As the dollar rose, the U.S. trade deficit began to widen, reaching a peak in 1987 of $152.1 billion. As the United States began to lose competitiveness, Americans began to import more products. The result was the loss of U.S. jobs at the same time as many U.S. companies were shifting plant locations to countries where labor was cheaper and major world markets were closer.

Between 1980 and 1983, the United States changed from the world's largest creditor to the world's largest debtor. As the need to fund the trade and budget deficits, called the "twin deficits," rose, the United States was forced to sell U.S. securities. The effect caused interest rates to rise to ensure that foreign investors would purchase these securities over non-dollar-denominated securities. As U.S. prices rose because the dollar was more expensive, U.S. manufacturers continued to lose jobs to foreign competitors.

By the mid-1980s, concerted American resistance to the high value of the dollar began to emerge. A need to reduce the value of the dollar to thwart the decline of U.S. manufacturing and balance relationships with American trading partners was emerging, particularly as it affected the Group of Seven industrialized countries, which was made up of the United States, Canada, France, Great Britain, Italy, West Germany, and Japan.

The Group of Seven—particularly Japan and West Germany, two of the strongest economies in the industrialized West—was also concerned that a strong dollar would create major problems for the U.S. economy. Job loss would continue, the U.S. economy would weaken, and as a result their largest export market would be less receptive to their products. The 45% rise in the dollar between 1980 and 1985 caused a loss of nearly 2 million U.S. jobs, most of them in manufacturing. A congressional study pointed out that the job loss was 1.5 million in the manufacturing sector and 500,000 in services and agriculture. As these concerns arose among the trading partners, policy coordination became one of the most important factors influencing interest rates as the Group of Seven attempted to deal with the high values of both the dollar and interest rates.

Some Factors That Boost the Dollar

First, improvement in the U.S. economy normally lifts the value of the dollar because foreign investors become more willing to invest in a United

States with a strong economy. Second, so long as inflation remains relatively modest and the U.S. economy grows, the dollar will continue to rise. Third, increases in oil prices create problems in the U.S. current trade accounts with both Japan and Germany, because oil is bought in dollars ("petrodollars"). Since these economies depend on oil to fuel their economies, the rise in the dollar increases the cost of purchasing oil in dollars, which in turn hurts their economies. Lastly, any increase in geopolitical tensions, particularly as they relate to the oil reserves of the Middle East, forces the dollar higher because the dollar is considered a safe haven during times of international crises.

The Factors That Make the Dollar Decline

Several important effects can bring down the value of the dollar. First, when the U.S. economy is in recession, the Federal Reserve Board lowers the federal funds rate and often the discount rate, to drive down short-term interest rates in an effort to stimulate the economy and reduce the value of the dollar against foreign currencies. Second, key U.S. and foreign governmental and financial leaders may "talk down" the value of the dollar when the U.S. economy is in a slump in order to increase U.S. manufacturers' competitiveness in foreign markets. For example, if the chair of the Federal Reserve Board testifies that because of the weakened U.S. economy, the Fed is considering lower interest rates, the dollar will move lower because lower interest rates make the dollar less competitive with other currencies. Third, pressures are brought on the U.S. government by American exporters to reduce the value of the dollar so that their products will be competitive in price with foreign products. Lastly, as the Japanese and German economies continued to grow, they began to raise interest rates to keep the attending inflation in check and their money growth from increasing too fast. As their interest rates rose, that increased the value of their currencies against the dollar, which declined.

What Happens When the Dollar Falls?

As the dollar falls, U.S. products become cheaper and more competitive with foreign products that are now more expensive than American products. Although the fall in the dollar allows U.S. manufacturers to compete more successfully, it also creates another problem. A falling dollar often leads to inflation, which causes U.S. interest rates to rise. However, if Americans feel that foreign products such as Japanese cars or stereos are of higher quality (they last longer with far fewer repairs and are competitively priced), they will keep buying foreign goods even if their prices rise. Rising inflation means that interest rates will also rise. The Federal Reserve Board is responsible for tightening the reins or restricting the supply of money to stop inflation, even if that means a slowdown in the U.S. economy. If the U.S. economy does slow down, the Federal Reserve Board will then loosen the reins and inject more money into the banking system.

A falling dollar can also create problems for other countries. Their exports, which are often priced in dollars, become less competitive. The result may be that these countries find themselves with less hard Western currency with which to pay their own foreign debts. If the dollar falls or is devalued, it also hurts industries that depend on a powerful currency to buy inexpensive parts and to stock their shelves with inexpensive finished goods such as electronics and computer equipment. If the dollar falls far enough, foreign investors are less attracted to U.S. securities such as U.S. Treasury bills, notes, and bonds. If the demand for U.S. securities lessens, this puts pressure on interest rates to rise high enough to ensure that foreign investors will continue to invest in U.S. securities.

International cooperation is an important element in trying to adjust the dollar to meet the needs of various countries. We will discuss the effect of international policy coordination and its effect on interest rates later in this chapter. Under the current international system of floating exchange rates among currencies, there is nothing to stop the financial markets from letting the dollar rise above the levels established by the Group of Seven countries. The market seems to be as interested in the psychological as in the fundamental factors that influence the value of the dollar and its effect on domestic and foreign interest rates. Some economists feel that the dollar's value is determined in speculative markets, such as those for stocks and bonds.

Market psychology can critically influence the way traders respond to domestic and foreign economic, fiscal, monetary, and political factors. These are the same factors that influence interest rates. There is a direct and significant relationship between the machinations of the dollar and the movement of both domestic and foreign interest rates. Any reported information on economic growth, inflation, unemployment, or the intentions of the Federal Reserve policy makers will influence both the dollar and global interest rates.

In theory, a weaker dollar makes imported goods more expensive in the United States and makes American exports more attractive abroad. So far, most foreign companies have kept price increases in the United States below the corresponding change in currency values by accepting lower profit margins and by cutting manufacturing and marketing costs. Their strategy has been to make less money in the short run in order to retain important market share in the long-run.

Many countries, particularly Japan, began to shift production capacity to the United States during the 1980s. Just look at the monthly reported auto sales in the United States. Of the 10 major companies in the Commerce Department's monthly number: Seven of them are Japanese manufacturers, because their plants are now located in the United States. Such companies can reduce some of the risk of currency fluctuations while at the same time maximizing American demand for well-made goods.

A continued fall in the dollar may also test the strength of the American consumer's addiction to cars, electronics, household appliances, and other items imported from Japan, Western Europe, and other Asian countries. At the same time, it could open the door to even more imports from South Korea and Taiwan, as it did in the 1980s and is now doing in the 1990s.

Foreign Interest Rates

When Japan or Germany becomes concerned about inflation because their economies are showing surging growth, U.S. financial markets become concerned about the possibility of these countries increasing their interest rates to thwart inflation. In the case of Germany, 15 other European countries have linked their currencies to the German mark. Therefore, whatever Germany does to push their interest rates lower or higher affects many other European interest rates, which in turn affects U.S. interest rates. If Japanese and German interest rates rise to combat inflation, U.S. interest rates will often rise to ensure that foreign investors will continue to fund the U.S. budget deficit. As foreign interest rates rise, especially the real interest rate (interest rate less inflation), U.S. securities become less attractive to foreign investors. *Barron's* publishes an excellent chart every week that tracks both short- and long-term foreign governmental interest rates. The corollary to foreign interest rates rising is the United States lowering its interest rates. For example, if the United States decides to cut interest rates in order to pull the U.S. economy out of recession, the Federal Reserve Board may cut the discount rate, with the result that the dollar declines against major currencies. That shift in the value of the dollar against foreign currencies makes dollar-denominated securities less valuable to investors. The result is that U.S. interest rates rise to ensure that foreign investors will continue to invest in U.S. securities. Another example is when the U.S. economy begins to show signs of recovery (job growth, decline in initial claims for unemployment insurance, a rise in durable goods orders, and an increase in housing starts). The result is a rise in the dollar as foreign investors become more positive about a growing U.S. economy. Then U.S. interest rates begin to rise because growth in the U.S. economy means that inflation begins to rise. The careful balance between foreign interest rates and the dollar and the effect of both on foreign economies vis-à-vis their relationship with the U.S. and its economy create an environment where international policy coordination becomes an important element in interest rates.

International Policy Coordination

Why is international policy coordination necessary? Policy coordination is necessary to rectify two difficult situations: controlling inflation and encouraging economic growth among trading partners. When finance ministers and sometimes the presidents and prime ministers of the major industrialized nations meet, especially the Group of Seven, the financial and business communities pay rapt attention because the meeting could affect the value of the dollar, which in turn would affect the U.S. economy and the movement of U.S. interest rates.

A Brief Review of International Policy Coordination in the 1980s

In September 1985, the Group of Five, or G-5 (the United States, Japan, West Germany, France, and Great Britain) met to deal with an overvalued dollar at the Plaza Hotel in New York City. The overvalued dollar had been widening both the U.S. trade deficit and the U.S. budget deficit. The finance leaders agreed to rectify the imbalances among the fiscal policies of the United States and its trading partners. Coordinated monetary policy was developed to allow both real and nominal interest rates to fall (the real rate of interest is the interest rate less inflation and the nominal rate is the real rate plus inflation). The United States, through the Federal Reserve Board, began to drive down the federal funds rate, which in turn helped to reinvigorate the U.S. economy, in which unemployment had reached 7%, inflation was below 3%, and gross national product was sluggish.

In February 1987, the Group of Five became the Group of Seven (G-7) by adding Italy and Canada to the original five. All seven met at the Louvre in Paris to try and stabilize exchange rates around the then-existing levels in order to prevent the dollar from depreciating further. At that time, U.S. gross national product was strong, inflation appeared to be rising, and the unemployment rate had fallen to about 6%. As a result of the agreement at the Louvre, the Federal Reserve Board began to push the federal funds rate higher in order to thwart inflation and moderate the U.S. economy's rapid growth. Both intermediate and long-term interest rates also began to rise steadily. The Group of Seven began to push their interest rates higher to thwart inflation in their own countries. The most significant result was the October 1987 stock market crash, which was preceded by a Japanese stock market crash. Too often, analysts are so involved with watching U.S. indicators that they sometimes neglect the movement of foreign interest rates. The attempts by the international financial community to meet periodically to review policies within their respective countries and how they affect their trading partners is often an important variant in examining the potential long-term movement in interest rates.

International Policy Coordination and the Dollar

One important way that foreign countries can manipulate the dollar to balance the problems of economic growth and inflation is through central bank intervention. The central banks of industrialized countries can establish a policy to intervene in the financial markets in an attempt to manipulate the value of the dollar in order to stimulate a given foreign economy. For example, if foreign central bankers flood the foreign exchange market with enough dollars, the price of the dollar can be driven down. Or these central bankers could buy dollars to drive the exchange rate up. However, the actual amount of buying and selling of the dollar, though enormous when compared with other transactions, is dwarfed by the overall trading of the dollar in one day. Traders might decide that intervention will drive the dollar down or up. They can simply do the opposite or the same to enhance or preserve the dollar relationship that is necessary for them to do business. The result is that the exchange rate could fall further or rise faster than the relatively small government intervention might suggest.

Trading in the dollar can often affect the movement of interest rates, depending on the reasons for the rise or fall. If the financial markets believe that there will be intervention to push the dollar down, then domestic interest rates will fall. Remember that a host of other factors may mitigate any deliberate attempt to move interest rates. By tracking the various factors that are influencing interest rates, one can often see why they will or will not move.

Some Issues Concerning Policy Coordination

Some analysts are doubtful about the appropriateness of focusing international policy coordination on monetary policy or the exchange value of the dollar, especially when various shocks affect exchange rates. These shocks include geopolitical events such as the Gulf war, a banking crisis, or a foreign stock exchange scandal. At times, nations have been forced to adjust to their own domestic inflationary problems apart from what was occurring in other countries. If the German economy, for example, exhibits strong growth, to the point where it may be overheating, German monetary policy makers may increase their Lombard rate (the rate the Bundesbank charges on short-term borrowings by commercial banks using securities as collateral) to help ease their own inflationary problems without too much concern for the effect on U.S. interest rates. Policy coordination may thus be difficult to achieve because of different national concerns about inflation and economic growth. No matter how difficult it is to achieve policy coordination, however, it is important for these countries to meet and discuss common problems of economic growth, inflation, and changes in the geopolitical climate in order to attempt reasonable growth in the Group of Seven economies and keep inflation at moderate levels. The financial markets are thus extremely careful observers of publicly held meetings of the Group of Seven. Interest rates often reflect both the talks themselves and the statements that may come out of such international meetings.

The momentous geopolitical changes necessary to reunite Germany and to integrate Eastern European economies into Western markets, as well as the breakup of the Soviet Union, and the reality of a new European Economic Community and its enormous market are making policy coordination far more difficult. Rising inflation and the extraordinary capital needs to provide new infrastructure in Eastern European countries and the former Soviet Union all involve the rise and fall of foreign interest rates, which in turn affect the rise and fall of U.S. interest rates. The juxtaposition of interest rates to encourage the flow of capital into these countries will be a major problem for the United States, which also needs to finance its own infrastructure, the U.S. budget deficit, and the U.S. trade deficit. These will be the key global issues of the 1990s. While many of these issues are subject to constant discussion among the major industrialized nations, the formal meeting of these countries can lend a psychological edge to juggling the concerns of international inflation and global economic growth.

10
Interest Rates, Psychology, and Politics

How Psychological Factors Influence Interest Rates

There is an old maxim about law: Law is just what the judges say it is. One can certainly say that interest rates are often only what the markets say they are. Markets are nothing more than human responses to events. In other words, financial markets reflect the responses of human psychology to an evaluation of economic events. These events include not only fundamental occurrences such as a recession, curtailment of oil supplies, war, and inflation, but also psychological and political events. Fundamental directions in global financial markets ultimately surface as a result of an intricate maze of interpretations. At some point, the statistics begin to show a consensus. That consensus is an emotional response to psychological effects and political decisions about how to invest in the financial markets. As trends become more apparent, interest rates adjust.

An important element in understanding interest rate trends is the psychological and political responses of key governmental decision makers to conditions not only in the U.S. economy but also in the economies of other major industrialized nations. Important people who influence interest rates include presidents, finance ministers, central government bankers, and highly placed governmental officials who can affect decisions about national economies, inflation, and interest rates. Their public statements, as reported in the media, affect the movement of interest rates.

Sometimes commentary by important but lower-level governmental officials is interpreted as the view of the President. For example, the chief White House economic advisor may comment to the media that interest rates should be lowered in order to invigorate the economy. In actuality those comments are simply another way of communicating the President's political message to the public when the President does not want to make a public statement for fear of causing harm in the financial markets. Comments like these can push interest rates in one direction or another as the financial markets try to interpret or react to what was said by whom, how important the official who made the comment is, and whether the comment is a tipoff that something will be done to move interest rates.

As factors begin to indicate a trend, such as a slowdown in the U.S. economy, at some point the psychology of the financial markets will be affected; then interest rates will move. There are many examples. If the United States is going to sell a large amount of new Treasury bonds to investors, the markets may become concerned that too much supply will become available. The announcement of the forthcoming auction is made one week in advance. Once that announcement is made public, the psychology of the markets takes over. Since the interest rate or coupon rate is not set until the day the Treasury bond is auctioned, neither is the yield which reflects the price that investors are willing to pay for the bond. Thus the yield on the bond will fluctuate until it reaches what market participants believe is the yield the bond must be sold at to induce both domestic and foreign buyers to purchase it.

Psychology moves interest rates in other ways as well. The chair of the Federal Reserve Board always plays an immensely important psychological role in the movement of interest rates. The reason is that any comment or testimony made by the chair of the Federal Reserve Board has enormous influence on the movement of interest rates because of the Fed's two goals of stimulating economic growth and keeping inflation low. The reason, as we have discussed before, is that the Fed has the authority to control the movement of short-term interest rates by manipulating the federal funds rate to increase or decrease the money supply, which in turn affects the availability of credit and the interest rates on that credit. When the chair of the Federal Reserve Board determines that a recession is ending and recovery beginning, and then publicly testifies that interest rates are still too high, the financial markets interpret this to mean that the Federal Reserve Board will lower interest rates. The worldwide importance of the actions of the Federal Reserve Board and therefore of any comments by the chair as to what the Fed may or may not do to meet its two goals can easily create a psychological climate in which interest rates will move. Sometimes even the vice chair can have a major effect on the movement of yields by saying something at an important meeting.

How Political Factors Influence Interest Rates

Politicians always demand lower interest rates in order to help them become reelected. What politician wants higher interest rates? What politicians want is lower mortgage rates so that everyone can buy a house, lower consumer rates so that people can buy a new car or washing machine, lower business loan rates so that a company located in their district can expand a plant and hire more people, and lower student loan rates so that parents can send their children to college. The only people who are not satisfied with lower interest rates are those who want to obtain a higher rate of return on their bond investments.

Every member of Congress is concerned about higher interest rates. Even at the pinnacle of government, the level of interest rates is part of a carefully calculated political strategy for achieving election or reelection to the presidency. For example, a President beginning a run for reelection has an intense desire for the economy to grow with hardly any inflation and low interest rates. Politicians hoping to unseat the President hope that interest rates will be high, the economy sputtering, and inflation rising so that they can point a finger and induce voters to elect a new President who can spur the economy, reduce inflation, and lower interest rates.

A good case of a politically motivated attempt to influence the movement of interest rates was provided by Secretary of the Treasury Nicholas F. Brady: "We would want to see the mortgage rates come down. And it seems to me now that inflation obviously has been checked, we should remove all impediments to returning this country to growth."*

There are many examples of foreign political leaders affecting U.S. interest rates. A Soviet official, for instance, announced that there would be large troop cuts in his nation in 1990. The result was that U.S. interest rates plummeted because the comments created the psychological feeling that the troop cuts would significantly reduce the threat of military escalation. A year later, U.S. short-term interest rates fell because the then highly visible Soviet foreign minister resigned from his post as a result of disagreements within the leadership. World markets interpreted that incident as a possible sign of major instability in that country. The result was a "Flight to Quality"—foreign investors ran to buy U.S. Treasury bills because U.S. securities are considered the safest in the world.

Public statements by leading central bankers in Germany or in Japan can play havoc with interest rates, not only in their respective countries

---

*Paul Duke, Jr., "Economy: Two Reports Indicate Easing of Recession," *The Wall Street Journal*, June 7, 1991, p. A2. Reprinted by permission of *The Wall Street Journal*, © 1991 Dow Jones & Company, Inc. All rights reserved worldwide.

but in the United States as well. A good example occurred in April 1991 before a meeting of the Group of Seven. Before the meeting the United States made it explicitly clear that it wanted interest rates lowered worldwide to help this country pull out of its recession. The President of the United States made the following public statement: "We want to see these interest rates down a little bit, and I think that would be good for the world economy, including our own."* However, Karl Otto Pöhl, the president of the German central bank, the Bundesbank, replied that "A cut in interest rates in Germany is not on the agenda. Calls for Germany to cut interest rates are, from our point of view, difficult to understand."† At the G-7 meeting, the members agreed to do nothing except to recognize what the United States was asking for while at the same time respecting what Germany would not do. According to one newspaper, this "burning the candles at both ends" compromise was "a medium-term strategy," and the ministers to the meeting had "agreed to monitor the situation closely and to take actions as needed within the coordination process with a view to achieving a sound recovery and a growing world economy."‡ According to one newspaper, the Secretary of the Treasury, Nicholas F. Brady, was insistent about the effect of high foreign interest rates on the U.S. recession: "Real interest rates [interest rates with the inflation rate subtracted] remain high in many countries, dampening investment and growth prospects."§

Following that rebuff at a G-7 meeting, the Federal Reserve Board lowered its discount rate to reinvigorate the U.S. economy. Of course, the President was quick to respond to the "lower the interest rates, and elect me again" syndrome: The President said (it was) "very good news" and "a very strong leadership role by the Fed."¶ Germany was also quick to praise the United States for lowering interest rates. One of the major newspapers reported a comment by a high-level public official in Germany's ministry of finance: "For the time being there's no possibility to say we can lower interest rates." Secretary Brady responded that "there is ample room

---

*Jonathan Fuerbringer, "U.S. to Push for Lower Rates at Group of Seven Meeting," *The New York Times*, April 26, 1991, p. D13. Copyright © 1991 by The New York Times Company. Reprinted by permission.

†Ibid.

‡Louis Uchitelle, "Plea by U.S. on Rate Cut Is Rejected," *The New York Times*, April 26, 1991, p. D1. Copyright © 1991 by The New York Times Company. Reprinted by permission.

§Peter Truell, "Brady Warns That High Interest Rates Cloud Prospects for Economic Recovery," *The Wall Street Journal*, April 30, 1991, p. A2. Reprinted by permission of *The Wall Street Journal*, © 1991 Dow Jones & Company, Inc. All rights reserved worldwide.

¶Alan Murray, "Economy: Fed Moves to Lower Short-Term Rates; Banks Likely to Follow with Cut in Prime," *The Wall Street Journal*, May 1, 1991, p. A2. Reprinted by permission of *The Wall Street Journal*, © 1991 Dow Jones & Company, Inc. All rights reserved worldwide.

for lower interest rates."* The result was that U.S. interest rates rose because of the apparent political conflict between Germany and the United States concerning the weak U.S. economic condition and Germany's rising inflation.

Another good example of interest rates playing an intriguing role in politics occurred at the 1991 spring meeting of the Business Council, composed of the leading executives of major companies. As reported in one newspaper, several of these key business people made comments about interest rates during a time when the U.S. economy was struggling to break out of recession. James Robinson, chairman of American Express Co., said: "The Fed should ease more and bring interest rates down." The chairman of General Motors, Robert C. Stempel, said: "It would be nice if the prime (rate) moved down another half point." Harold Poling, chairman of Ford Motor Co., said: "I was disappointed the countries couldn't reach an agreement on interest rates."† These comments were another way of putting pressure on the White House to lower interest rates.

A key source of political conflict is how independent the Federal Reserve Board is of the desires of the White House. The Fed is always trying to sustain economic growth and keep inflation low, and also trying to maintain its independence from White House political rhetoric. The give and take between these two highly charged positions is often reflected in a move in interest rates, because the financial markets do not like conflicts at high levels of government.

Summary

Both psychology and politics affect the movement of interest rates and impact on the financial markets. The important point is that any effort to understand the dynamics of interest rates and the factors that influence them over periods of time must consider the psychological and political nuances. The psychology of the financial markets often reflects what participants feel about the state of the U.S. economy, inflation, and interest rates. The politics of the moment reflect what business and elected officials feel is the right direction for the nation to go, whether moving out of recession by lowering interest rates, quelling inflation by raising interest rates, or ensuring election to public office. Readers should pay close attention to testimony of the chair of the Federal Reserve in particular, and to what the President says about interest rates. Sometimes rhetoric becomes action.

---

*Ibid.

†Alan Murray, "Economy: Top Executives Urge Fed to Trim Rates," *The Wall Street Journal*, May 13, 1991, p. A2. Reprinted by permission of *The Wall Street Journal*, © 1991 Dow Jones & Company, Inc. All rights reserved worldwide.

11
Setting Up the Interest Rate Charts

Introduction

So far we have discussed the various factors that affect interest rates, and how to interpret them. In this chapter we begin to describe the process of putting the parts together. The instrument for accomplishing this goal is a series of interest rate charts, particularly a weekly interest rate chart. These charts are the linchpin of the process. They present a framework within which one can not only track the specific factors and see the movement of selected interest rates, but also interpret what has happened to interest rates. The charts are simple to use and take a minimum of time to complete. The weekly interest rate chart is filled out each day using one or more of the four newspapers we have described. Normally, one should be able to enter the selected data in 15 minutes or less, and then take another 15 minutes to interpret what has occurred. At the end of the week, only a few minutes will be needed to make judgments about the week's activities, because the necessary thinking process will have been begun as the week progressed.

Each of the interest rate charts we will use occupies one page. Each consists of key signs relating to the impact of economic, monetary, fiscal, global, political, and psychological factors on the trends in interest rates. The charts can be easily set up on a computer using any of the common spreadsheet programs. Also, a graphics program can be used to illustrate trend lines, if desired. Those who wish to complete the charts by hand should use a pen with a "very fine" point. Sometimes, when a major event—such as a dramatic rise in the consumer price index or a drop in the federal funds rate—occurs, I write about it in more detail. To do this, I have several options. First, I can use the blank space at the bottom of the chart or, when more space is needed, the back of the chart. I always use a red pen to circle a particular indicator that I believe has a major influence on interest rates. If, for example, the producer price index shows a third straight decrease, or the National Association of Purchasing Management index declines below 45% for the first time in years, I will highlight the entry with a red pen. This is a good way to focus on key events that directly affect the movement of interest rates. As one begins to use the monthly and the quarterly interest rate charts, these red notations become the fundamental way to go through the weekly interest rate charts to ascertain the major factors that influenced interest rates, and then transpose them onto both the monthly and quarterly interest rate charts. These other charts also have plenty of room in which to make all types of notations or add more commentary about certain indicators, or to express in more detail your own comments or interpretations of what is happening or may happen in the future.

For analyzing interest rates, I use several different charts—a weekly chart, a monthly chart, and a quarterly chart. Each of these charts summarizes a particular time period over which interest rates will react or not react to a given set of factors. I also use a select group of indicators to monitor the movement of interest rates. However, as you become more familiar with using the charts, other indicators may be used in addition to, or perhaps instead of, the ones I have selected.

The Interest Rate Notebook

I suggest using a three-ring notebook to keep the charts together, dividing it into three sections for the three types of charts: weekly, monthly, and quarterly. In addition, various articles may be collected and incorporated that include detailed explanations of a particular factor, reviews of the economy, explanations of interest rates, or any other information that may prove helpful in coming to a conclusion about a particular factor. Further, a section may be used to keep useful illustrations from the various publications. Even if you maintain the charts themselves on a computerized spreadsheet, a notebook is still a good way to keep information about interest rates that can be referred to from time to time. If you keep the interest rate charts in the notebook, articles and illustrations showing interest rate yields or the various factors can be placed in the section that includes the weekly charts or in separate sections. The importance of using an interest rate notebook is to keep all the information together for ready reference.

The Weekly Interest Rate Chart

The weekly interest rate chart includes not only considerable information but also enough space to make relevant comments about what happened in a given week. Setting up and filling in the chart the first time may take a few weeks, because of the need to obtain maturity dates for the interest rates and in order to become comfortable with using the chart. The exact amount of time will depend on when the chart is started as well as the user's familiarity with the newspapers being used. Once the chart is set up, however, the process of filling it in will steadily become easier and faster.

We will use "current" yields, the current coupon interest rates and exact maturities of a select group of U.S. Treasury bills, notes, and bonds consisting of the 3-month Treasury bill, the 2-year Treasury note, the 10-year Treasury note, and the 30-year Treasury bond. The reason for using these specific U.S. Treasury securities relates to when they are sold at public auction. The auctions take place weekly, monthly, or quarterly, depending on the type of security: Treasury bills are auctioned weekly, the 2-year Treasury monthly, and the 10- and 30-year Treasuries quarterly. These time periods allow one to see how specific interest rates react to economic, inflation, monetary, and political factors. As these securities are tracked from day to day, week to week, month to month, and quarter to quarter, trends will develop. The yields of these securities change day to day, but the coupon rate or interest rate remains the same until a new Treasury bill, note, or bond is auctioned by the U.S. Treasury Department. Remember that the yield represents the daily reaction of an interest rate to the various economic, inflation, monetary, and political factors we have discussed.

Let us now begin to look more closely at the weekly interest rate chart we will be using (see Fig. 11-1). Listed down the first column on the left are general interest rates and specific factors that will affect the movement of interest rates. As one gains experience in using the chart, other factors may be added, such as mortgage rates, the municipal bonds index given each day except Saturday in the "Key Rates" chart in *The New York Times,* or other municipal indices such as those published in *The Wall Street Journal* or in *Investor's Business Daily.* Information about the Japanese stock market, specific corporate bonds or indices, money market instruments such as the Donohue index, or the futures index for the 30-year Treasury bond (published by the Chicago Board of Trade and found in all of our publica-

WEEKLY INTEREST RATE CHART

Week of _____	Mon	Tues	Wed	Thurs	Fri	Key Interest Rate Factors Yields: U=Up D=Down N=Neutral
Comments						Monday to Friday Difference 3 Mon. T-Bill in Basis Points 30 Yr. T-Bond in Basis Points Key Factors
Federal Funds Rate						
3 Mon. Treas. Bill						
2 Year Treas. Note						
10 Year Treas. Note						
30 Year Treas. Bond						
Gold (COMEX)						
Yen in Dollars						
Mark in Dollars						
CRB						Key Factors Overlooked
Japan 10 Year Bond						
German 10 Year Bond						
Stocks - Dow Indust.						Current Interest Rate Trend
WTIC Oil Price						

Figure 11-1. Weekly interest rate chart.

tions) may be added or substituted for some of the other factors. What is important to keep are the first five interest rate factors: the federal funds rate, the 3-month Treasury bill, the 2-year Treasury note, the 10-year Treasury note, and the 30-year Treasury bond (sometimes called the "long bond" or the "bellwether bond"). These are the key rates. Other factors can be substituted for any of the remaining factors. The gold indicator is taken from the New York Commodity Exchange, or Comex. The yen and mark are values for dollars in foreign currency. CRB refers to the Commodity Research Bureau futures index. And the WTIC oil price is the West Texas Intermediate Crude futures price. All of these statistics are commonly used in the financial markets as indicators. Obviously, we have selected only a few of the indicators, but these are the ones I have used over many years. Others can of course be used instead.

At the top of the interest rate chart, on the far left, is a space in which to note the week being covered, such as Week of June 24, 1991. Next along the top is shown each individual day, beginning with Monday. Below each day is a blank space. In this space should be entered the factors that are being reported during that week, such as factory orders, retail sales, consumer price index, or testimony by the Federal Reserve chair to Congress.

[Note: I suggest that at this point you make sure you have handy copies of The New York Times (Sunday, Monday, any other day, and Saturday editions), *The Wall Street Journal* (Monday and one other day's edition), *Investor's Business Daily,* and *Barron's.* As I explain where to find the specific numbers, refer to the newspapers as an aid in the learning process.]

One can find the daily factors in each of the journals we are using to track relevant information. In *The New York Times,* Sunday edition, in the Business Section under "Business Diary," located on the second page, is a chart on the bottom right entitled "This Week's Numbers." This chart lists on a day-by-day basis what indicators are going to be reported during the week. Also in the Monday edition of *The New York Times* is a chart entitled "Economic Calendar," which also gives the week's economic indicators. In Monday's edition of *The Wall Street Journal,* on the second page of Section A is a subsection called "Economy." Under this heading a chart called "Tracking the Economy" includes another chart called "Statistics to Be Released This Week." *Investor's Business Daily* includes a column on the first page entitled "This Week Ahead." This column is more comprehensive than the others, as it includes important conferences by chief executives of major companies, specific happenings, as well as foreign dignitaries who may be meeting with the President of the United States. When the chair of the Federal Reserve Board is testifying before a congressional committee, this is also noted. For each day is listed the major economic, monetary, or fiscal indicators that will be reported during the week. In addition, the prior month's number is normally given as well.

Again, just below each day on the chart, enter the specific indicator to be released, putting the month first, then the abbreviation for the factor. Thus May durable goods orders is entered as May DGO; the May producer price index is entered as May PPI; and September factory orders is entered as Sept FO. Sometimes I just enter the number of the month; i.e., 5 FO for May factory orders. The calendars in the various publications also give the prior month's number, so I also enter that on the chart. For example, just below the factory orders notation, I would put a slash and to the right of it the previous month's number: /+0.4. When an indicator is reported, the article in which it is discussed includes the prior month's figure; then I put the current month's number to the left of the slash. For example, under May CPI I would put the May figure, then a slash, and the prior month's figure (0.4%/0.2%). Many times I will also include the annual rate, such as 6.2%, below these numbers. As each month's number is reported, the annual rate of the CPI changes accordingly. I therefore include the core rate of the CPI as well. Again, one can enter as much information as is needed to explain the indicator. Any additional commentary can be placed at the bottom of the chart or on the back of it. If the indicator has reached a yearly high, and if there is room, I may put it in that column under that specific reporting day. Otherwise, when I work on the key interest rate factors section, I note that information or sometimes put it on the back of the chart, particularly if these indicators are significantly important to the movement of interest rates. For example, one might put on the key indicator section or on the back of the chart that industrial production for that month was the highest of the year, or that durable goods orders for that month had plummeted to its lowest in 2 years, or that the chair of the Federal Reserve Board had said that the probability that the board would lower interest rates any further is remote. In almost every case, the need for these special notations is easily recognizable because of the enormous press that such occurrences are given. In other cases, a particular comment by an individual might take on special significance in your interpretation of a specific indicator. There is then every reason to enter it somewhere on your interest rate chart. Perhaps most important, your own interpretation should be highlighted or underlined with a red pen.

Just under "Week of" is a space "Comments." In this space one can enter almost any notation about interest rates. Examples might include a note that the Federal Reserve Board appears to be easing because the federal funds rate has been about 25 basis points lower than the current level; or that the Group of Seven major industrialized countries will be meeting over next weekend to discuss the rising dollar or the effect of interest rates on their economies. A follow-up note might be that last week's overlooked factor of a rise in German bond yields ought to be checked at the end of the week to see if a continued trend is developing that might affect U.S. interest rates. One might want to note a comment by one of the Federal Reserve Board members that there is enough liquidity in the market, signaling that the Federal Reserve Board will probably not lower interest rates for the time being; or the Japanese finance minister's comment that Japan is concerned about rising inflation, which implies that the Japanese central bank may raise Japan's short-term rates.

Major Treasury note and bond auctions are announced the week before the auction. Often Treasury auctions push yields higher in the hopes of attracting major buyers. As you begin to gain more knowledge about the factors that move interest rates, you will want to enter this information in the comment section. Most times I will note the day on which a particular U.S. security will be auctioned. Once the security is sold, I can fill in the new interest or coupon rate plus when the security matures. For example, suppose a new 2-year U.S. Treasury note was auctioned at 7.00% to mature on June 1995. On the weekly interest rate chart it would look like this: 2 YR Auction, 7% 6/95. Then I enter that coupon rate and maturity in the space for the 2-year note, so I will always have the coupon or interest rate and the maturity date in case I need it.

The next section we will discuss, called "Key Interest Rate Factors," is located on the right side of the chart. The first two numbers are the movement of two key interest rates over a week: the 3-month Treasury bill and the 30-year Treasury bond, both measured in basis points. Remember that yields are measured in basis points, or one one-hundredth of a point.

Therefore, if yields of the 3-month Treasury bill move up 6 basis points between Monday and Friday, you would write down +6 bp. If they declined 6 basis points, you would write either –6 bp or (6 bp).

Next on the right side is a section entitled "Key Factors." Here is where you summarize the week's interest rate events. At the same time, when you note a key factor, enter U, D, or N at the far right to indicate whether the indicator moved yields up, down, or was neutral. Remember that yields represent the daily reactions of interest rates to the factors reported in the newspapers. At a later time, the yields will be seen to be trending in a particular direction. That is when interest rates will increase or decrease to reflect the past movement of yields. Thus the symbols can imply either a possible trend or simply the reaction of yields to the publication of that factor. In other words, if durable goods orders rise for the second straight month, you would write "U" to the right of this factor. The "U" means that this particular indicator implies strength in the economy, which means that inflation is possible. If inflation is expected to rise, yields will rise, so the "U" symbol is put next to the particular indicator. I circle them so that they will stand out. The implication is that if the economy continues to grow, interest rates will rise, reflecting the rising trend in the yields of the current interest rates. It is also important to remember that as yields rise, the price of the bond being tracked will decrease. This inverse relationship is constant.

Each key factor should carry one of the three symbols to its right, for example, (1) CRB heading down—D. Remember that a decline in the CRB means that inflation is coming down as based on the Commodity Research Bureau's futures index. Another example is (2) German bond yields rising—U. The rise in the 10-year German government bond yields would signify that inflation is growing in Germany as its economy grows. This could mean that the German central bank may raise German interest rates to stem inflation. The result could mean that U.S. interest rates may rise in order to compete against the higher yield of the German government bonds. So if yields are moving up, when the next 10-year German bonds are sold, their coupon or interest rate will be higher than the previous month.

The section called "Key Factors Overlooked" can be important. Perhaps the Dow has been rising steadily. That could spell trouble for the bond market. If the stock market is moving up because the U.S. economy is continuing to show growth, then inflation is also rising, and therefore interest rate yields will rise. Another possibly overlooked factor might be a continuation of a steady rise in WTIC oil prices over several weeks. That too might signify rising inflation. Clearly, there are many other possibilities. Many times there is no need to put any factor in this section. It all depends on your interpretation of the information in the weekly interest rate chart.

The last section on the right is called "Current Interest Rate Trend." At this juncture, it is a good time to pause to reflect on what is being shown on the weekly interest rate chart. Then put your thoughts under this column. Maybe short-term interest rates have been rising in reaction to a tightening by the Federal Reserve Board that is reflected in a rise in the federal funds rate. Perhaps the U.S. economy is beginning to slow down as reflected in some of this week's economic indicators and in the decline of the 30-year Treasury bond yield. There is enough space to indicate what the trend appears to be for that week.

Note that if you prefer to work from weekly numbers by using the last-day-of-the-week figures in *Barron's* rather than the day-to-day numbers of the other newspapers, that is a reasonable way to track the movement of interest rates. The significant drawback is that you do not see how the interest rates react to a given indicator on a given day. I prefer the 5-day approach because it tells me more about how interest rates are reacting to many different factors.

The Federal Funds Rate

Of particular importance is how to obtain the interest rates we will track on the weekly chart. First consider the federal funds rate. Over time you will learn the current level at which the Federal Reserve Board wishes to keep the federal funds rate, by reading the various articles that discuss the Fed and its actions. Keep a note on the chart about the current level. Often I put it under the federal funds line on the chart. Then, if the federal funds rate appears to be below the current level for several weeks, one can sense that the Fed may try to stimulate the U.S. economy by adding money to the banking system to provide more funds to loan to businesses. In *The New York Times* (except on Saturday) the "Key Rates" chart in the "Credit Markets" column reports this figure, giving "Yesterday," "Previous Day," and "Year Ago" numbers.

In *The Wall Street Journal*, the daily closing figure for the federal funds rate is on the first page of Section C, "Money & Investing." On the left side of the first page of that section is a page-length chart called "Markets Diary." The third section down, entitled "Interest," gives the federal funds rate as "Fed Funds (NY Fed, Babcock Fulton Prebon)." Beneath that title is a chart showing the movement of the federal funds rate over about a year and a half. To the right of that chart is another chart showing the weekly movement of the federal funds rate with the prior day's number on the top left and the change over the day before at the top right of the line chart.

In *Investor's Business Daily*, the federal funds rate appears on the page that lists the yields of Treasury bills, notes, and bonds. At the bottom of the page, in the lower left-hand corner, is a chart called "Money Rates." In the left-hand column of the chart, below both the prime rate and the discount rate, is the federal funds rate, including the close (see Fig. 11-2). To obtain

Money Rates

Prime Rate 8.50	**Commercial Paper (range):**	**Eurodollar Rates:**
Base interest rate charged by major U.S. commercial banks on loans to corporations.	Dealers:	(Secondary Market)
	30-180 days 5.57-5.55	Overnight....................5.5625-5.6875
Discount Rate 5.50	Corporate Issuers:	1 month 5.625-5.75
Rate charged by Federal Reserve System on loans to depository institutions.	30-270 days 5.56-5.54	3 months 5.625-5.75
	Discount rate for unsecured notes of top-credit corporations sold directly or through dealers.	6 months 5.75-5.875
Federal Funds Rate:		1 Year.......................5.9375-6.0625
High 5.5625 Low 5.50 Close 5.50		Rates paid on dollar deposits outside the U.S.
Rates on overnight loans among financial institutions.	**Certificates of Deposit:**	
	($100,000 minimum)	**London Interbank Offered Rates:**
Bankers Acceptances:	30 days 5.36	3 months 5.75
30 days...................................5.57	90 days 5.42	6 months 5.875
60 days...................................5.56	180 days 5.55	The average of rates paid on dollar deposits.
90 days...................................5.53	Rates paid on new certificates of major commercial banks, usually in blocks of $1 million or more.	**Treasury Bill Auction Results:**
120 days...................................5.80		3 months (as of Aug 12)................5.30
150 days...................................5.55	**Broker Call Loans** 7.25-8.00	6 months (as of Aug 12)................5.39
180 days...................................5.53	Rate charged on short-term loans to brokerage dealers backed by securities.	Average discount rate for Treasury bills in minimum units of $10,000.
Discount rate on business credits backed and sold by banks to finance trade.		**Source: Telerate Systems Inc.**

Figure 11-2. (*From Investor's Daily, August 19, 1991, p. 31.*)

a trend of the movement of the federal funds rate, one can look in the upper right-hand part of that page for a chart called "Selected Interest Rates." The chart shows the movement of the federal funds rate, the discount rate, and the 3-month Treasury bill for about a year and a half.

In *Barron's*, the federal funds rate appears in the statistical section entitled "Market Laboratory/Economic Indicators," on the right side under the chart called "Money Rates," "Federal Funds," and then the row entitled "Average Effective." It gives the "Latest Week," "Previous Week," and "Year Ago Week." One can also use the "Average Weekly Auction" number.

The 3-Month Treasury Bill

In *The New York Times*, the daily yield for the 3-month Treasury bill can be found in several different places, in the "Key Rates" chart in the "Credit Markets" column in Section D, Business Day, or the second section of the Saturday edition of *The New York Times*. The 3-month Treasury bill in the "Key Rates" chart is given as a discount yield. That particular yield does not equate to an equivalent bond yield. One can either use the discount yield or the bond equivalent yield, so long as there is consistency. There is an easy way to obtain the bond equivalent yield. On most Mondays, except holidays, 3- and 6-month Treasury bills are auctioned or sold to the public. On Tuesday, all the publications we use quote the statistics related to that sale. Since the 3-month Treasury bill is auctioned every week, it is an excellent indicator of what factors are influencing the movement of short-term interest rates. One of the results of the auction is the maturity date of that 3-month Treasury bill. You could enter the maturity date on your chart just under the space for the 3-month Treasury bill. Then find the chart called "Treasury Bills, Bonds and Notes." It is usually located either on the page before the "Credit Markets" column or sometimes on the same page as the "Credit Markets" column. In that chart, on the left-hand side, is a column entitled "Treasury Bills." Look for the maturity of the current auctioned 3-month Treasury bill and move to the right-hand column titled "Yield." Yield here means bond equivalent yield. Remember that the 3-month Treasury bill is auctioned each week so you must change the maturity date every week.

In *The Wall Street Journal*, the 3-month Treasury bill data can be found on the first page of Section C, "Money & Investing," right where we found the federal funds rate, in the "Markets Diary" under "Interest." Just below the federal funds chart is a column headed "Issue." Just below that is the "3-month T-bill" discount yield showing its "close" for the prior day. To find the bond equivalent yield of the 3-month Treasury bill, turn to the chart called "Treasury Bonds, Notes and Bills." Using the maturity date of the 3-month Treasury bill, look for the column called "Treasury Bills," which is located at the bottom of the chart on the right. The current 3-month Treasury bill is in bold type to help the reader locate it.

In *Investor's Business Daily*, the 3-month Treasury bill is given in the discount rate mode at the same place as the federal funds rate, in the chart called "Money Rates," where one can find both Monday's auction results at the discount yield on Tuesday and the yield of the current 3-month Treasury bill thereafter until the next auction. (See Fig. 11-2.) The illustration in the upper right-hand corner gives the analyst a long-term view of the movement of the 3-month Treasury bill over about a year and a half. It can also be found in the chart entitled "Treasury Bills, Bonds and Notes," usually found to the left of the "Selected Interest Rates" chart.

In *Barron's*, the 3-month Treasury bill is found on the same page as the federal funds rate under "Market Laboratory/Economic Indicators." In the same column, below the federal funds rate, is a section called "Treasury Bills," where you will find the listings based on weeks. The 3-month Treasury bill matures in 13 weeks. Find the line that says "13 weeks, Coupon Equivalent Yield (date)"; the first number is the bond equivalent or coupon yield as of the last day of the week. This figure can be used, but following the daily movement gives a better handle on the reaction of the 3-month Treasury bill to daily indicators. One can also find the 3-month Treasury bill discount in the "Review and Preview" section in the front of the journal. On the left-hand side, just under column head "Last Week," one can find three figures. The last one is the 3-month Treasury bill. The number is also given in the statistical section entitled "Bonds/Government," under the heading "U.S. Treasury Bills."

The 2-Year Treasury Note

I use the 2-year Treasury note because it is auctioned every month, so it is an excellent indicator of how interest rates are reacting to the various indicators. For example, if the daily yields of the 2-year Treasury note have been rising right up to the next auction of the 2-year Treasuries, then it is more than likely that the new 2-year Treasury will be sold at a higher coupon or interest rate to reflect the rise in the past month's yields. Since it is auctioned each month during the third week of the month along with the 5-year Treasury note, one can obtain the maturity date and enter it on the chart.

Assuming that you begin your chart before the auction takes place, you can almost always find the 2-year Treasury note in the commentary in the "Credit Markets" column of *The New York Times*. About the only time that it may not be in that column is when the discussion centers about the auction of the new 2-year Treasury. Once an auction is held, the next day there is the chart in the "Credit Markets" column that displays the movement of the 2-year Treasury note for a number of months. The results of the auction are given below the chart. Look for the maturity date and enter it on your chart. For example, you might put down 6¾%, (the coupon or new interest rate) followed by a small space, and then the maturity, 5/95. If the yield of the 2-year Treasury note is not given, find the "Treasury Bills, Bonds and Notes" chart. Just after the figures on the Treasury bills are the yields for both notes and bonds under the heading "Bonds & Notes." Look for the maturity, now May 95, then the coupon which is 6¾%, and then to the far right for the yield.

In *The Wall Street Journal*, the "Credit Markets" column will often mention the 2-year yield along with that of the 30-year Treasury bond and the 10-year Treasury note. Again, if it is not noted, you may have to wait a day or so to pick up the maturity and yield. Make sure you enter the maturity on your chart so that in case you cannot find it one day, you can look it up in the "Treasury Bonds, Notes and Bills" chart.

In *Investor's Business Daily*, the "Credit Markets" column often gives the yield on the 2-year note. Make sure that you note on the weekly interest rate chart the coupon and maturity of the 2-year Treasury when you locate it. Once those elements of the 2-year note are known, you can look it up in the chart that lists the daily yields of Treasury bills, bonds, and notes, usually found on the following page.

In *Barron's*, the 2-year Treasury note is listed in the statistical section, but it is also sometime mentioned under the "Capital Markets" column. The subsection in the statistical section under "Bonds/Government" is called "U.S. Treasury Notes and Bonds." It gives the rate, then the maturity, and finally, on the far right, the "Ask Yield." If you have the maturity and the coupon rate, finding the yield is easy.

The 10-Year Treasury Note

Both 10- and 30-year Treasury notes and bonds are auctioned every quarter. Because these Treasury securities come under such close scrutiny, they are always mentioned in all the publications. The 10-year Treasury note is normally mentioned in the "Credit Markets" columns of both *The New York Times* and *The Wall Street Journal. Investor's Business Daily* sometimes mentions the 10-year Treasury note. With all the publications we use, once you know the coupon and the maturity of the 10-year Treasury bond, you can look up the yield in the charts that list the Treasury bills, notes, and bonds. These are usually found on the same page or perhaps the page before or the page after the "Credit Markets" columns of all the daily publications. Again, once the auction takes place (during the first week of February, May, August, and November), you should carefully note the coupon and the maturity on the weekly interest rate chart for future reference. Once the coupon and the maturity are known, a check of the appropriate columns can be made as we did for the 3-month bill and the 2-year note. Finding the rates of the 10-year Treasury in the other publications is the same as finding the 2-year Treasury note.

The 30-Year Treasury Bond

The 30-year Treasury bond, the "long bond," is one of the central interest rates that all the financial markets watch. As such, it is called the "bellwether" bond. Because of the close scrutiny it receives, the long bond is listed in several places in our publications. In *The New York Times*, it is always mentioned in the "Key Rates" chart in "Credit Markets"; in the "Credit Markets" column itself; on the first page of Section D of the "Business Day" page of the Business Section, in the left-hand corner in the column called "Business Digest" in the box called "Bonds"; and under "Treasury Bills, Bonds and Notes," usually a page or so before or on the same page as "Credit Markets."

In *The Wall Street Journal*, the 30-year Treasury is listed on the first page of Section C, "Money & Investing," in the column called "Tuesday's Markets" (or whatever day you are reading with reference to the day before); in the "Credit Markets" column, particularly under the "Treasury Securities" subheading; or, if one knows the coupon and the maturity, in the "Treasury Bonds, Notes and Bills" chart.

In *Investor's Business Daily*, the "Credit Markets" column always gives the yield of the long bond. If you already know the coupon rate and the maturity, you can also locate it under the listing of Treasury bills, bonds, and notes, found usually on the following page.

In *Barron's*, the long bond is listed in the same section as the Treasury bills and notes in the statistical section. Also, it is always discussed in the "Capital Markets" section under the "Current Yield" column. In addition, you can find the long bond as part of the chart entitled "Box Score—Performance" in the same article plus as part of the chart called "U.S. Long Rates," always located at the bottom of the page where the "Current Yield" article is located. Also, it can be found in the "Review and Preview" section under "Last Week."

Before we move on to the next indicator to track, we should discuss how to locate these interest rates if you are just starting to put data on the interest rate chart. For example, take the 2-year Treasury. If it is now 1993, add 2 years (that is, 1995). Find the listing of yields under the chart titled something like "Treasury Bills, Notes, and Bonds." Since the 2-year Treasury is auctioned in the third week of every month, you have to use a little common sense. Say you are starting in the second week of the month of July 1992. Look in the year for the month of June 1994. Because there are usually several Treasuries that mature in that month, you have to select one. Even if you are not sure, you will find that the yields are nearly the same or carry only one or two basis points in yield difference. Therefore, you can use one of the bonds until the next auction in the third week of the month. Make sure that when the next auction occurs, you put onto the interest rate chart both the coupon and the maturity. Once you have done that, you will always have the current 2-year Treasury note. Finding the yield for the 10-year and 30-year Treasuries is the same.

Gold

The next indicator on the interest rate chart is gold, from the Comex or Commodity Exchange in New York City. In *The New York Times,* the number can be found in Section D, "Business Day." The best way to locate it is to find in this section the chart entitled "World Gold." One can normally find it directly under the "Foreign Exchange" chart. Ten lines down is the "NY Comex spot month" price. Some analysts prefer to use the NY Republic National Bank gold price, which is found just below the NY Comex gold price. The difference between the two is usually minimal. In *The Wall Street Journal,* the price of gold can easily be found on the front page of Section C, "Money & Investing," under "Markets Diary" on the left side of this page. About three-quarters down is a chart called "Commodities," where you will find three of the commodities to be tracked at their closing prices: the CRB futures index, gold (Comex spot) in troy ounces at the close, and oil (West Texas Intermediate Crude) in barrels (bbl).

In *Investor's Business Daily,* the price of gold can be found on the page of futures prices in the chart called "Precious Metals." The first price is on the line "Gold (CMX)." Move to the right, where the price is located below the column "Close." You can also find the price of gold in another chart, usually located on the preceding page and called "Spot Prices," under the category "Gold" (see Fig. 11-3). In this chart the prices are given for the day before and for one day before that.

Spot Prices

Foods

	Wed	Tue
Butter AA Chi. lb.	1.0325	1.0325
Broilers dressed lb.	5537	5525
Eggs large white NY Doz.	.74	.74
Flour Minn. Std Spring Patent cwt	10.75	10.70
Coffee parana ex – dock NY per lb.	.66	.66
Coffee medlin ex – dock NY per lb	.87	.86½
Cocoa beans Ivory Cost $ mtrc tn	1172	1206
Cocoa butter African styl $ met tn	2894	2929
Sugar No. 11	9.40	9.55
Hogs Omaha 1 – 2 200 – 250 lb avg cwt	48.00	48.50
Feeder cattle 500 – 600 lb Okl av cwt	90.50	90.50
Pork bellies 12 – 14 lb Midwest v cwt	.35½	.35½

Grains

Corn No. 2 yellow Chi processr bd	2.59½	2.61
Soybeans No. 1 yellow	5.73	5.74¾
Soybean meal Decatur ton	186.00	185.00
Wheat No. 2 soft	3.07¼	3.04¾
Wheat N. 1 dk nthn 14pc – pr Mpls.	3.14¼	3.17¼
Wheat No. 2 hard KC.	3.16	3.16

Fats & Oils

Coconut oil N. Orleans lb.	.20½	.21½
Corn oil crude dy mill Chi. lb.	.29¾	.29¾
Soybean oil crude Decatur lb.	.20	.20¼

Metals

Aluminum cents per pound LME	57.1	56.9
Antimony bulk 99.5 pct NY per lb.	2.00	2.00
Copper electrolytic per lb.	1.1345	1.1320
Silver Handy & Harman	3.920	3.930
Lead per lb.	.33	.36
Pig Iron fob fdry buff gross ton	213.00	213.00
Platinum per troy oz. NY (contrct)	344.00	344.00
Platinum Merc spot per troy oz.	341.50	331.50
Mercury per flask of 76 lbs.	100.00	100.00
Steel scrap No. 1 heavy gross ton	87.83	87.83
Tin Metals Week composite lb.	3.6105	3.6199
Zinc (HG) delivered lb.	.5225	.5275

Textiles & Fibers

Cotton 1 – 1 – 16 in. strict low middling	64.98	64.49
Wool fine staple terr Boston lb.	2.30	2.30

Miscellaneous

Rubber No. 1 NY smokd shts lb.	.44½	.44½
Hides heavy native steer lb.	.75	.75

Petroleum — Refined Products

Fuel oil No. 2 NY hbr bg gl fob	.6160	.6140
Gasln nl prm RVP NY hbr bg gl fb	.7185	.7330
Gasoline unl RVP NY hbr bg gl fob	.6555	.6720
Prices provided by Oil Buyer's Guide		
x – prices are for RVP grade of gasoline		

Petroleum — Crude Grades

Saudi Arabian light $ per bbl fob	17.50	17.60
North Sea Brent $ per bbl fob	19.90	20.00
West Texas Intermed $ per bbl fob	21.75	22.00
Alask No. Slope del. US Gulf Coast	18.40	18.80

Gold

Hong Kong late:	$355.15, up $0.60
London morning fixing:	$355.30, up $1.50
London afternoon fixing:	$354.50, up $0.70
London late:	$354.40, off $0.10
Paris afternoon fixing:	$355.64, up $0.03
Frankfurt fixing:	$355.27, up $0.68
Zurich late afternoon:	$354.10, up $0.10
	$354.60 asked
NY Handy & Harman:	$354.50, up $0.70
NY Engelhard:	$355.75, up $0.70
NY Engelhard fabricated:	$373.54, up $0.74
NY Comex gold spot month close Wed.	$353.90, off $0.50
NY Republic National Bank 4 p.m. Wed.	$354.25, off $0.10

Gold Coins

Maple Leaf, 1 troy oz.	$382.00 up	$ 1.75
Mex. 50 Peso, 1.2 troy oz.	$461.75 up	$ 2.25
Aus. 100 crown, .9802 troy oz.	$364.50 up	$ 1.75
American Eagle, 1 troy oz.	$382.00 up	$ 1.75
Krugerrand, 1 troy oz.	$356.00	. . . .
China Panda 1989, 1 troy oz.	$383.00	. . . .
b – bid		a – asked.
n – Nominal		r – revised.
n.q. – not quoted.		n.a. – not available.

Figure 11-3. (*From Investor's Daily, August 29, 1991, p. 19.*)

In *Barron's*, the price of gold can be found in the statistical section under "Commodities Futures" the section entitled "N.Y. Commodity Exchange." The dollar price we are using is found toward the right. You can also find the gold price in the section called "Barron's/Market Week" under the heading "The Trader." At the end of this section is a chart called "Vital Signs." On the right side of the chart at the bottom is the listing for "Gold (CMX nearby futures)" with the "Last Week" and "Week Ago" numbers.

The Japanese Yen and the German Mark in Dollars

In *The New York Times*, one can find the two currencies in the "Currency Markets" column, on the left side of the page. Within the column is a chart called "Foreign Exchange," with the date just below the title. The listing is by country: "Japan (Yen)" and "Germany (Mark)." The second group of numbers to the right is titled "Dollar in Fgn. Currency." The left column is the day before, and the column to the right is two days before.

In *The Wall Street Journal*, the quickest way to locate the two foreign currencies in dollars is again on the first page of Section C in the "Markets Diary" chart called the "U.S. Dollar." Just below the chart are the currencies. Look for the column head "Late NY," then "Japanese yen (per U.S. dollar)" and "German mark (per U.S. dollar)."

In *Investor's Business Daily*, both the yen and the mark can be found in the chart entitled "Foreign Exchange Rates" (see Fig. 11-4). Just look for the particular country and move to the right under the column "Dollar to Fgn. Currency" to find the dollar in both the mark and the yen. The number on the left is the day before, and the number on the right is the day before that.

In *Barron's*, again find the "Commodities Futures" page in the statistical section. On the far left is a listing called "Foreign Exchange" listed by country: "Germany (Mark)" and "Japan (Yen)." Move to the second column from the left, which is entitled "U.S. $ in Foreign Currency."

The Commodity Research Bureau Index of Futures Prices

In *The New York Times*, the Commodity Research Bureau (CRB) futures index can be found on the same page as the currencies and gold prices. At the top of the page right in the middle is a set of statistics with the title "Futures." There are two columns of figures. The column to the right is entitled "Commodity Research Bureau Index" and has three sections: "Today," "Previous Day," and "Year Ago." The first section gives the prior day's figure for the CRB.

In *The Wall Street Journal*, again use the first page of Section C, "Money &

Foreign Exchange Rates

Currency	Fgn. Currency In Dollars 8/28	8/27	Dollar In Fgn.Currency 8/28	8/27
Prices as of 3:00 p.m. Eastern Time.				
Rates for trades of $1 million minimum.				
f-Argentina	.000100	.000101	9957.0	9957.0
Australia	.7855	.7847	1.2731	1.2744
Austria	.0803	.0803	12.45	12.45
c-Belgium	.0278	.0278	35.97	35.97
Brazil	.0026	.0026	379.35	369.35
Britain	1.6910	1.6815	.5914	.5947
30-day fwd	1.6834	1.6737	.5940	.5975
60-day fwd	1.6764	1.6673	.5965	.5998
90-day fwd	1.6697	1.6605	.5989	.6022
Canada	.8770	.8763	1.1402	1.1411
30-day fwd	.8749	.8742	1.1430	1.1439
60-day fwd	.8731	.8723	1.1454	1.1464
90-day fwd	.8709	.8702	1.1482	1.1491
y-Chile	.003530	.003530	340.96	340.96
Colombia	.001545	.001545	647.36	647.36
Denmark	.1476	.1480	6.7730	6.7550
z-Ecuador	.000918	.000918	1089.79	1089.79
ECU	1.1724	1.1724	.8530	.8530
d-Egypt	.3023	.3023	3.3078	3.3078
Finland	.2336	.2336	4.2800	4.2800
France	.1697	.1686	5.8920	5.9320
Germany	.5758	.5722	1.7368	1.7475
30-day fwd	.5741	.5705	1.7420	1.7527
60-day fwd	.5724	.5658	1.7471	1.7675
90-day fwd	.5707	.5673	1.7523	1.7627
Greece	.005206	.005206	192.10	192.10
Hong Kong	.1288	.1288	7.7655	7.7655
y-India	.0386	.0386	25.930	25.930
Indonesia	.000510	.000510	1961.00	1961.00
Ireland	1.5385	1.5385	.6500	.6500
Israel	.4255	.4255	2.3500	2.3500
Italy	.000766	.000766	1305.50	1306.50
Japan	.007323	.007305	136.55	136.90
30-dy fwd	.007312	.007293	136.76	137.11
60-dy fwd	.007302	.007284	136.95	137.29
90-dy fwd	.007294	.007276	137.09	137.43
Jordan	1.4472	1.4472	.69100	.69100
Lebanon	.001119	.001119	894.00	894.00
Malaysia	.3596	.3596	2.7805	2.7805
z-Mexico	.000304	.000304	3290.00	3090.00
Netherlands	.5074	.5077	1.9710	1.9695
N. Zealand	.5730	.5730	1.7452	1.7452
Norway	.1458	.1462	6.8570	6.8410
Pakistan	.0403	.0403	24.81	24.81
y-Peru	1.2618	1.2618	.79250	.79250
z-Philippines	.0378	.0378	26.46	26.46
Portugal	.006680	.006680	149.70	149.70
Saudi Arabia	.2667	.2667	3.7500	3.7500
Singapore	.5802	.5802	1.7235	1.7235
So. Korea	.001364	.001364	733.10	733.10
So. Africa	.3473	.3473	2.8790	2.8790
Spain	.009174	.009179	109.00	108.95
Sweden	.1571	.1576	6.36700	6.34865
Switzerland	.6590	.6577	1.5175	1.5205
30-day fwd	.6568	.6563	1.5225	1.5238
60-day fwd	.6564	.6551	1.5234	1.5265
90-day fwd	.6551	.6538	1.5264	1.5295
Taiwan	.0375	.0375	26.70	26.70
Thailand	.03900	.03900	25.71	25.71
Turkey	.000218	.000218	4589.00	4589.00
U.A.E.	.2723	.2723	3.6727	3.6727
f-Uruguay	.000479	.000479	2120.00	2120.00
z-Venezuela	.0168	.0168	59.6000	59.6000
Yugoslavia	.04429	.04429	22.58	22.58

ECU: European Currency Unit, a basket of European currencies. The Federal Reserve Board's index of the value of the dollar against 10 other currencies weighted on the basis of trade was 93.14 Wednesday, off 44 points or 0.48 percent from Tuesday's 93.58. A year ago the index was 85.32.

c-commercial rate, d-free market rate, f-financial rate, y-official rate, z-floating rate.

Figure 11-4. (*From Investor's Daily, August 29, 1991, p. 25.*)

Investing," under the "Markets Diary" listing on the left-hand side of the page under "Commodities." Directly to the right of the title is "CRB Futures Index (1967 = 100)." Below that is a chart showing the movement of the CRB for about a year and a half (see Fig. 11-5). To the far right is the day-to-day within a week movement of the CRB. At the top of this weekly chart is the CRB figure to be entered on the interest rate chart.

In *Investor's Business Daily*, the CRB index can be found on the page with the futures prices at the top, similar to *The New York Times*. Within the box the CRB is given as high (Hi), low (Lo), and close (CL). Also note the chart that tracks the CRB for more than a year and a half. Use the CL figure.

In *Barron's*, the CRB can be found in two places. The CRB index appears in the "Barron's/Market Week" section under "The Trader." The figure is listed in the "Vital Signs" chart on the right side under "Inflation" (CRB Futures Index). *Barron's* also includes the CRB figure in the statistical section under "Market Laboratory/Bonds" at the bottom of the page to the left, as "CRB/Commodity Research Bureau Index of Futures Prices," listed by futures contract day. The last contract date is the figure to be entered on the interest rate chart.

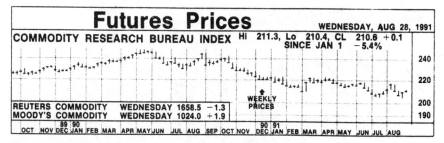

Figure 11-5. (*From Investor's Daily, August 29, 1991, p. 19.*)

Japanese and German Government Bond Yields

For our weekly interest rate chart we will use the 10-year Japanese and German government bond yields. These are the longest maturities that these governments issue. Therefore, if we want to compare foreign yields to U.S. Treasury yields, we must use the 10-year U.S. Treasury for comparative purposes. *The New York Times* and *Investor's Business Daily* do not provide a daily listing of these yields. However, on each Monday in the "Business Day" section or Section D on the second page is an excellent chart that includes these yields. The chart is "World Economies," which we have discussed before. It includes key statistical information for the past week for six major industrial countries, the United States, Japan, Germany, Britain, Canada, and Mexico. The chart is easily identified by the use of each country's flag. The second row from the bottom is called "10-Year Government Bond (Weekly %)." Under each of the two countries we are tracking are the current yields.

In *The Wall Street Journal*, the only daily quotes of foreign government bonds are found in Section C, "Money & Investing," in the column called "Bond Market Data Bank," which notes the date of the information directly to the right of the title. About three-quarters of the way down this chart is a section called "International Government Bonds" (see Fig. 11-6). There are four subsections: Japan, United Kingdom, Germany, and Canada. The Japanese 10-year government bond yield is found with a little, but easy, investigative work. For example, if the current year is 1992, 10 years would be 2002. Looking down the Japanese subsection, one does not find a bond with the maturity of 2002. But upon a closer look, one might find a maturity of 3/00, which is the closest bond to 10 years. Compared to the other maturities, that is the current Japanese 10-year government bond. Also, the Japanese assign a number to each bond issue. Periodically the Japanese government will issue a new 10-year government bond. One can learn about such a new issue by reading the credit markets columns of any of our publications. To find the yield, just look to the last column

INTERNATIONAL GOVERNMENT BONDS
Prices in local currencies, provided by Salomon Brothers Inc.

COUPON	MATURITY (Mo./yr.)	PRICE	CHANGE	YIELD*	COUPON	MATURITY (Mo./yr.)	PRICE	CHANGE	YIELD*
JAPAN (3 p.m. Tokyo)					**GERMANY** (5 p.m. London)				
#89 5.10%	6/96	93.910	− 0.342	6.59%	6.00%	8/93	94.450	− 0.192	8.96%
#59 7.30	12/93	101.543	− 0.072	6.57	6.00	10/92	96.420	− 0.177	9.14
#108 4.80	6/98	89.894	− 0.795	6.66	6.75	9/97	90.050	− 0.570	8.74
#129 6.40	3/00	99.069	− 0.930	6.54	9.00	1/01	101.950	− 1.140	8.49
#15 6.70	3/11	99.704	− 1.020	6.72	8.88	1/96	99.820	− 0.271	8.71
UNITED KINGDOM (5 p.m. London)					**CANADA** (3 p.m. EDT)				
10.00%	4/93	99.969	+ 0.094	9.99%	9.50%	6/10	96.300	− 0.200	9.93%
9.00	10/08	93.125	− 0.219	9.82	9.25	10/96	99.950	+ 0.830	9.26
13.50	9/92	103.469	+ 0.062	10.07	9.75	6/21	98.050	− 0.200	9.95
10.00	11/96	99.813	+ 0.125	10.02	9.00	6/93	99.950	+ 0.150	9.02
10.00	2/01	99.781	− 0.062	10.02	9.75	12/01	99.950	− 0.050	9.76

*Equivalent to semi-annual compounded yields to maturity

Figure 11-6. (From The Wall Street Journal, August 20, 1991, p. C14. Reprinted by permission of The Wall Street Journal, © 1991 Dow Jones & Company, Inc. All rights reserved worldwide.)

within each of the four subsections under "Yield"; for the Japanese bond we are looking at the yield is 6.54%. For the German 10-year government bond yield, use the same procedure for locating the current 10-year government bond as we did for the Japanese government bond. All you have to do is find the bond that is closest to the 10-year maturity. For the German bond the yield is 8.49%.

In *Barron's*, foreign bond yields are found in the statistical section under "Market Laboratory/Bonds" at the bottom of the page under the title "J.P. Morgan Overseas Government Bond Index." This index is a weekly, as is *The New York Times* index. To the far right of that index is a column with the title "-Yield-" which has a subhead called "%" under which you can find both the Japanese and German 10-year government bond yields by finding the first column entitled "Country" to locate the nations.

Stocks—The Dow 30
Industrial Average

We use the Dow 30 Industrial Average as the indicator of the U.S. stock market. In *The New York Times* that number appears on the first page of Section D, "Business Day," under the listing on the left side of the page called "Business Digest." Just below the title to the far left is the Dow 30 Industrial Average, plus the change from one day to the next. In addition, one can also find the Dow listed under "Market Indicators" under the heading "New York Stock Exchange Issues," with a chart called "The Dow: Minute by Minute." That chart shows the daily change from the previous day, then the "Close," which is the figure you want to put into the interest rate chart.

In *The Wall Street Journal*, on the first page of Section C, "Money & Investing," in the "Markets Diary" column, the first chart is called "Stocks Dow Jones Industrial Average," with a chart to the right showing the daily movement on a day-to-day basis with the figure we use on the top of the daily chart. The chart to the left shows the movement of the Dow Industrial Average for about a year and a half up until the week of the current month. There are other places to find the figure, such as on the same first page of Section C in the column that discusses the prior day's stock and bond market activities called "Tuesday's Markets" if it is discussing that particular prior day. One can also find the figure on the second page in the daily column called "Abreast of the Market," which includes the hour-by-hour movement of the Dow. Furthermore, on the same page on the right is the "Stock Market Data Bank," which includes all the major stock indices, with the first one being the "Dow Industrial Averages," under which you will find "30 Industrials" followed by "Close."

In *Investor's Business Daily*, the Dow 30 Industrial Average is found in the column entitled "Inside the Market," usually found between the third and fifth pages, and in the series of charts on another page called "General Market Indicators." The third chart from the top, right after the title "Dow Jones Industrials," gives the day, the average, the number of points up or down, and the percent change from the day before.

In *Barron's*, the Dow Industrial Average appears in the "Traders" column under "Vital Signs." The first number on the left-hand side is the figure we need, called "DJ Industrials" under "Friday's Close." You also can find the figure in the "Review and Preview" section under the heading "Last Week" and subheading "Dow Industrials." If you are interested in finding what stocks make up the Dow Industrial Average, you can find the listing in the statistical section on the page titled "Market Laboratory/Stocks" under the heading, "Components—Dow Jones 65 Stock Averages," and the subheading "Industrials."

Oil Prices

We use the West Texas Intermediate Crude futures price index, called the WTIC index. This commodity is traded on the New York Mercantile Exchange (NYMEX) and is given as crude oil for delivery in the next month. For example, if you are looking for the price in October, the price given will be the futures contract due in November. In *The New York Times*, you can find the particular oil price we use on the first page of Section D, "Business Day," in "Business Digest" with the heading "Oil Nymex Spot." That number is the West Texas Intermediate Crude price. The same number also can be found as part of the column called "Futures/Options," in the listing of "Cash Prices" with the date of the prior day just below the title. Move to the last section called "Petroleum"; under "West Texas Intermed $ per bbl fob," you can find the figure we use in the number column to the left, which is for the day before. The column next to it is the previous day's figure.

In *The Wall Street Journal*, the same number is given on the first page of Section C, "Money & Investing," in the "Markets Diary" under "Commodities," where we found the CRB and gold price. Just below the gold price is "Oil (W.Tex.int.crude), bbl," with the closing price first. You can also find the same number in the Section C column called "Commodities" in the chart called "Oil Prices," which is located on the right side of the page under "Domestic." The first figure is called "W. Tex Int Cush" and is located directly to the right under the column that gives the previous day's figures. The chart also lists the figures for the day before the previous day and a year ago.

In *Investor's Business Daily*, the West Texas Intermediate Crude oil price can be found in the same "Spot Prices" chart as the gold price, under "Petroleum—Crude Grades" (see Fig. 11-3). Here the prior day's close and the day's close before that are given.

In *Barron's*, one can find the oil price in the same "Vital Signs" chart as we used to find the Dow Jones Industrial Average, the CRB, and the price of gold. Look for the heading called "Crude Oil (NYM nearby futures)" for the closing Friday number. You can also find the oil price in the statistical section called "Commodities Futures" under the heading "N.Y. Mercantile Exchange." The subheading is "Crude Oil." The third dollar figure to the right is the one you want. Just check it against the figure you found in the "Vital Signs" chart to be sure it is the correct figure.

Summary

We have now discussed all the factors that appear on the weekly interest rate chart. Again, as experience is gained, you may wish to add other factors or to replace some factors on the chart. I strongly suggest that you keep the specific interest rates, however. Economists, financial analysts, portfolio managers, businesspeople, and many other users of interest rate information have their own statistics that they follow. But all relate to these basic interest rates. What we are trying to do is obtain an indication of what is happening. For example, some analysts use the long bond futures index as an important indicator. One could also add mortgage rates, foreign stock market indexes, and the municipal bond buyer 20 bond index of the 20 most actively traded general-obligation or tax-backed municipal issuers as factors to follow. What you use depends on both your particular need and the time available to locate information and enter it on your particular chart.

The Monthly Interest Rate Chart

The Data

The monthly interest rate chart is shown in Fig. 11-7. The basis for setting up the data portion of the monthly interest rate chart is the weekly interest rate chart. Using the same data, the monthly chart takes each of the four or five weeks (depending on the month) and determines what happened in those weeks. One can also use a spreadsheet program to calculate the numbers, not only for the monthly but also for the quarterly interest rate chart.

There are several ways to show the weekly changes on the monthly chart. I average the 5 days of the week to obtain the weekly numbers. For example, for each week on the monthly chart, I average five daily yields of the 3-month Treasury bill. Then I note the change between the first and last weeks. Another method would be to take each of the Friday numbers and put that into the weekly column, so that when you calculate the change, you are using the close of the first week against the close of the last week of that particular month. This method is least time-consuming, but I prefer the simple averaging method because if you use Friday, then when a major indicator such as employment is reported, it could easily

MONTHLY INTEREST RATE CHART

Month of _____	Week 1 Average	Week 2 Average	Week 3 Average	Week 4 Average	Change	Key Interest Rate Factors Yields: U=Up D=Down N=Neutral
	Comments					
Federal Funds Rate						
3 Mon. Treas. Bill						
2 Year Treas. Note						
10 Year Treas. Note						
30 Year Treas. Bond						
Gold (COMEX)						
Yen in Dollars						Key Factors Overlooked
Mark in Dollars						
CRB						
Japan 10 Year Bond						
German 10 Year Bond						Current Interest Rate Trend
Stocks - Dow Indust.						
WTIC Oil Price						

Figure 11-7. Monthly interest rate chart.

skew the average (since employment is always reported on the first Friday of the month except when a holiday occurs). Also, when an indicator is reported, the financial markets often show volatility until they settle down. Perhaps, instead of using the close of each Friday, one could use the close on Monday of the first week and the close on Monday for each of the following weeks except the last week, when one would use the close at Friday. Obviously, there are many methods for calculating these changes.

Interpreting the Factors

The section to the right of the monthly interest rate chart, entitled "Key Interest Rate Factors," is obtained from the weekly interest rate charts. Basically, I take each of the weekly charts and circle or mark in red the most important factor or factors that occurred during that week. Then I put these factors in the monthly interest rate chart, noting the symbols for yields moving up, down, or remaining neutral on the far right-hand side. I do the same for the section called "Key Factors Overlooked." Having entered this information on the monthly interest rate chart, I then sit back and review what the key factors have been during that particular month. Then I determine the current interest rate trend in the last section. I use the comments section just above the data for elaborating the current interest rate trend in more detail. Or I add important comments that I wish to review when creating the next month's or quarter's chart.

The Quarterly Interest Rate Chart

The Data

The quarterly interest rate chart is shown in Fig. 11-8. Using the monthly interest rate charts and assuming use of the averaging method, take each of the weeks and average them to determine an average for the particular month. Then establish the change from month 1 to month 3 and enter that result in the change column. If you are using a spreadsheet program, calculation will be quite easy. If you want to use a moving average, all the data is there. All you need to do is use the formula for creating a moving average in the same way as you would determine the average formula within the spreadsheet.

Interpreting the Factors

The same method of finding the more important factors for the monthly interest rate chart is used to find the key factors for the quarterly interest

QUARTERLY INTEREST RATE CHART

Quarter _____	Month 1 Average	Month 2 Average	Month 3 Average	Change	Key Interest Rate Factors Yields: U=Up D=Down N=Neutral
Comments					
Federal Funds Rate					
3 Mon. Treas. Bill					
2 Year Treas. Note					
10 Year Treas. Note					
30 Year Treas. Bond					
Gold (COMEX)					
Yen in Dollars					Key Factors Overlooked
Mark in Dollars					
CRB					
Japan 10 Year Bond					
German 10 Year Bond					Current Interest Rate Trend
Stocks - Dow Indust.					
WTIC Oil Price					

Figure 11-8. Quarterly interest rate chart.

rate chart. Take each of the monthly charts, and circle or mark in red the most important factors. Then write or type them onto the quarterly chart, noting the symbols for yields moving up, down, or remaining neutral. The same method is used to indicate key factors overlooked. Again, sit back and review the key factors and then determine a current interest rate trend. Use the "Comments" space above the data for more detailed information in terms of prospective trends.

There is no doubt that one can create four quarterly charts, a 6-month chart, and finally a yearly chart. The same methods would be used for all these charts. The longer the time period, the more it will take to think through what is happening. But that is the fun part of this entire exercise. The combination of the data and the interpretation of the many key factors on the movement of interest rates is precisely what these charts can help you with in deciding the direction or the trend of interest rates. I strongly suggest that you watch for different views and opinions about what is happening, so that when you are thinking about the trend of interest rates, you do not become caught in the consensus view without considering other points of view. Look at the data, check the factors overlooked, weigh the differing opinions against the data, and then make your own decision as to what the key factors are and what effect they have had and will have on the movement of interest rates.

12
Charting Interest Rate Trends

In this chapter I will fill in several charts and discuss my interpretations of a particular week, 3 months, and a quarter that have actually taken place. In this way, you will be able to see how data is gathered and what interpretations I drew from the charts. As we discuss the charts, I will comment as if I was reading the daily and weekly information on the day I filled them out. The description of the weekly interest rate chart will be based on day-to-day activities from Monday to Monday. How many of the four publications are used to collect the data is a matter of individual preference, based mostly on the amount of time available. I want to stress that the reader *can* use only one of the publications if time is very limited. While none of the publications provides all the necessary information on a daily basis, each does provide it all during the course of a week.

In this chapter I have used all the publications in order to provide the most comprehensive approach to executing the process. In Chap. 11 we discussed where each piece of data can be found in each publication. I normally use at least one of the three daily newspapers in the early morning to fill in the appropriate blanks on my chart. If time permits, I go through the other dailies, particularly the important columns about interest rates, later in the day. Using only one of the publications, it takes a maximum of 15 minutes to enter the data on the chart and another 15 minutes to interpret the factors. Sometimes less time is needed, depending on how many factors have been reported. As you become efficient in using the charts, the time needed to perform the work should become shorter.

The Weekly Interest Rate Chart

Monday, June 24, 1991

The New York Times.   The first week we will cover begins on June 24, 1991, with a reading of Monday's edition of *The New York Times*. The filled-in weekly interest rate chart we will have at the end of the week is shown as Fig. 12-1. Refer to it as we locate and enter the various factors. I first turn to the second page of the Business Section to look at the chart entitled "World Economies." I usually clip this chart and keep it in my interest rate notebook for further reference. The three countries I review quickly are the United States, Japan, and Germany. I look particularly at the 10-year government bonds of these three nations, their respective inflation rates, and the exchange rates, none of which show much change from the previous week.

Next I turn to the "Credit Markets" column, which carries a typical

WEEKLY INTEREST RATE CHART

Week of June 24, 1991	Mon	Tues	Wed	Thurs	Fri	Key Interest Rate Factors U=Up D=Down N=Neutral
Comments Uncertainty on recovery. Watch Germany. Chief banker resigns; new chief extremely hard on inflation; could push rates up later.		May Dur 3.8/3.6 2nd big rise 2 yr Treas	GNP Fin 2.8/1.9 5 yr Treas	May Per Income 0.5/0.1 spd 1.1 claims -17,000 431,000	May LEI up 4th stg mon 0.8/0.4	Monday to Friday Difference 3 Mon. T-Bill in Basis Points (5) 30 Yr. T-Bond in Basis Points (10) Key Factors 1. CRB trending down; positive D for inflation. Weak economy.
Federal Funds Rate	5.65	5.73	6.00	5.63	5.81	2. LEI up for 4th straight mon. U
3 Mon. Treas. Bill	5.75	5.74	5.70	5.70	5.70	3. Durable Goods up for 2nd U straight month
2 Year Treas. Note	6.88	6.90	7.02	6.96	6.90	4. German bond yields rising; U but they decided to keep rates firm.
10 Year Treas. Note	8.31	8.32	8.33	8.29	8.22	5. Personal income up; 4th U stgt rise;Highest since fall 1990; spending up.
30 Year Treas. Bond	8.50	8.50	8.51	8.48	8.40	Savings rate to 3.5% from 4.5%; shows consumers spdg.
Gold (COMEX)	363	365.60	365.90	366	368.10	6. Claims below 500,000. U Key Factors Overlooked
Yen in Dollars	138.75	138.70	138.40	137.96	137.53	U.S. budget deficit widened to U record number; S&L to blame.
Mark in Dollars	1.7820	1.7940	1.7875	1.7948	1.8075	
CRB	210.29	210.84	211.23	209.09	208.46	
Japan 10 Year Bond	6.78	6.75	6.75	6.77	6.78	
German 10 Year Bond	8.19	8.21	8.24	8.28	8.30	
Stocks - Dow Indust.	2913.01	2910.11	2913.01	2944.93	2906.75	Current Interest Rate Trend
WTIC Oil Price	19.98	20.05	20.05	20.48	20.56	Temporarily down but if economic indicators continue to show strength with mod infl. long end will rise.

Figure 12-1. Weekly interest rate chart for the week of June 24, 1991.

headline: "Views Differ on Increase in Rates."* The opening sentence suggests that market participants are very concerned about whether the economy will start to recover, and if it does whether inflation will begin to rise enough to push up interest rates. The article goes on to discuss the Federal Reserve Board's possible actions over the next several months, the recent meeting of the G-7 countries as they review the 20% rise in the value of the dollar as a reflection of the rise in interest rates, and a preview of specific factors that will be reported during this week. One sentence catches my eye. Gilpin notes that, in the statement of the G-7 countries, they said that even though lower interest rates are important, the economic conditions of particular countries have to be understood. In other words, if one country's economy is sluggish, interest rates might have to be lowered; while in another country with a growing economy, interest rates might have to be pushed up. Since Germany and Japan are the two major countries to watch because of their significant influence on the United States, what their central bankers do to either thwart inflation or to spur their economies will have an effect on U.S. interest rates. What the effect will be depends on many other factors as well. But most important, since the chart tracks the yields of both the longest German and the longest Japanese government bonds, I should be able to pick up what might happen as I track these specific interest rates. Throughout the article, varying views by economists or participants in the bond market are given. This column serves as an excellent view of the past week as well as of prospects for the coming weeks. These views provide some perspective on what may or may not happen.

I pull out my chart and, using *The New York Times'* "Economic Calendar," fill in the indicators that will be reported during the week under their respective days. Then I look at the Monday chart, "Current Interest Rates," which shows how both short- and long-term rates have been moving from December 1990 through the last three weeks of June 1991.

I read one other article about gold. Since the chart tracks gold prices on the New York Commodity Exchange (COMEX), it is worth reading. The article points out that, in the opinion of some analysts, gold is less important today as an inflation hedge because of four things: (1) the use of computers has brought about the globalization of financial markets, so that tracking gold prices is far quicker and easier than before; (2) other investments are now available, particularly option and future contracts, as a hedge against inflation or as a financial means of offsetting a contrary movement of stocks and bonds; (3) the reduced tensions between the West

---

*Kenneth N. Gilpin, "Views Differ on Increase in Rates," *The New York Times*, June 24, 1991, p. D5.

and the East; and (4) the minimal likelihood that a worldwide financial crisis will occur. However, the article does make it clear that other analysts believe that gold still has considerable value as an indicator; the controversy appears to be only what that value is.*

The Wall Street Journal.   I next turn to *The Wall Street Journal* and Section C, "Money & Investing." First I find the chart called "Bond Market Data Bank" so that I can fill in Friday's Japanese and German 10-year government bond yields, given in the small chart entitled "International Government Bonds." Then I find the "Credit Markets" column, written today by Tom Herman. I usually fill in the Treasury interest rates and the other factors over the weekend from *The New York Times*, because it is published on Saturday and *The Wall Street Journal* is not. I could also fill in the Treasury figures on Sunday using *Barron's* or on Monday from either *The Wall Street Journal* or *Investor's Business Daily*.

I notice on the first page of *The Wall Street Journal* an excellent chart showing unemployment claims from mid-1988 to mid-1991. I check the "Tracking the Economy" column,† which includes the "Statistics to Be Released This Week" chart; I check the information against the data on my chart obtained from *The New York Times*. *The Wall Street Journal* chart adds a few important facts. It provides the release date of the indicator, the actual figure for the previous month or week, and the current consensus expectation of what the figure will be when it is released. I often clip this chart and keep it for reference. "Tracking the Economy" also contains a brief discussion of the personal income indicator that will be released on Wednesday, including a good illustration that shows personal income from mid-November 1990 to mid-May 1991. Next I review the rest of the column for any additional information to supplement what I read in *The New York Times*.

Next, I turn to the "Credit Markets" column, written today by Constance Mitchell.‡ Despite its title, this particular article offers little new information on interest rates. But I do check the "Treasury Yield Curve" and the "Bond Yields" chart in the "Credit Markets" column. The first chart shows how steep the current Treasury yield curve has become since last Friday, 1 week ago, and 4 weeks ago. It shows that as of last Friday, short-term rates were around 6.70% and long-term yields at 8.50%, a spread of 180 basis points. The lower short-term yields are a result of a decline in the federal funds rate, which is controlled by the Federal Reserve Board. The long-term yields are high in reaction to possible recovery of the U.S. econ-

*Jonathan Fuerbringer, "Fewer Investors Find Haven in Gold," ibid., p. D1.

†"Tracking the Economy," *The Wall Street Journal*, June 24, 1991, p. A2.

‡"Corporate Bond Issuance Surges as Treasurers Conclude That Interest Rates Are Bottoming Out," Credit Markets, ibid., p. C17.

omy and concerns about rising inflation. The "Bond Yields" chart shows the movement of AA-rated utilities, long-term Treasuries, and municipals from December 1990 to mid-June 1991. The sloping yield curve is evident in all three of these securities.

I next turn to the "Foreign Exchange" column, written by Candace Cummerbatch.* She discusses the current strength of the U.S. dollar and the ability of the central bankers to deal with that strength. This Monday column often reviews the past week's activities in the dollar markets. In today's column, Cummerbatch notes the meeting of the G-7 nations in London the day before. Their concern is the strong dollar, which has risen recently against other currencies in reaction to the possibility of the ending of the U.S. economic recession.

Monday's "Commodities" column contains no information of value concerning interest rates. Before leaving *The Wall Street Journal,* however, I look at the front page of Section C to check the Commodities Research Board futures index chart, which shows the movement of the CRB from December 1990 through May 1991. Clearly it has moved downward, indicating the effects of the recession on the price of both agricultural and industrial commodities included in the index.

Investor's Daily. Upon beginning to read *Investor's Daily,*† I notice an excellent chart on the first page on mortgage rates from January 1990 to June 1991. It shows clearly the effect of the recession on mortgage rates, which began to move down sometime in April 1990, from around 10.50%, to approximately 9.80% by June 1991.

Before I read the "Credit Markets" column, I flip through the paper and notice an article describing the views of high-ranking business executives gathered in Beaver Creek, Colorado.‡ Most appear to be quite pessimistic about the recovery, despite recent economic reports that a recovery may be beginning. Others are less so, believing that recovery will occur soon, but at a much slower pace than had been expected. To me it seems that nobody is quite sure what is going to happen or when it is going to happen. That opinion is clearly reflected in the long-term Treasury rates, which have risen tentatively in the face of uncertainty as to how weak the recovery will be—not how strong it might be.

---

*Candace Cummerbatch, "Dollar Appears Strong Enough to Resist Intervention to Knock Currency Lower," Foreign Exchange, ibid., p. C10.

†*Author's note:* In mid-1991, when the analysis discussed in this chapter was done, *Investor's Business Daily* was called *Investor's Daily.* In order to be accurate, then, when this newspaper is referred to in the context of filling out the interest rate charts, it will be called *Investor's Daily.*

‡"U.S. Recovery Is Months Away, Global Business Leaders Believe," *Investor's Daily,* June 24, 1991, p. 7.

Next to this article is another that describes how wide the U.S. monthly budget gap has become, reaching a record $53.32 billion for May. This is an issue that should be noted on the weekly interest rate chart under "Key Factors Overlooked," because of the potential for an upward movement of interest rates if the financial community decides to pay attention to it. If the deficit continues to widen, the U.S. Treasury will have to borrow more, and that means higher interest rates. I briefly skim the column entitled "Foreign Exchange," which says about the same as the two other newspapers.

The "Credit Markets" column is written by Phil Hawkins.* He notes that a recent Salomon Bros. report expressed the opinion that the 30-year U.S. Treasury will rise to 9.00% (about 50 basis points from current yields on the "long bond") because of fears of a U.S. economic recovery and the lack of buying of Treasuries by foreign investors, among several reasons. The main point of Hawkins' commentary is concern about the forthcoming auction of U.S. Treasury securities: $12.5 billion of 2-year notes and $9.25 billion of 5-year notes. At what level interest rates will end up in response to these large issuances of Treasury borrowings is a source of uncertainty in the financial markets. The yields on current bonds will tend to stall until the results of the auction take place. Who will buy these notes and at what interest rate will trouble the market until the actions are completed.

Before leaving *Investor's Business Daily,* I usually check the several interest rate charts entitled "Selected Interest Rates." One key rate on the chart today shows a sharp decline in 90-day CD rates, from a high of about 9.50% in August 1989 to a low of 6.00% by June 17, 1991.

Tuesday, June 25, 1991

The New York Times. On Tuesday, I start my interest rate review by filling in the appropriate data on my weekly interest rate chart. Using *The New York Times,* I look at the first page of "Business Day," or Section D. To the far left is "Business Digest," listing key numbers and articles in this section.† At the top of this chart are several numbers I use on the interest rate chart: the Dow 30 Industrials, the dollar vs. the Japanese yen, and bonds (30-year Treasuries). I then flip to the page where the futures statistics are located to find the Commodity Research Bureau index, which is at the top of the page. To the left is the listing called "Foreign Exchange."‡

---

*Phil Hawkins, "Most of Recent Gain Is Erased Putting Yield Back above 8.5%," Credit Markets, ibid., p. 30.

†"Business Digest," *The New York Times,* June 25, 1991, p. D2.

‡"Foreign Exchange," ibid., p. D19.

From this chart I take the dollar in foreign currency numbers for the German mark. (Remember, I already took the dollar versus the yen from the front page of "Business Day.") I next decide to read the "Currency Markets" column, which has a lead headline entitled "Dollar Down amid Concern about Rates and Polices."* The article notes that the fall in the dollar resulted in part from a statement issued from the G-7 meeting in London, held over the weekend to discuss the recent 20% rise in the dollar, and in part from concerns that Germany might raise its interest rate, which would make the mark more valuable and soften demand for the dollar as well as other currencies. The statement from the G-7 countries said that they would intervene only "if necessary." The currency markets were unsettled by that statement, because it left doubt as to what the G-7 countries would do if the dollar continues to climb. In the view of U.S. participants, if the dollar continues to rise, it might stop any beginnings of a recovery because the higher the dollar, the more expensive U.S. goods are priced compared to foreign products.

I flip down to the "Futures/Options" section, which contains no information concerning interest rates. However, on many occasions this column will talk about oil or gold prices and the events that create changes in their prices. Further, within this column is the numbers chart called "Cash Prices." At the bottom is the listing of petroleum prices. I look for the West Texas Intermediate price. One can either use this oil price number or the one on the front page of "Business Day," in the upper left-hand chart we noted before.

Back one page is the "Credit Markets" column. I put down on my chart the important numbers in the chart called "Key Rates," including the federal funds rate, sometimes the 30-year Treasury instead of using the number on the first page, and lastly the 3-month Treasury bill. This particular rate is a discount rate, and I change it to a bond equivalent rate or use the statistics in the chart entitled "Treasury Bills, Bonds and Notes." Each Tuesday (except holidays), *The New York Times* prints a chart showing the results of the weekly Treasury bill auction. This simple chart provides an excellent view of short-term rates from March 1991 to the present. At the end of the "Credit Markets" column is a listing of all the results of the auction for both the 3- and the 6-month Treasury bills. I note on my chart the maturity of the 3-month Treasury bill and then check in the "Treasury Bills" column we noted before. When you look at it, you will see that the first group of numbers is called "Treasury Bills" and lists by date, bid and ask discount yields, change from the previous day, and finally yield, which means the bond equivalent yield. Using the bond equivalent yield

---

*"Dollar Down amid Concern about Rates and Policies," Currency Markets, ibid., p. D19.

allows for more accurate comparison with the other U.S. Treasury interest rates we use on the weekly interest rate chart.

Now I start to read through the "Credit Markets" column,* which today appears to be short of things to say, perhaps because of a dull Monday. However, it does mention another drop in the Commodity Research Bureau's index of 21 leading spot commodity prices, and the Japanese stock scandal that is currently on the front pages of world financial journals and newspapers. The drop in the CRB implies that inflation is down, and the Japanese stock scandal suggests that Japanese investors may well place funds in the U.S. Treasury market until this mess is resolved. Some concerns are related to this week's auction of 2- and 5-year U.S. Treasury notes, as to whether the large supply will force yields up to entice buyers. Other than that, today's column offers little else. Since no indicators were released on Monday, I now pick up *The Wall Street Journal* and pull out its business section.

The Wall Street Journal. I turn first to the page-long chart called "Bond Market Data Bank," which shows the date 6/24/91.† There are a number of inset blocks of statistics, including "Major Indexes," "Corporate Bonds," "Tax-Exempt Bonds," "Mortgaged-Backed Securities," "Guaranteed Investment Contracts," "International Government Bonds," "Total Rates of Return on International Bonds," and "Eurodollar Bonds." The chart I need is called "International Government Bonds." Under Japan, I look for the current 10-year government bond, which is listed as "#129" with a coupon of 6.40% and maturing in March 2000 or 3/00. Moving across that line to the yield (6.78%), I enter that number on my weekly interest rate chart. Then I move over to Germany for the 10-year government bond, which in this case is the 9.00% coupon maturing on January 2001 or 1/01. The yield is 8.19%. If the Japanese or the Germans issue a new 10-year government bond, one can always find a discussion of it in the various columns of the sources we use.

If I purchased *The Wall Street Journal* instead of *The New York Times*, I can obtain the same information as I got from the *Times*. The key column is "Credit Markets," written today by Kevin Donovan and Christopher B. Wilcock.‡ The article talks about one economist, Mitchell Held of Smith Barney, Harris Upham & Co., who notes that the lack of activity in the Treasury market is attributable to the closing of the books for the quarter.

---

*Kenneth N. Gilpin, "Short-Term Notes Down Slightly," Credit Markets, ibid., p. D18.

†"Bond Market Data Bank, 6/24/91," *The Wall Street Journal*, June 25, 1991, p. C16.

‡Kevin Donovan and Christopher B. Wilcock, "Bonds Finish Mixed as Investors Are Reluctant to Change Positions Ahead of End of the Quarter," Credit Markets, ibid., p. C19.

Portfolio managers do not like to trade at the end of the quarter, so little activity results despite important factors coming to the market. Under the subhead "Treasury Securities," I can find the yields from Monday's activity in the 2-, 10-, and 30-year Treasuries to put on the chart. The *Journal* also publishes the results of the 3- and 6-month Treasury auction. I can enter either the discount rate or the bond equivalent yield, but I prefer the latter.

I skim through the other pieces in the "Credit Markets" column, including "Corporate & Junk Bonds," "Municipal Securities," "Mortgage & Asset-Backed Securities," and lastly "Foreign Bonds." I pay particular attention to this information, because of the strong relationship between German and Japanese government bond interest rates and U.S. government bond interest rates. In this section one can always learn if a new foreign government bond will be issued. Today's comments concern the scandal in the Japanese stock brokerage firms and its effect on the current Japanese "No. 129" 10-year government bond, which has declined in yield.

I then return to the first page of Section C to look at "Market Diary," in order to obtain the other information I need to fill in my chart. In the "Interest" chart, I find yesterday's federal funds rate with a nice little chart inset showing the movement of the federal funds rate from Monday to Monday. Also, I take the 3-month Treasury bill yield and put it onto my chart. In the chart "U.S. Dollar," I find the Japanese yen and German mark figures listed under "Close" in the first column and put them on my chart. Below that chart is the commodities chart, which shows in pictorial form the movement of the CRB futures index (1967 = 100) from December 1990 to June 1991, and next to it the weekly movement of the CRB from Monday to Monday, with yesterday's closing number on top. Also listed in this chart are gold (Comex spot) and oil (W.Tex.int.crude) prices under "Close." Both of these numbers are put on the weekly interest rate chart.

I next look for the "Foreign Exchange" column, which discusses the aftereffects of the meeting of the G-7 countries over the past weekend. The one comment I pick up from this column is by British Prime Minister John Major concerning the dollar's future. His comments to the French newspaper *Le Figaro* are quoted in this column: The Prime Minister was concerned about the large need for capital for reconstructing Germany and the need at the same time to mitigate inflation, which would justify the raising of short-term interest rates.* This means that the German central bank may raise interest rates to quell inflationary pressures in the country. That could spell trouble for U.S. interest rates. The remaining comments in the

---

*Alwyn Scott, "Dollar Drifts Lower after G-7 Officials Fail to Take Strong Stand on Currency," Foreign Exchange, ibid., p. C13.

column are similar to those in *The New York Times*. In the "Commodities" column, a key comment may have an effect on interest rates in the future. The column notes that corn futures prices are rising because of forecasts for hot and dry weather across the Midwest at a critical time for development of corn. This means that the cost of grain may increase, thus forcing up the producer price index. This in turn would mean inflation, and could push U.S. interest rates up in the future. I make a note on the chart to keep a watch on this development. However, an offsetting factor is that wheat requires hot, dry weather, as noted in the column. Maybe one will cancel the other out.

As no economic, fiscal, or monetary factors are reported on Monday, there is no need to look specifically at the second page of Section A.

Investor's Daily. Upon picking up *Investor's Daily*, I turn first to Phil Hawkins's "Credit Markets" column, but there is nothing here that has not been covered in the other newspapers. Next I look at the "Foreign Exchange" column, looking for further information about the G-7 meeting. Here again the stress is the concern that Germany will raise interest rates, which would make the German mark more valuable at the expense of the dollar and other currencies. I check my chart to see if I have noted that possible development. I will also keep a close eye on the movement of the German 10-year government bond yields for the week to see what happens. There is an excellent chart tracking the value of the dollar expressed in German marks on the first page of *Investor's Daily*, so I clip it for future reference.

Wednesday, June 26, 1991

The Wall Street Journal. I first pick out *The Wall Street Journal*'s numbers to fill in the spaces in my weekly interest rate chart, mostly from the "Markets Diary" in Section C, "Money & Investments." By looking at the charts in the "Markets Diary" column, I notice the continued decline of the CRB from early June. This implies that inflation may be coming down. I note this on my chart.

Next I turn to the "Credit Markets" column.* The text notes an important peculiarity of the bond market. Three key economic figures were reported the day before, all indicating that recovery is occurring: May durable goods orders were up, the Conference Board's June consumer confidence index rose, and May existing home sales increased. Ordinarily,

---

*Constance Mitchell and Kevin Donovan, "Treasury Long Bond Ekes out Small Gain despite More Signs of an Economic Recovery," Credit Markets, ibid., June 26, 1991, p. C10.

yields would also rise, as all these factors imply inflation. However, since this week will end the second quarter, portfolio managers are reluctant to change positions at this time. Thus yields will probably not move very much until the first week of July. A quick look at the "Treasury Yield Curve" in the "Credit Markets" column shows results over the past week compared to 4 weeks ago. I also note that three key economic indicators will be reported during the first week in July: the June index of the National Association of Purchasing Management and the June unemployment rate and employment numbers.

In reading the column I pick up only the previous day's yield on the 30-year Treasury. However, since the 2-year Treasury note was auctioned the day before, I note its maturity date on my chart. In that way, I can track the 2-year note from any of the Treasury listings in *The Wall Street Journal*, *The New York Times*, or *Investor's Business Daily*. It is better to put down the maturity dates of these U.S. Treasury securities on the weekly interest rate chart because if the "Credit Markets" columns of the respective newspapers do not include a particular yield, one can always go to the U.S. Treasury bills, notes, and bonds chart to locate the yield.

Before turning to the "Foreign Exchange" column, I take off the Japan and German bond yields from the "Bond Market Data Bank" to put on my chart. The "Foreign Exchange" column has several comments I begin to reflect on.* The issue of the dollar seems to be a key global factor. The dollar's rise, based on signs of U.S. economic recovery, is double-edged. The first edge: If the dollar continues to climb, it will depress other world currencies, making the prices of their products cheaper than U.S. products. If that continues, it would dampen the attempt of the U.S. economy to recover sufficiently by making U.S. products more expensive than those of other countries. When foreign currencies decline in value, it raises inflation, and this in turn pushes foreign interest rates upward, which slows the growth in foreign economies. The second edge: At the same time, the strength in the U.S. dollar raises U.S. interest rates as it reflects the growing strength of the U.S. economy, thereby making U.S. securities cheaper to purchase than foreign securities. Then cash flows back into the U.S. bond market to buy U.S. Treasury securities that support the U.S. trade deficit. However, the article notes that the G-7 countries might attempt to bring down the dollar. The problem is that the precise action that the G-7 might initiate is known only to the G-7 countries, despite speculation about what the levels should be, particularly for Japan and Germany. Thus the key issue is that there was no unequivocal statement by the G-7 that

*Alwyn Scott, "Dollar Puts in Mixed Showing as Fears Persist over Possible Concerted Action," Foreign Exchange, ibid., p. C11.

they would coordinate policy to bring down the dollar, and that made the foreign exchange markets jittery. Before leaving Section C, I skim the "Commodities" column, but there is nothing here concerning interest rates.

Back at the front page, I look at the chart showing durable goods orders from mid-1988 through mid-June 1991. Just from looking at the chart, it is clear that durable goods orders have risen for two straight months. Now I check the articles on page 2 of Section A under the heading "Economy." The first concerns durable goods orders, which showed a rise of 3.8% in May after rising 3.6% in April.* The article notes that despite the rise over the last 2 months, orders were still 6.1% below their level in May 1990. Reading further down into the article, the volatile transportation segment of the total figure rose a large 11.5% after falling 3.1% the previous month. Excluding the transportation orders, durable goods orders rose only 1.4% in May after a sharp rise of 5.9% in April. Therefore the rise, while important to sustaining the feeling that recovery is underway, also shows that it is happening slowly.

Further on in the article, the key component called orders for non-defense capital goods rose 4.2% after having fallen in each of the 4 previous months. Remember that this component indicates manufacturers' plans to invest or increase production. Also, shipments rose by 1% after rising 4.6% in April. Importantly, the backlog of orders is not picking up. Taken together, these numbers show that while durable goods orders are increasing, the pace is extremely slow. This indicator is still leaving the bond markets a little hesitant about the reality of the U.S. economic recovery.

In the same article, the Conference Board's consumer confidence index climbed to 78 in June from a revised 76.4 in May. This adds to the positive view about the U.S. economy. However, one of the economists quoted in the article notes that the rise is from a very low level. Fabian Linden, the Executive Director of the Board's Consumer Research Center, suggested that even though consumer confidence was on the rise, it was still at the point that indicated only very slow growth in the economy.

Another article on the same page discusses the sharp rise in existing home sales by 6% in May.† The feeling expressed in the article is that the rise is another step in the continued improvement in the housing market, and therefore a sign of U.S. economic recovery. However, there are some

---

*Paul Duke, Jr., and Kevin Pritchett, "Durable Goods Orders Rose 3.8% in May; Consumer Confidence Climbs Steadily," ibid., p. A2.

†Mitchell Pacelle, "Existing-Home Sales Grew 6% in May as Gradual Housing Recovery Continued," ibid., p. A2.

doubts expressed (as there always are) that much more information needs to be reviewed. These pessimists believe that rising interest rates, which have moved from 8.00% in February to 8.50% by June, and the serious lack of lending by the banking industry will stunt housing growth, and therefore slow the U.S. recovery.

All in all, *The Wall Street Journal* is articulating the view that a U.S. economic recovery is occurring but at a very slow pace. Once I diagnose an economic indicator that shows reviving growth, I continue to find offsetting components. Also, the U.S. recovery has to be weighed in the context of the rise of the dollar against foreign currencies.

The New York Times.   Next I turn to *The New York Times.* The first page of "Business Day" includes the headline "Durable Goods Orders Up 3.8% in May."* The first tidbit of information I pick up is that the April figure was revised up to 3.6% from 3%, and that the May figure was larger than expected. Again, the focus is on orders for nondefense items, which posted a 4.2% rise in May after a 10% drop in April. The article notes the doubters who still believe that the U.S. economy will slow down again. They believe that high consumer debt, a rising tax burden resulting from the rise in tax rates in states throughout the United States, and the continued caution by banks to lend funds will keep the U.S. economy growing slowly if at all. From my work analyzing the municipal bonds issued by states and cities nationwide, I strongly agree with that comment.

Also on the same page are two articles on consumer confidence and existing home sales. A key point made concerning consumer confidence is that this was the tenth straight month in which consumers had a lower opinion about current economic conditions. Since the consumer is a vital part of economic recovery, this particular aspect of the index supports the "slow recovery" view. However, the index also shows more optimism about the prospects for economic recovery in the months ahead, supporting the "recovering U.S. economy" view. At most, the controversy between the two points of view appears to be continuing from week to week. I make note of the dichotomy on my weekly interest rate chart.

The article on May sales for existing homes had nothing to add to what I had already gleaned from *The Wall Street Journal,* that lower mortgage rates and a slight rise in consumer confidence are beginning to encourage buyers in the housing market. However, as we pointed out earlier, interest rates have been rising. Maybe the rise will be short-lived. Also, this is the tail end of spring, when the buying season begins to pick up.

*Robert D. Hershey, Jr., "Durable Goods Orders Up 3.8% in May," *The New York Times,* June 26, 1991, p. D1.

I next turn to the "Credit Markets" column. Kenneth N. Gilpin, who writes this column, notes that according to many analysts, most economic reports were showing that economic recovery appears to be slow, at least.* I put down the rates for the newly auctioned 2-year Treasury note and the 10- and 30-year Treasuries, checking the latter against what I already had on my weekly interest rate chart. *The New York Times* illustration shows the average rates of the 2-year Treasury auctions since January 1990 through this last auction in bar-chart form. I clip the chart for future reference. The "Current Markets" column simply confirms what I already know about the rise in the dollar as a reflection of U.S. economic recovery.

Investor's Daily. In *Investor's Daily*, an illustration on p. 1 entitled "Existing Home Sales" shows the rise in this indicator over the past 4 months. This illustration also shows the indicator's moves from 1984 through mid-June 1991. The accompanying article† notes that inventories were much lower than in previous business cycles because producers were better able to balance consumer demand with production. Within the article, a little presidential pronouncement is proffered to encourage consumer confidence. The President's spokesperson, Marlin Fitzwater, suggested that the sharp rise in durable goods orders did not mean that the recession was over, but was merely one of several indicators that showed that the nation was very slowly coming out of economic malaise. The article highlights the "unfilled orders" component of the total figure, which declined by 0.1% in May, thereby possibly shutting off the recovery.

The "Credit Markets" column discussed the same items as the other newspapers.

Thursday, June 27, 1991

Investor's Daily. Today I begin my interest rate review with *Investor's Daily*. On the first page is a clearly delineated chart showing the movement of the gross national product (GNP) since 1980 though the end of the first quarter in March 1991.‡ The final revision of the GNP showed a drop of 2.8% annual rate for the first 3 months of 1991. To the right of the

---

*Kenneth N. Gilpin, "Treasury Issues Narrowly Mixed," Credit Markets, ibid., p. D15.

†Laurie Marmor, "Upturn Continues in Durable Goods Orders," *Investor's Daily*, June 26, 1991, p. 36.

‡*Author's note:* The U.S. Commerce Department did not publicly change the gross national product to the gross domestic product until December 1991, when it reported the preliminary third quarter figures. Therefore, for the remainder of this chapter gross national product (GNP) will be used.

illustration is a key article discussing GNP for the first 3 months of 1991, not what has begun to occur in the second 3 months, when indicators appear to be showing an end to the recession and a possible recovery of the U.S. economy.* The article points to a reduced amount of inventories as a key aspect of GNP. This important component of GNP is a strong sign of the potential for economic recovery, because inventories are so low that if demand picks up or consumers show a willingness to purchase, products will have to be produced to fill up inventories to meet the increased demand. As demand rises, both industrial production and capacity utilization factors will pick up in later months. Other components of GNP show that imports declined, as they would in a recession, but exports increased, showing that our trading partners were still buying. Thus, the final revision of the GNP figure showed all the attributes of a recession. The new indicators for the second 3 months of 1991 are displaying a possible change from recession to recovery, although the jury is still out on deciding exactly what is happening to the U.S. economy. Bond yields moved hardly at all when the advanced GNP was reported, since the information applies to the past which is already figured into the current yields of U.S. Treasury securities.

On the same page as the article on GNP is an analysis of current indicators and concerns that the economy may return to recession.† Based on conversations with several economists, the author points out Federal Reserve Board fears about inflation, which have prevented interest rates from being pushed lower. Furthermore, the author makes a key point that both states and cities nationwide have been planning to raise taxes to make up substantial losses in revenues that include sales, personal, and corporate taxes against sharply rising expenditures in the health and public safety categories. As many of these entities have a fiscal year ending in June, the total result of all the taxes to be raised will be an important issue to follow. In my work as head of municipal bond investment research for the Bank of New York, I strongly believed that the U.S. economy will continue to show slow growth because of the substantial difficulties that key industrial states are having generating operating revenues. These states include California, New York, Michigan, the entire Northeast, as well as many other states. The opposite view is articulated by David Bostian, chief economist and investment strategist at Jesup, Josephthal & Co. in New York. He believes that the dramatic change in countries leading to the revi-

---

*Dana Manning, "Pockets of Strength Seen amid Weak Profits," *Investor's Daily*, June 27, 1991, p. 1.

†Laurie Marmor, "Favorable Data Don't Preclude So-Called Double-Dip Recession," ibid., p. 27.

talization of democracy and capitalized economies will bring about long-term world growth. He believes that capital investment will be the underlying force that will encourage strong global economic growth. All this might put enormous pressure on interest rates, because strong growth normally means high inflation, which pushes up interest rates. It is my own opinion that revitalizing East Europe and the renewed efforts for establishing an economically unified Europe and Central and North America are issues to be considered in these extraordinary changing times. However, these changes will take considerable time in developing. Nevertheless, watching these changes and how they will influence U.S. interest rates is part of the process this book is about.

The "Foreign Exchange" column of *Investor's Daily* points out that the fall of the dollar the day before resulted from a fear that Germany would raise its interest rates to restrain its inflation.[*] Again, raising its interest rates would induce a flow of capital into Germany as investors buy the higher-yielding German government bond at the expense of U.S. Treasury securities, which must compete by raising interest rates to prevent an outflow of dollars to Germany.

Today's "Credit Markets" column just reviews Wednesday's market activity in both the Treasury and corporate bond markets.

The New York Times. With *The New York Times*, I start by looking for the numbers to fill in the blanks in my chart, using the figures at the top of the "Business Digest" column on the front page of Section D, "Business Day." I next turn to the "Credit Markets" column to catch up on the previous day's market activities and to find out what analysts are thinking about interest rates. Today's article implies that the market is basically sleepy because not much is happening to stimulate its juices.[†] The column does include a chart tracking the average yields on yesterday's auction of the 5-year Treasury note from 1988 through June 1991's auction. Again I decide to clip this chart for future reference. The author notes that there appears to be a beginning spotlight on the forthcoming June employment numbers, which will not be released until July 5, a week from this Friday. This implies that not much activity can be expected until then, as market participants normally place great emphasis on the components of the employment number because it may give a clue as to whether the Federal Reserve Board may or may not reduce short-term interest rates further.

I look for and find the yields for the 2-, 10-, and 30-year Treasury issues,

---

[*]"Dollar Falls on German Outlook; Comex Gold Climbs $1.30/Ounce," Foreign Exchange, ibid., p. 25.

[†]Kenneth N. Gilpin, "U.S. Issues Are Narrowly Mixed," Credit Markets, *The New York Times*, June 27, 1991, p. D20.

as well as check the "Key Rates" chart for the federal funds rate and the discount yield of the 3-month Treasury bill of the day before.

The "Currency Markets" column reinforces the data I reviewed in *Investor's Daily* in the "Foreign Exchange" column. I then pick up the dollar in foreign currency numbers for the German mark and the Japanese yen. Then I look at the top of the page for the little chart called "Commodity Research Bureau Index (CRB)" and put the CRB of the day before on my chart. There is nothing about interest rates in the "Futures/Options" column, so I look for the price of gold in the "Metals" chart to put onto my chart.

Lastly, I review *The New York Times* article on the GNP figure.* The chart accompanying the article is also excellent, as it depicts the GNP since 1987 through the first quarter of 1991. One can clearly see the two down quarters which officially mean a recession. The article also reinforces what was said in *Investor's Daily* and also notes the importance of the forthcoming July 5 employment numbers.

The Wall Street Journal. I turn to Section C in *The Wall Street Journal* to obtain the yields on the Japanese #129 government and German government 10-year bonds and put them on my chart. Then I move to the "Commodities" column, which today discusses the CRB index in detail because it has moved lower over the past several weeks despite a few ups and downs, and 16% since the beginning of the year.† The drop in the CRB means that inflation is constant and should not rise even if the Federal Reserve Board decides to lower short-term rates another notch. The "Foreign Exchange" column also notes the concerns about the German central bank raising its interest rates to quell inflation in that country.

Next I find the "Credit Markets" column, which points out that the GNP figure had no effect on bond yields.‡ However, the wait for Thursday's weekly claims for unemployment insurance is making the bond market a little nervous. If claims are down, that would be a short-term sign that the U.S. economy is showing a bit of recovery. If claims rise, it would mean that the U.S. economy is still weak and laying off more people. Within the column is a good illustration showing the movement of short-term interest rates from January 1991 to mid-June. The sharp drop in all the rates sparked by the downward movement of the federal funds rate has taken

---

*"G.N.P. Fell 2.8% in Quarter, Showing Severity of Slump," ibid., p. D2.

†Elyse Tanouye, "CRB Index Rebounds from Its Monday Low, But Analysts Say the Rise May be Short-Lived," Commodities, *The Wall Street Journal*, June 27, 1991, p. C12.

‡Kevin Donovan and Anita Raghavan, "Bonds Post Slim Gains amid Investor Anxiety over Five-Year Note Sale, Today's Labor Data," Credit Markets, ibid., p. C18.

the 3-month Treasury bill from above 6.50% to just above 5.50% since January.

Lastly, I return to Section A to look at the GNP bar chart on the front page, which depicts GNP from 1986 through the first quarter of 1991. The related article reaffirms what the other newspapers have said.* Further down on the same page is an article about the Conference Board's "Measure of Business Confidence" index for the second quarter of 1991.† It jumped to 55, the highest reading since the 1988 third quarter, after having measured 33 in the fourth quarter of 1990, then a 10-year low according to the article. The survey covered more than 50 chief executive officers in many different industries across the United States. A reading above 50 indicates that positive responses outnumbered negative ones during the second quarter. This index simply adds support to those analysts who believe that the recovery has begun. Yields did not react to this article, but I felt it was worth noting on my weekly interest rate chart.

Friday, June 28, 1991

The Wall Street Journal.   After having put numbers from *The Wall Street Journal* on my chart, I turn back to the first page of Section A to look at the personal income chart for a moment, and then turn to page 2 of Section A to read about consumer spending and personal income for May under the "Economy" heading.‡ Personal spending rose 1.1% from the prior month. According to the article, spending occurred in both durable and nondurable goods. Personal income rose 0.5% in May, 0.1% in April, and 0.4% in March. Analysts are now saying that the continuing rise in personal income is another sign of recovery. To encourage the positive psychological feeling, President Bush's chief economic advisor, Michael Boskin, Chair of the White House Council of Economic Advisors, suggested that the rise in personal income over the past 3 months is a sign that the economy is beginning to recover. Adding to the good cheer about recovery was another drop in unemployment claims of 17,000, to 431,000. The article notes that the average level of claims for the past 4-week period ended this week was 429,750 compared to the prior 4-week period at 433,250. The decline in unemployment claims is a clear sign of possible recovery in the making. These indicators added to the rise in durable goods orders and the increase in existing home sales as still more fuel for the recovery point of view.

---

*"GNP Profits Data for the First Quarter Revised Downward," ibid., p. A2.

†"Business Confidence Index Jumps to Three-Year High," ibid.

‡Paul Duke, Jr., "Shopping Spree Gave Economy a Boost in May," Economy, ibid., June 28, 1991, p. A2.

Adjacent to the article on personal income and spending is the lead article, "Fed Officials Gearing Up for Conflict on Money-Supply Targets for Next Year."* Because of the importance of the Fed and these targets, especially M2 (M1 or cash in circulation and nonbank travelers' checks plus money-market mutual funds), reading this article is important to gain an understanding of what analysts are thinking about the money supply and its relationship to interest rates. A good illustration of the money targets shows them from 1990 through 1991. The Fed will be meeting next week (the first week in July) to decide the money targets for 1992. According to the article, money targets have again become more important than adjusting interest rates by manipulating the federal funds rate. There are two sides to the argument concerning the growth of money supply or M2 and its effect on the U.S. economy. Some analysts feel that the current targets of 2½% to 6½% should be higher to produce more money growth and thereby help to sustain the U.S. economic recovery. Others feel that higher targets will not only produce economic growth but also inflation. This would push interest rates higher, which in turn would stall any chance for a sustained U.S. economic recovery. The important issue is at what level the money targets such as M2 will be set. The article will serve as a good guideline for what happens. Remember that whatever the Fed decides will not be known publicly for about 6 weeks. I clip the article for future reference, because it also shows the specific views of key Fed members who speak for both sides.

Next I turn to the "Credit Markets" column. The headline is intriguing: "Bond Prices Rise as Investors Decide to Ignore Indications That Economy Is Picking Up Steam."† The authors felt that interviews with a number of economists seemed to indicate that no one had any clear conviction as to why yields were declining or prices rising. With indicators clearly showing some signs of either the recession ending or recovery starting, yields should have risen higher, particularly after yesterday's figures on personal spending, personal income, and unemployment claims were reported. Again, analysts pointed out that since it is the end of the quarter, portfolio managers normally square their books and do not buy securities. Also, some analysts feel that these recent numbers are in line with expectations, and therefore not significant enough to warrant any reaction in yields. Still others feel that the yields rose in overreaction to the first piece of news that represented the possibility of a recovery, and that stronger data is needed for yields to move higher.

---

*Alan Murray, "Fed Officials Gearing Up for Conflict on Money-Supply Targets for Next Year," Economy, ibid.

†Anita Raghaven and Robert Sherman, "Bond Prices Rise as Investors Decide to Ignore Indications That Economy Is Picking Up Steam," Credit Markets, ibid., p. C17.

The "Foreign Exchange" column noted that the Bundesbank, the German central bank, had announced no interest rate adjustment.* The exchange markets had become quite skittish about whether the German central bank would raise its discount rate higher than 6.5% and its Lombard rate above 9%. Apparently the exchange market was more concerned about the possible raising of German interest rates than the possibility of a U.S. economic recovery. One member of the German central bank made it clear, however, that there was room to raise rates if it felt that inflation was moving too high. The rise in the dollar was also attributable to concerns about the civil war in Yugoslavia. This is a good example that when global turmoil occurs outside the United States, the dollar rises as investors prefer to purchase U.S. securities based on the historical monetary and economic stability of the United States. Add to this the apparent beginnings of a U.S. economic recovery, and the dollar has the potential to rise more. If that happens, interest rates may well react and fall as more foreign investors purchase U.S. Treasury bonds and other securities.

The trend appears to indicate that interest rates may continue to rise based on the possibility of U.S. economic recovery. On the other hand, they may decline if the dollar continues to rise high enough to thwart the recovery. Which direction interest rates go may well hinge on which of these two views predominates.

Investor's Daily. Today's issue of *Investor's Daily* leads with the key story that the President's chief economic advisor believes that the evidence is strong enough to declare the recession is over.† After discussing the personal spending and income figures, the article notes that Robert Forrestal, President of the Atlanta District office of the Federal Reserve System, spoke about aging baby boomers who were now past their household-formation years. This means that housing starts will not rise as fast as in past years, thereby affecting all the subsidiary industries that make up the housing industry, such as appliances, furniture, building materials, and so forth.

Both the "Foreign Exchange" and "Credit Markets" columns had little to say today about interest rates.

The New York Times. In *The New York Times,* the "Credit Market" column has the most appropriate headline to signify the importance of the

---

*"Mark Is Driven Lower by News Barrage as Dollar Rises against Most Currencies," Foreign Exchange, ibid., p. C11.

†Laurie Marmor, "Bush's Economist Declares Recession Is Over," Our Economy, *Investor's Daily,* June 28, 1991, p. 1.

global factor: "Prices Up after German Decision."* The article notes the German central bank decision not to raise its interest rates. Then the discussion centers about the third largest rise in personal consumption in the last 4 months, which is a plus factor for the U.S. economic recovery view. Several analysts quoted in the article are quick to point out that personal income has not risen as fast as personal consumption, and if personal incomes do not rise higher, that would be a negative for the U.S. economy. If this view became the public perception, interest rates would have an excuse to move lower.

The "Credit Markets" column also includes the week's statistics from the Federal Reserve. The other newspapers also give this information, but I like *The New York Times* chart, which shows that M2 rose 4.9% at an annual growth rate during the last 3 months, 4.4% during the past 6 months, and 3.4% during the past 12 months. These figures are within the Federal Reserve Board's target for M2 of between 2.5% and 6.5%. The other two columns of importance—"Currency Markets" and "Futures/Options"—contained little new information today.

On page 2 of the "Business Day" section are several important articles. The first is an editorial by Leonard Silk about the issue of U.S. economic recovery. Mr. Silk always provides perspective. In this article, he summarizes the consensus view that recovery is apparently taking shape. He feels that there are still structural problems in several industries which depend on other industries. He states that "The economy is like a vast network or matrix. Troubles in one industry cause troubles in others: The computer industry depends on banks, insurance, retailing and the airlines. Publishing, hard hit by a fall off in advertising, depends on financial services, retailing, airlines and computers." He feels that "The recovery now getting under way must still overcome such structural resistance. But there appears to be little reason to expect an inflationary upsurge or tightening of Fed policy that would cause the recovery to collapse."† My only concern about his comments is that global factors such as German inflation and Japanese economic growth tend to impact on what happens in the United States when one least expects it. I always attempt to guard against taking a view of interest rates based only on what is happening in the United States and ignoring what is happening elsewhere in the world.

Another article on the second page of the business section concerns the personal income and personal spending indicator reported the day before. Nothing new here after reading the other two newspapers and looking at the data.

---

*Kenneth N. Gilpin, "Prices Up after German Decision," Credit Markets, *The New York Times*, June 28, 1991, p. D13.

†Leonard Silk, "Soft Landing, Soft Recovery?", Economic Scene, ibid., p. D2. Copyright © 1991 by The New York Times Company. Reprinted by permission.

Saturday, June 29, 1991

The New York Times.   Because *The New York Times* publishes on Saturday, I can use it to find most of the information I need on my weekly interest rate chart except the yields on the German and Japanese 10-year government bonds. Also, this is the first chance I have to review Friday's activities. In Saturday's edition there are only two sections. "Business Day" is in the second section. One of the key articles today concerns the reporting of the May Index of Leading Economic Indicators, which rose for the fourth straight month.* Ordinarily, this trend toward economic recovery would be enough to push yields upward to reflect the potential for inflation if the economy continues to improve. In May's report, 8 of 11 indicators rose, which means that the rise in the index was widespread. A key aspect of the three indices is that the Index of Coincident Indicators, which moves at the same time as the economy, rose for the first time since June 1990. But the Index of Lagging Indicators fell 0.9%, meaning that maybe the recovery is yet to be. Another way of looking at this indicator is that one may wish to worry less about what is being reflected in the May statistics and more about what the June statistics will bring in the way of economic and inflation interpretations. In any case, yields headed down instead of upwards. Why?

On turning to the "Credit Markets" column, the reason for the downward instead of upward trend in yields unfolds. Today's column says that a stronger dollar and slumps in Tokyo and European stock markets helped push the yields down.† Also, the CRB index continued to head down, a good indicator of inflation. With these factors, there were considerable buyers of U.S. Treasury issues. In other words, the rise in the May Index of Leading Economic Indicators was largely ignored.

The "Currency Markets" column added some more support for a further decline in yields.‡ There was nervousness about the turmoil in Yugoslavia and what effect it might have on Germany's economy, which helped push the dollar higher at the same time that foreign investors were upset that Germany was bringing back a withholding tax on interest income. Many sold out of German marks to buy dollars.

Today's reflection on Friday's happenings appears to create more confusion than anything else. Clearly, the potential for a recovery in the U.S.

---

*Robert D. Hershey, Jr., "More Signs of Recovery in May Data," ibid., June 29, 1991, pp. 2, 36.

†H. J. Maidenberg, "Prices of Long-Term Treasury Bonds Soar," Credit Markets, ibid., p. 42.

‡"Dollar Mostly Up, but Mark Is at Center of Day's Activities," Currency Markets, ibid., p. 43.

economy was overshadowed by events in Europe which apparently pushed U.S. interest rates down.

Sunday, June 30, 1991

The Sunday Edition of *The New York Times*. The "Business" section of the Sunday edition of *The New York Times* provides the first review of the past week. Now I can begin to sit back and reflect on the week's events as they influenced interest rates. With the weekly interest rate chart in front of me for reference, I can refer to the comments made on the week's factors and assumptions about the trend in interest rates. Normally, I pull out several weeks of charts in order to obtain a broader view of what has been happening.

I start by looking over the "Business Diary" section, edited by Joel Kurtzman.* This review is an excellent way to obtain information on what has happened during the past week if you happened to miss a day's reading. Particularly useful are the illustrations accompanying the brief descriptions of the reported economic and inflation indicators. In this Sunday's column, the charts are quite telling. The illustration depicting GNP for the past several quarters shows decline in two quarters—the fourth of 1990 and the first of 1991. These two consecutive declines technically are considered to indicate a recession, as determined by the Business Cycle Dating Committee of the National Bureau of Economic Research. Another illustration, of the Index of Leading Economic Indicators, shows four straight rises, including two monthly increases in the first 2 months of the second quarter of 1991, indicating a possible recovery in the second quarter. That illustration is followed by a report of the May durable goods orders, which shows declines from January through March, reflecting in part the GNP for the first quarter, and then two consecutive rises in the first two months of the second quarter. Clearly, one can make a good case for the possibility of recovery. But the nagging question is whether it will be slow or fast or relapse into a recession (economists would call this a "double-dip" recession). This data is reflected on the weekly interest rate chart.

Next I take a quick look at the chart called "Data Bank/June 30, 1991," at the bottom of the page. All the indicators of the past week are given but also those for the past 3 months. Next to the "Data Bank" chart is the "This Week's Numbers" chart. Sometimes I use this information to begin filling out the weekly interest rate chart for the forthcoming week. This particular chart is very helpful in that it also gives the previous month's figure for

*Joel Kurtzman (ed.), "Business Diary," *The New York Times*, Sunday edition, June 30, 1991, "Business" section, p. 2.

those indicators to be reported during the week. Also, a chart at the bottom entitled "This Week's Developments" notes that the Federal Open Market Committee of the Federal Reserve Board will meet on Tuesday and that minutes of the last Federal Open Market Committee, held in May, will be released.

Barron's. On either Sunday or Monday, I pick up a copy of *Barron's*. This newspaper provides a good way to review the factors of the past week that have influenced interest rate trends as well as some of the statistics on the weekly interest rate chart. In the column entitled "Review and Preview," the week's past events, mostly political events, are highlighted. I note that the issue of fiscal difficulties in many states will soon pause, as most state budgets are due by the end of the fiscal year on June 30. Because of the squeeze on revenues, many states are trying to establish how much in tax increases will have to be made as well as how much to cut expenditures in various programs and how many employees might have to be laid off. To the right on this page are news briefs that also highlight factors in which we are interested, including in this case the May durable goods orders and the May Index of Leading Economic Indicators. For a more thorough review, I turn to the "Capital Markets" section.

In the "Capital Markets" section, I first take a quick look at the illustrations at the bottom of the page, which include both global short and long rates. Looking at this illustration, one can see that yields on the current German government long-term bond rose in late June, reflecting concern about the possibility of raising German interest rates to stem inflation as growth in the German economy continues. To the right of these illustrations are two illustrations that depict both the U.S. short and long rates. The short-rate illustration clearly shows the dramatic drop in the federal funds rate and its effect on both 1-month commercial paper and 3-month Treasury bill rates. But I also note that U.S. long rates trended upward slightly, reflecting the possibility of an imminent recovery in the U.S. economy. In other words, as we have said before, the Federal Reserve can manipulate short-term interest rates but not long-term interest rates. Long-term rates reflect broader concerns about global factors as well as domestic factors.

Also in the "Capital Markets" section is a column entitled "Current Yield," written by Randall W. Forsyth.* Today, Forsyth appears to be scratching for the determining factor concerning interest rates and he comes up with one. Last Friday, the Purchasing Management Association of Chicago reported an unexpected drop in its June index. That may have

---

*Randall W. Forsyth, "Flight to Quality—or Quantity?", Capital Markets, Current Yield, *Barron's*, June 30, 1991, p. 36.

been the cause of the decline in yields on Friday. Forsyth believes that this particular index is a leading trend indicator for determining the direction of the U.S. economy because it a regional sector of the nationwide NAPM index. Since the index dropped, it indicates that the U.S. economy has not recovered as yet. Forsyth goes on to say that a slight gain is expected in Monday's report of the total index. In fact, the overall NAPM index rose sharply from 44.5 in May to 50.9 in June.

But Forsyth is amused as to what actually happens to interest rates. He describes the January prognostications of economists about interest rates: on average they should be headed down sharply based on the recession. To date, bond yields have risen instead. Forsyth then gives an excellent review of the past 6 months' activity. This is a good way to reflect on what has been happening, by tracking the various indicators and making over-all comments on the weekly, monthly, and quarterly interest rate charts. Forsyth briefly discusses predictions by several key economists. Obviously there are a multitude of views concerning inflation, global interest rates, recovery in the U.S. economy, and politics. The column also includes an illustration entitled "Rate Forecasts: Next 6 Months," which I clip and keep for future reference. Incidentally, the chart notes that the actual federal funds rate was 5.75% by the end of June 1991. The forecasts ranged from a low of 5.90% to a high of 9.75%. The closest forecast, made at the end of December 1990, was 5.90%. The actual 30-year Treasury rate at the end of June 1990 was 8.41%. Here the forecasts ranged from a low of 6.80% to a high of 10.75%. The closest to the actual rate of 8.41% was 8.25%. So much for predictions.

I will now wait for Monday's review columns in *Investor's Daily, The Wall Street Journal,* and *The New York Times* to complete the past week's actions and numbers on the weekly interest rate chart. The only remaining day to consider is the forthcoming Monday. While that is not part of the previous week, the reason for including it is twofold: First, *The Wall Street Journal* and *Investor's Daily* do not publish on Saturday; and second, Monday also serves as a review of the previous week's activities for the above two newspapers but especially *The New York Times,* because it publishes on Saturday.

Monday, July 1, 1991

Investor's Daily. As soon as I pick up my *Investor's Daily* I notice an excellent chart in "Business News Digest" on the rise and fall of the Commodity Research Board futures index from 1984 to June 1991.* It shows the sharp drop in commodity prices in May and June 1991, supporting the

---

*"Commodity Prices Tumble," Business News Digest, *Investor's Daily,* July 1, 1991, p. 1.

contention of several analysts that inflation is coming down. The front page also carries an article on the May Index of Leading Economic Indicators. I notice a comment by Michael Boskin, Chairman of the White House Council on Economic Advisors; he feels that the recession has ended, unless factors that the Council has not forecasted show otherwise.* The article echoes what was said in Saturday's edition of *The New York Times.*

The "Credit Markets" column refers to the political problems in Yugoslavia, the Chicago Purchasing Management index, the fall in the CRB index, and difficulties of major U.S. banks.† The latter comment has been mentioned as another reason yields have trended downwards as a reflection of the major concern about the U.S. financial system.

The "Foreign Exchange" column mentions the German withholding tax on income interest and the Yugoslavian political crisis as reasons why foreign investors sold marks and bought U.S. dollars, because the dollar is viewed as a safe haven in times of foreign political stress.‡

The New York Times.   On the second page of *The New York Times* is a chart entitled "World Economies," which reviews a number of key indicators for six of the major industrialized countries: the United States, Germany, Japan, Britain, Canada, and Mexico.§ The statistics include their inflation rates, industrial production, exchange rates, and yields on their government long bonds. I review the chart in relation to my weekly interest chart. Often I clip this chart for future reference.

Next to the chart on world economies is a good article on the possibility of Japan's central bank lowering its short-term rate.¶ Should this happen, the United States would react positively, because the U.S. Secretary of the Treasury has been urging both Japan and Germany to cut their interest rates to help in stimulating their economies, even at the risk of inflation.

The "Credit Markets" column deals with the current U.S. banking crisis as a thorn in the side of a U.S. economic recovery from recession.# Unless the banks lend, the recovery will be far slower than anticipated. The column notes that the problems with sharp earnings losses by the major U.S.

---

*Laurie Marmor, "Indicators in May Posted Fourth Gain in Row," Our Economy, ibid.

†Phil Hawkins, "Issues Post Gains in Active Trade as Buyers Make Move to Safety," Credit Markets, ibid., p. 28.

‡"Dollar Up Sharply against Mark as Germany Mulls Dividend Tax," Foreign Exchange, ibid., p. 27.

§"World Economies," *The New York Times,* July 1, 1991, p. D2.

¶James Sterngold, "Japan Rate Cut Is Said to Be Near," ibid.

#Kenneth N. Gilpin, "Banking Gloom Clouds Outlook," Credit Markets, ibid., p. D7.

banks is a long-term question in conjunction with the lack of lending. But of more current concern is the forthcoming report on Friday on the U.S. unemployment rate and employment numbers. Because it will be July 4th week, the reaction to these indicators may not occur until the following week.

The Wall Street Journal.   The first item I see on the front page of *The Wall Street Journal* is an illustration showing the dramatic rise in the Index of Leading Economic Indicators. Next I read through "The Outlook" column, which discusses free trade among the trade blocks in Europe, Asia, Latin America, and Canada. Next I turn to the "Economy" column, which discusses the May Index of Leading Economic Indicators. The key point made is that the fourth rise in the index is a clear trend that recovery is occurring.* The "Tracking the Economy" chart focuses on Friday's unemployment rate by giving a brief description of the indicator and what the consensus appears to be. I also check the "Statistics to Be Released This Week" chart and corroborate it with the data I put on my weekly interest rate chart from the other newspapers.

Moving on to Section C, "Money & Investing," I turn to the "Credits Markets" column after finding the yields of the Japanese and German 10-year government bonds in the "Bond Market Data Bank" statistical column. On Monday the "Credit Markets" column begins on the front page of Section C. Today's article concerns junk bonds, U.S. Treasuries and interest rates, but little about interest rate trends is given.

Finally, I turn to the "Foreign Exchange" column, since nothing much that would affect interest rates is mentioned in the "Commodities" column. Here the prognosis is that the dollar will be stronger in the third quarter of 1991 because of concerns about German inflation as they deal with the unification of the two Germanies.† The concern is what the G-7 nations will do to prevent the dollar from becoming too strong, which would negate the U.S. economic recovery because it would make U.S. products more expensive and foreign products cheaper. Will the G-7 intervene and push the dollar down with the possibility of pushing U.S. interest rates up? Traders in the foreign currency market are also concerned about what both the U.S. and foreign countries will do about interest rates. All this leads to uncertainty in the foreign exchange market, or at least caution about how high the dollar will rise.

---

*Paul Duke, Jr., "Leading Indicators of the Economy Advanced in May," Economy, *The Wall Street Journal*, July 1, 1991, p. A2.

†Melinda Amberg-Vajdic, "Stronger Dollar Is Seen in 3rd Quarter, but Yen May Show Climb, Survey Says," Foreign Exchange, ibid., p. C10.

Summary—The Weekly
Interest Rate Chart

Now that all the numbers have been entered in the weekly interest rate chart, we can analyze what has been happening during the week of June 24. My comments under "Key Factors" are as follows (see Fig. 12-1). (1) The downward trend in the CRB indicates that inflation is going down. Therefore, yields will trend down. (2) The fourth straight rise in the Index of Leading Economic Indicators means that yields should rise; this implies that a U.S. economic recovery is under way. That encourages the possibility of inflation, which push up yields. (3) Durable goods orders for May showed a big rise. This indicator also should push up yields. (4) German government bond yields are rising, reflecting concern about German inflation with the concomitant possibility of a rise in German short-term interest rates.

A particular factor overlooked in my judgment was a record widening of the U.S. budget deficit. That means the U.S. will have to issue more Treasury notes and bonds to fund the deficit. That usually spells trouble for interest rates, as they will have to rise in order to persuade foreign investors to purchase U.S. securities. In summary, my current interest rate trend, based on the information in the weekly interest rate chart, is that yields will decline temporarily, but if economic indicators continue to show a recovery, they will head upward, particularly in the long end of the yield curve. If the recovery is slow, yields will rise hesitantly.

The foregoing review represents a considerable amount of reading, but one can focus on much less. Sometimes you may want to look at only one of the sources, at other times all of them. There are an infinite array of possibilities for tracking the data and acquiring knowledge about what factors are influencing interest rate trends. In most cases, I will read at least two of the major newspapers, because that gives me a perspective not only on trends in interest rates but also on what is happening to the domestic and foreign economies, exchange rates, inflation, and politics worldwide. For the most part, all the factors that one must attempt to understand in order to manage money, conduct business, or influence policy at local, state, national, and international levels are found in these newspapers (note, though, that The Wall Street Journal is the only one that carries the daily yields of both the Japanese and German government bonds).

The Monthly Interest
Rate Chart

As an exercise in compiling the monthly interest rate chart, I will use the months of April, May, and June 1991, that is, the second quarter of 1991. From the information in the weekly charts, I can easily fill in the monthly interest rate charts. Usually, after each week, I begin to fill in that week's column of each particular monthly chart. You should note that I average the yields of the 5 days of each week for the number to be placed on the monthly chart. However, you can also use Friday's closing yield and the other numbers for that day. The method of how to compute these weekly figures for the monthly chart is an individual choice. After filling in all the blanks, note the change from Week 1 to Week 4 on the monthly chart in the column titled "Change." Some months have 5 weeks because there are 31 days instead of 30 days. In that case, I simply put the changed numbers immediately to the right of the other numbers.

The next step is to review the comments on each of the weekly charts. Determine the key factors that were influencing interest rates during that week. One method for incorporating these comments in the monthly interest rate chart is to begin putting down the one or two key factors that most influenced interest rates during that week. Then move onto the next week until you have completed the 4 or 5 weeks' worth of commentary and interpretation.

April 1991

For the month of April 1991 (see Fig. 12-2) I felt that the indicators being reported showed the possibility that the recession had ended and that re-

MONTHLY INTEREST RATE CHART

Month of April 1991	Week 1 Average	Week 2 Average	Week 3 Average	Week 4 Average	Change	Key Interest Rate Factors Yields: U=Up D=Down N=Neutral

Comments						1. Beginning signs recession ending.
						   a. March NAPM up U
						   b. March CPI down D
						   c. March Ind. Prod. & Cap. N
						      Util. might be at bot.

Uncertainty about whether recession has ended despite a few indicators that were positive. Long end is not moving as a result. CRB key factor in that it indicates moderating inflation. Question as to whether Fed will lower the Federal Funds Rate (currently below 6.00%).						

Federal Funds Rate	6.20	5.70	5.75	5.88	5.75	2. Dollar rising forcing Mark U
						   down putting inflationary
						   pressure on Germany.

3 Mon. Treas. Bill	5.91	5.74	5.75	5.81	(10)bp	3. G-7 rejects U.S. request U to lower interest rates.
2 Year Treas. Note	6.95	6.91	6.90	6.93	(2)bp	
10 Year Treas. Note	8.01	8.00	7.98	8.08	7 bp	
30 Year Treas. Bond	8.21	8.20	8.15	8.24	3 bp	
Gold (COMEX)	$359.62	$363.06	$359.88	$355.74	(3.88)	
Yen in Dollars	137.57	136.12	136.22	138.41	0.84	Key Factors Overlooked
Mark in Dollars	1.6731	1.6769	1.6902	1.7508	.077	1. CRB Index trending downwards.

CRB	220.99	220.85	219.41	217.77	(3.22)	2. Fed Funds rate appears to
						   be heading down. Maybe a
						   signal of an easing.

Japan 10 Year Bond	6.63	6.66	6.61	6.67	.04 bp	
German 10 Year Bond	8.22	8.20	8.27	8.27	.04 bp	Current Interest Rate Trend
Stocks - Dow Indust.	2844.36	2898.45	2977.27	2928.22	2.84	Short end down; long end up. Uncertainty about recession
WTIC Oil Price	$19.68	$20.80	$21.51	$21.19	1.51	ending and recovery starting. Dollar strength could hurt U.S. economy. States have large deficits.

Figure 12-2. Monthly interest rate chart for April 1991.

covery was beginning. But I also remained cautious about the strength of
what appeared to be the nascent recovery. While some factors moved up,
others moved down. For example, the National Association of Purchasing
Management index rose in March, the March jobs picture was revised upward, and the March consumer price index was down, indicating that inflation was moderating. All these key indicators were signs of a beginning
recovery.

Several other important factors were reported. The Group of Seven industrialized countries rejected Treasury Secretary Nicholas F. Brady's re-
quest to lower international interest rates in order to help the U.S.
economic recovery. (We discussed this conflict in Chap. 10.) The lower U.S.
interest rates and the higher foreign interest rates were drawing capital
from the United States to other countries. More important, the United
States wanted to be sure that these nations' economies were not being
hampered by high interest rates, which make it more difficult to import
U.S. goods. Another important factor was the continued rise of the dollar
against other countries' currencies, particularly Germany's. If the dollar
continued to rise, it would create opposite results. The stronger the dollar,
the higher U.S. interest rates move. This elevation would induce more investment in U.S. securities. On the other hand, the stronger the dollar, the
higher U.S. prices become, which if allowed to continue would make them
less competitive with foreign goods in terms of price. One other factor I
noticed was that the federal funds rate had been heading lower during the
4 weeks of April 1991. That could mean a drop in the federal funds rate to
5.75% from the current level, set by the Federal Reserve Board at 6.00%.

Before making an overall comment on the month of April 1991, I reviewed the monthly changes. What I gleaned from these numbers was
that short-term interest rates trended downward while long-term interest
rates trended upward. I also noticed that the Commodity Research
Bureau's futures index headed down by a large 3 points plus. My overall
view was then set forth in the "Comments" column on the monthly interest rate chart. I felt that there was a clear case of uncertainty in the marketplace, as evidenced by the rise in long-term interest rates compared to the
drop of the short-term numbers. Remember that the Federal Reserve
Board does not control the long end of the yield curve. It responds to
many stimuli outside the ken of the manipulations of the Federal Reserve
Board.

May 1991

After putting in the numbers, I sorted through the weekly interest rate
charts to determine the key factors involved in influencing interest rates

for the month of May. May is one of the months with 5 weeks, so I made a sixth column so that I could put in the change from the first to the last week in May (see Fig. 12-3).

For the second month, I felt that the downward trend in the CRB index was being overlooked. This trend bode well for the inflation. A key indicator was the cut in the discount rate by the Federal Reserve Board to 5.5% and another drop in the federal funds rate to 5.75%. Remember that in April it appeared as if the federal funds rate was heading down. Another important indicator was that the psychology of the financial markets was leading to the view that the recovery was on its way, despite the usual opposite view by some analysts. This meant that interest rates would increase.

In my "Comments" space, I begged the question of whether the recovery had actually begun, as state governmental officials were still struggling with deficits, including enormous ones in California, New York, Texas, Connecticut, and New Jersey. My belief was that these big states with substantial economies in a weakened condition would deter any strong recovery. For example, California's economy, at approximately $700 billion, the seventh largest in the world and of course the most significant in the United States, was in recession. The governor and the state

MONTHLY INTEREST RATE CHART

Month of May 1991	Week 1 Average	Week 2 Average	Week 3 Average	Week 4 Average	Week 5 Average	Key Interest Rate Factors Yields: U=Up D=Down N=Neutral		
Comments								
Key issue still is when will recovery occur. Many mixed views. Fed did cut Discount Rate and lowered Fed Funds Rate level to help pull U.S. economy out of recession.						1. Fed cuts discount rate D to 5.50% and lower FFR to 5.75% level.		
						CHG.		
Federal Funds Rate	5.82	5.68	5.82	5.65	5.72	(10)	2. Psychology: Market D uncertain on recession	
3 Mon. Treas. Bill	5.67	5.64	5.59	5.59	5.62	(5)	ending. Fact. Ordrs rose, consum confid. dn,	
2 Year Treas. Note	6.81	6.81	6.81	6.74	6.62	(19)	Apr LEI up 3rd mon row.	
10 Year Treas. Note	8.00	8.04	8.05	8.06	8.04	4	3. Dollar rising.	
30 Year Treas. Bond	8.18	8.23	8.31	8.27	8.26	8		
Gold (COMEX)	354.58	356.84	357.96	356.52	362.27	7.7		
Yen in Dollars	137.64	138.36	138.10	137.93	137.91	0.27	Key Factors Overlooked	
Mark in Dollars	1.7330	1.7274	1.7060	1.7154	1.7172	(0.166)	CRB Index appears to be trending down meaning	
CRB	216.07	215.33	214.77	216.02	215.00	(1.1)	lower inflation.	
Japan 10 Year Bond	6.65	6.61	6.59	6.61	6.60	(5)		
German 10 Year Bond	8.21	8.28	8.28	8.23	8.15	(6)	Current Interest Rate Trend	
Stocks - Dow Indust.	2914.50	2925.47	2891.46	2904.50	2989.12	74.62	Short end flat; long end up because of uncertainty.	
WTIC Oil Price	21.19	21.67	20.93	21.14	21.22	0.03		

Figure 12-3. Monthly interest rate chart for May 1991.

legislature were in a tense and difficult struggle to find revenues to offset enormous expenditures, including health care, that are for the most part a nationwide problem. This factor would have the effect of impinging on the recovery of the U.S. economy.

June 1991

For the month of June 1991, again some indicators reported for the previous month of May were showing improvement. The Index of Leading Economic Indicators rose for the fourth straight month, durable goods orders increased for the second month in a row, and retail sales were up (see Fig. 12-4). The CRB index fell more than 7 points in June alone. I decided to check back to April and found that since the beginning of the first week in April, the CRB index had fallen 11 points—a dramatic drop, indicating that inflation was coming down. This would be a strong positive for economic recovery. Overall, for the month of June there were signs of evident improvement within the U.S. economy. But there was enough uncertainty to push long rates upward.

MONTHLY INTEREST RATE CHART

Month of June 1991	Week 1 Average	Week 2 Average	Week 3 Average	Week 4 Average	Change	Key Interest Rate Factors Yields: U=Up D=Down N=Neutral
Comments						1. CRB heading down which is a D positive for inflation.
More nascent signs of an economic recovery. CRB still heading down. Fed now holding steady based on indicators showing positive signs. But uncertainty still dominating market psychology as long end of Treasury curve continues to rise.						2. Some signs of recovery.
Federal Funds Rate	5.81	5.70	5.71	5.76	5.75	a. LEI up for 4th strgt mon. U
3 Mon. Treas. Bill	5.73	5.74	5.75	5.72	(1)bp	b. Durable goods orders up U second strgt month.
2 Year Treas. Note	6.83	6.99	6.90	6.93	10 bp	c. Retail sales rise. U
10 Year Treas. Note	8.18	8.28	8.30	8.29	11 bp	
30 Year Treas. Bond	8.39	8.49	8.49	8.48	9 bp	d. Fed holding steady. U
Gold (COMEX)	362.00	370.42	367.80	365.52	3.52	
Yen in Dollars	139.33	141.21	139.73	138.30	(1.03)	Key Factors Overlooked
Mark in Dollars	1.7531	1.7829	1.7991	1.7932	0.4	None
CRB	217.36	215.53	212.91	209.98	(7.38)	
Japan 10 Year Bond	6.61	6.75	6.78	6.77	16bp	
German 10 Year Bond	8.19	8.20	8.18	8.26	7bp	Current Interest Rate Trend
Stocks - Dow Indust.	3009.69	2977.17	2971.15	2917.56	(92.13)	Short rates flat to up; long rates upwards based on signs of
WTIC Oil Price	20.63	19.84	20.88	20.22	(.41)	economic recovery.

Figure 12-4. Monthly interest rate chart for June 1991.

The Quarterly Interest Rate Chart—Second Quarter 1991

The data entered onto the quarterly interest rate chart (see Fig. 12-5) was determined the same way as the monthly interest rate chart, by taking each month and averaging the 4 or 5 weeks of each of the figures. Again, one can also use the beginning of the month of April to the end of the month of June to determine the number. Or one can use the average of the first week with the average of the fourth or fifth week if so desired.

The numbers showed the following. While the federal funds rate was pushed down another 25 basis points to 5.75%, the actual fluctuations of the federal funds rate rises above or below that target rate. The short end of the Treasury yield curve declined 7 basis points, while the long end or 30-year long bond rose 26 basis points. Clearly, the Federal Reserve Board was trying to stimulate the U.S. economy despite resistant U.S. banks that did not lend enough to suit the needs expressed repeatedly by the chair of the Federal Reserve Board. The CRB index on my chart declined by more than 5 points, but if one considers the beginning of April to the end of June, it declined a sharp 11 points. Oil prices remained at the $20/barrel

QUARTERLY INTEREST RATE CHART

Quarter 2nd 1991	Month 1 Average	Month 2 Average	Month 3 Average	Change	Key Interest Rate Factor. Yields: U=Up D=Down N=Neutral
Comments					1. Key issue is whether the U.S. U economic recovery will be sustained.
Some strong signs of recovery with moderating inflation though the second quarter. Dollar's strength could be a problem. G-7 nations meeting may have an effect on interest rates. Fed holding firm after cutting the discount rate and lowering the level of the Fed Funds rate. Psychology positive.					2. The CRB Index continued to D head downwards. This is a strong positive for inflation.
Federal Funds Rate	5.88	5.74	5.75	–	3. Psychology is positive for U recovery.
3 Mon. Treas. Bill	5.81	5.62	5.74	(7) bp	4. Key indicators (NAPM, LEI, and Durable Goods Orders) up U for more than one month.
2 Year Treas. Note	6.92	6.76	6.91	(1) bp	
10 Year Treas. Note	8.02	8.04	8.26	24 bp	5. Fed holding steady.
30 Year Treas. Bond	8.20	8.25	8.46	26 bp	6. Bank lending hurting recovery. D
Gold (COMEX)	359.58	357.63	366.43	6.85	
Yen in Dollars	137.08	137.99	139.64	2.56	Key Factors Overlooked
Mark in Dollars	1.6978	1.7198	1.7821	.843	Large budget deficits of large states may keep recovery slow.
CRB	219.73	215.44	213.95	(5.78)	
Japan 10 Year Bond	6.64	6.61	6.73	9 bp	
German 10 Year Bond	8.24	8.23	8.21	(3)bp	Current Interest Rate Trend
Stocks – Dow Indust.	2912.25	2925.01	2968.89	+56.64	Short end remaining flat while long end is trending upwards.
WTIC Oil Price	$20.80	$21.23	$20.39	(0.57)	

Figure 12-5. Quarterly interest rate chart for the second quarter of 1991.

level for the quarter. The dollar rose against both the Japanese yen and the German mark. Overall, the stock market rallied by 56+ points because of the assumption that the U.S. economy was recovering.

Then I searched through the three monthly interest rate charts for the key factors, circling them in red. I felt that there were six key factors creating some positive but uncertain indicators of a potential U.S. recovery. (1) The key issue was whether the recovery had started, and if so, whether it would be a slow recovery. (2) The CRB Index continued to head downward, and (3) the psychology for a U.S. recovery was positive. That meant that stocks were heading up, while the U.S. Treasury long bond increased because of fears of inflation. (4) The key indicators for the second quarter, including the National Association of Purchasing Management index, the Index of Leading Economic Indicators, and durable goods orders, rose for more than 1 month. (5) The Federal Reserve Board was holding short-term interest rates steady. (6) The lending of money by banks was still tight, which was hurting the attempt of the U.S. economy to recover. An overlooked factor was the enormous fiscal strain on the largest states, which, in my opinion, might forestall a U.S. economic recovery.

Overall, I noted in my "Comments" space that there were strong signs of a modest recovery with moderating inflation through the second quarter. The strength of the dollar was a concern because of its potential negative effect on U.S. competitiveness with foreign countries. That would be a positive for U.S. Treasury yields. But the dominant factor appeared to me the psychology factor, which was incorporated in the rising yields in the long end of the U.S. Treasury curve by the 26 basis points. A possible concern was the forthcoming Group of Seven meeting in July, which might have enormous effect on world geopolitics, including whether the G-7 countries will assist the Soviet Union, and if so, in what way. Also, whether these countries will try to stop the rise of the dollar and lower their respective interest rates were matters of concern lending to an atmosphere of uncertainty mixed with a budding positive psychology about the prospects of a U.S. economic recovery.

Summary

As you can see, there are many ways to obtain the data to fill in the three types of charts. You could as easily develop a chart for 6 months as well as a yearly interest rate chart. How you compute the numbers, particularly for the monthly and quarterly charts, is entirely up to you. Notice that at the bottom of the left-hand side of all the charts is a blank row. Here is an opportunity to put in another statistic that you may wish to follow—perhaps mortgage rates, a municipal bond yield index, a corporate bond yield index, the 30-year Treasury futures price index of the Chicago Board of Trade (CBT), or any other indicator that might have particular relevance to you.

The main point of the weekly, monthly, and quarterly interest rate charts is that they create an opportunity to evaluate the factors that influence interest rates in a simple fashion using everyday, easily accessible information as reported in the newspapers. You do not have to use all of the publications. One will suffice, although then you may give up seeing other interpretations of the factors being reported. But time to conduct this review is as important as the process itself. The goal of this book is to ensure that the process of tracking these factors will remain the same even if these factors change in importance or if new ones are developed to assist in determining trends in interest rates.

13
Conclusion

The goal of this book has been to establish a workable and easily applicable process within which one can understand the movement of interest rates. The tracking method to achieve the goal is based on using a weekly interest rate chart followed by both a monthly interest rate chart and a quarterly interest rate chart. The process will be able to adapt to changes that will no doubt occur in the definition of the various economic, inflation, monetary, fiscal, global, and political factors that determine the movement of interest rates. Various governmental agencies continue to study revising the components of these factors so as to bring them more in line with changes in the structure of the U.S. economy or to find new components. As the financial markets become more global and as the U.S. economy both reacts to changes in its own economic structure and adapts to changes in the world economic structure, interest rates will influence and be influenced by these changes. Although we use four newspapers, only one is necessary to fill in the information.

We began this process by defining interest rates in Chap. 1 and by distinguishing in Chap. 2 between yields and interest rates as they affect U.S. Treasury securities as well as other types of interest rates such as mortgage rates and business and consumer lending rates. Yields reflect the current coupon rate of a U.S. security. For example, say the current 2-year U.S. Treasury note has a 7.00% coupon rate or interest rate with a maturity of September 1994 and is priced at par or 100 or $1.00 for every $1000 of face value. Technically, as the price of the bond rises, the yield declines. That is a constant relationship. Market conditions are the determining force as to why yields move up or down. Since these 2-year notes are auctioned every month by the U.S. Treasury Department, the possibility exists that the coupon rate or interest rate will change at the next month's U.S. Treasury auction. Why? Between one month and the next, the U.S. economy continues to show considerable strength along with a further rise in inflation. Yields of the 2-year Treasury note continue to rise over that time based on the expectation by financial market participants, including traders, portfolio managers, economists, and market analysts, that inflation will continue to rise because of the strong growth of the U.S. economy. The result is that at the next month's auction, the coupon rate of the prior month at 7.00% would rise to 7.25% to reflect the financial markets' demand that rising inflation represents more risk and thus requires a higher interest rate to compensate for that risk. As inflation pervades the U.S. economy, the costs of borrowing to purchase new homes or businesses also rises. The result is that mortgage rates and business lending rates also rise. By using selected U.S. Treasury securities, one can watch the effect of changes in the condition of the U.S. economy and the impact of related factors on the yields of these securities in order to understand trends in the movement of interest rates.

We also discussed the linkages among the variety of factors. Linking together economic, inflationary, fiscal, monetary, and global factors is an important part of the process. The linking together of the variety of factors ultimately establishes a pattern in the movement of interest rates. As each of the economic factors is reported, they begin to relate to one another. For example, if durable goods orders fall, capacity utilization declines, unemployment rises, initial claims for state unemployment insurance increase, consumer confidence indices plummet, and inflation indices begin to decrease, then the interest rates will begin to decline and this will be reflected in the interest rates used on the charts.

In Chap. 3 we discussed how to obtain the important information necessary to track the movement of interest rates. We described four newspapers that provide the requisite data, *The Wall Street Journal*, *The New York Times*, *Investor's Business Daily*, and *Barron's*. The importance of this discussion is to show that all the information necessary to understand the factors influencing the movement of interest rates is readily available to any reader. In most instances, these publications can be purchased not only in the United States but throughout the industrialized world, particularly in major financial and business centers. Readers who do not work in the New York metropolitan area can certainly substitute their local newspapers for *The New York Times*, particularly in larger cities. In addition, coverage of the financial markets within these newspapers continues to expand, including more information on the economic, inflation, monetary, fiscal, and global factors that affect interest rates. I consider these four newspapers a base of necessary data. Other sources can be used, including other weekly and monthly U.S. and foreign newspapers and commonly recognized business magazines. The point is that all the essential information is publicly available. In this chapter we stressed using the many illustrations and charts that are available, including those that depict various changes in factors over a period of months or years and the changes in interest rates over a period of months. We pointed out that it makes sense to clip some of these illustrations to put into an interest rate notebook for future reference. We emphasized the important articles and columns that discuss interest rates. In particular, we discussed the "Credit Markets" columns of *The Wall Street Journal, The New York Times,* and *Investor's Business Daily* as the central source for what is happening to interest rates here and in foreign countries. In addition, the "Capital Markets" column in *Barron's* provides a weekly perspective on how interest rates affect domestic and foreign bond markets. We described how the various factors are reported and where to look for other key articles that will help in understanding the influences on interest rates. This chapter served as a means of introducing the general material needed to begin the understanding of interest rates.

In Chaps. 4 and 5 we described and evaluated the important factors related to the U.S. economy and inflation and their effects on the movement of interest rates. We separated the specific economic and inflation factors into their component parts, because many times the components are actually more important than the total number that is highlighted in the newspapers. It is thus important to read the entire article, and not just extract the number in the headline. Often a revised number for the preceding month has more significance than the current one. It is easy to miss relevant points that directly affect interest rates if one does not read the article in its entirety. In our discussions of each factor, we also pointed out some of the problems in interpreting the results. Understanding these problems is vitally important to understanding how the factors affect the movement of interest rates as well as to determining whether a trend is actually developing—for example, the repeated revisions of many of these numbers because of the way data is collected, the effects of weather, and the effects of different seasons on some of the factors. As these changes are smoothed out, a significant point arises that cannot be stressed enough: *One month does not make a trend.* The reader must track several months of reporting of these factors to obtain the insights necessary to make intelligent financial, business, and personal decisions based on the movement of interest rates. All these factors ultimately link together to form a trend. For example, if housing starts and new home sales decline, retail and automobile sales decrease, and industrial production and factory orders slow down over several months, along with moderating inflation as expressed in the producer price index, then ultimately interest rates will move down.

In Chap. 6 we discussed the monetary system and the Federal Reserve Board in general in order to understand how it works. The twin goals of the Federal Reserve Board to sustain economic growth and keep inflation down were highlighted. We described several distinct interest rates that are either manipulated or controlled by the Federal Reserve Board, including the federal funds rate, the discount rate, and the prime rate. Special emphasis was placed on the use of the federal funds rate as one of the key indicators that affect the movement of interest rates. The federal funds rate can be tracked on a daily basis and is a key factor by which the Federal Reserve Board can indicate policy changes in pursuit of its twin goals.

In Chap. 7 we discussed the effects of the U.S. budget deficit and the need to fund it with U.S. Treasury securities. The amount of Treasury securities necessary to fund it is large enough to create situations in which yields and interest rates rise or fall based on the demand for these securities. Market conditions force yields up or down before each auction of these securities, so the coupon or interest rate is not determined until the auction. That interest rate is affected directly by the perceptions of market participants about the current and future condition of the U.S. economy and inflation. We also discussed the issue of taxation and how it affects the need for capital in the United States and the effect of that need on interest rates.

In Chap. 8 we began to discuss global influences on U.S. interest rates. We evaluated a number of global issues that have a direct influence on interest rates. These issues provide the context within which to understand the effects of several other major factors on the movement of interest rates. Following the discussion of these global issues, we highlighted the U.S. foreign trade deficit. By explaining the conditions through which it was created and the problems it creates for the U.S. economy, we tried to show how it influences interest rates. Our evaluation of the U.S. trade deficit also served to make an important point. Today the trade deficit has declined substantially and has a lesser focus than it did several years ago. However, that we still have a trade deficit does not diminish the concern that it may again become a dominant factor in evaluating the movement of interest rates. When one least expects it, a factor of apparently less importance may take on enormous importance. Keeping abreast of the U.S. foreign trade deficit is critical to understanding trends in U.S. interest rates.

In Chap. 9 we concluded our discussion of the global environment by considering the relationship of the dollar to other currencies, the effect of foreign interest rates on U.S. interest rates, and the attempts at international policy coordination to deal with problems of national economies, the value of the dollar, and the relationship among the interest rates of the key industrial nations of Japan, Germany, and the United States. The significance of the dollar in its relationship to other currencies, particularly the Japanese yen and the German mark, was highlighted. Further, we discussed how the dollar affects the U.S. economy, as well as its relationship to major foreign industrialized economies. We then talked about the interrelationship between U.S. interest rates and foreign interest rates, again with special emphasis on the 10-year government bonds of both Japan and Germany. We noted that the rise or fall of one often affects the rise and fall of the others. The concluding section of this chapter considered the issues of international policy coordination among the Group of Seven industrialized nations: the United States, Canada, Germany, Japan, France, Great Britain, and Italy. We noted that with the changes in Eastern Europe and the former Soviet Union, this group of major nations as well as others may expand in the future. The policies of the G-7 concern the relationship of the dollar to their currencies, the relative balance of economies, monetary policies as they relate to inflation in their countries, and the effects of changes of interest rates on their respective economies. The main point in discussing the global factors is to emphasize the importance they have in evaluating trends in U.S. interest rates.

Chapter 10 discussed the impact of politics and psychology in the movement of interest rates. We highlighted the effects of presidential elections on the movement of interest rates and the significant influence of the White House in "talking down" interest rates, as well as its relationship to the Federal Reserve Board, the central bank of the United States. We noted how the financial markets are driven by psychological responses to what is happening to the U.S. economy and inflation as well as the U.S. budget deficit. While it is clearly impossible to quantify the political aspects of interest rates, it is still important to understand that key individuals in government, business, and finance can affect how many people feel about the current level of interest rates. I therefore feel strongly that politics is a key factor in the movement of interest rates that must be considered along with the specific economic, inflation, monetary, fiscal, and global factors we have discussed throughout this book. The movement of interest rates is tied directly to psychological responses to these factors. How the reader perceives the trend of these factors and how interest rates react to these trends is key to understanding how interest rates fluctuate.

Chapter 11 described in detail the three charts that serve as the data-gathering and interpreting basis for evaluating all the factors we discussed in previous chapters. The three charts are the weekly, monthly, and quarterly interest rate charts. Most of the discussion was directed at taking the reader through the weekly interest rate chart. We described specifically how to locate the factors that are entered on this chart, and precisely where they can be found in each of the newspapers discussed in Chap. 3. The three charts provide not only consistency in tracking the selected factors but also appropriate space for interpreting them. By creating an interest rate notebook, the user can keep these charts handy so that continued interpretation can take place. Within the notebook one can keep important articles about trends in interest rates, as well as illustrations and charts that show what is happening to interest rates, including yield curves of the various U.S. Treasury bills, notes, and bonds that are found in all of the newspapers and depictions of the various factors over periods of time from several months to several years. When taken together, the interest rate notebook plus all of the charts can provide the essential information for understanding interest rates.

Chapter 12 provided insight and interpretation of an actual week, 3 months, and a quarter. In this chapter I described not only how I use the interest rate charts but how I interpret the data. The purpose of the chapter was to provide an example of the process in action. My interpretations may differ from someone else's; the important point is that the process is the same no matter who uses it.

I wish to emphasize that it is the *process* that is the key to understanding the movement of interest rates. What economists, stock, bond, commodities, currency, and cash management portfolio managers, business executives, and individuals handling their own personal finances want to know about the movement of interest rates can be learned by understanding how the process described in this book works. Readers need not worry that this process will be out of date in a few years. The process will be able to follow changes. These changes will require only that some of the economic and inflation factors reported by the various governmental and private services may have to be revised. Of equal importance, the changes that have happened in Eastern Europe and in the former Soviet Union, as well as what might happen in other geopolitical regions, can be followed using this process. Change is constant, but constant changes can be understood as one practices the process.

As a lecturer at The American Institute of Banking, I have been teaching a course entitled "Influencing Interest Rate Trends" for a number of years. At the beginning of the course I tell my students that I am going to describe four personal maxims that will mean success in the course if all are rigorously followed. All of these maxims are critical underpinnings of the process of understanding interest rates. First I tell them that the ability to think is the most important asset the student has. Second, I advise them to use their intuition to pull the pieces together, since the pieces are often larger than the whole interest rate pie. Third, there is no substitute for hard work. The hard work comes in putting down the information of the interest rate charts, interpreting the information on them, and keeping abreast of changes. And lastly, the only way to achieve the goals of using the first three maxims is to have fun. So enjoy the process, and let me know how this process of understanding the movement of interest rates is working for you.

Glossary

Auto Sales: Total monthly unit sales of ten major manufacturers of automobiles and light trucks.

Beige Book: The economic summary review of the 12 regional districts of the Federal Reserve Banking System, published approximately every 6 weeks in preparation for the Federal Reserve Board's Policy Meeting. Also called Tan book.

Capacity Utilization: Measures the output and changes in productivity levels at factories. Referred to as the operating rate of factories.

Commodity Research Bureau Futures Index: An inflation indicator based on a futures index that measures the hourly movement of the price of 21 commodities. The price is predicated on what the buyer bets is the price of each of the commodities for future purchase. Called the CRB index.

Construction Spending: The amount of funds spent on building industrial plants, warehouses, offices, and shopping centers, single- and multifamily housing, and national and local government buildings.

Consumer Borrowing: An inflationary indicator consisting of various types of installment credit owed by consumers, mostly on a monthly payment basis.

Consumer Confidence Index: Results of a monthly survey conducted by the Conference Board and consisting of a survey of 5000 households, which measures what people think will happen to the economy over the next 6 months.

Consumer Price Index: An inflationary index measuring the rise or fall in prices that consumers pay for a "market basket" of goods.

Consumer Sentiment Index: Results of a survey conducted by the University of Michigan's Institute for Social Research, which measures consumers' opinions about both the current and the future outlook for the economy as it affects their personal financial decisions. Based on 500 monthly telephone interviews of households nationwide.

Consumer Spending: An inflation indicator that measures personal outlays for all types of consumer spending except interest payments on consumer debt.

Coupon Rate: The interest rate that the borrower pays to a bondholder for use of the money lent to an issuer. I refer to the coupon rate as the *interest rate*.

CPI: See *Consumer Price Index*.

CRB: See *Commodity Research Bureau Futures Index*.

Crude Goods Index: The prices for goods that enter the production chain for the first time, such as raw cotton.

Current Account: The broadest measure of U.S. trade, including both trade in goods and services as well as specific financial transfers.

Current Yield: The yield based on the actual market price of a bond, the coupon rate, and the maturity, stated as a percentage.

Discount Rate: The interest rate established by the Federal Reserve Board in which each of its respective 12 regional banks charges depository institutions when they borrow from the discount window at these Federal Reserve Banks.

Durable Goods Orders: "Big ticket" or expensive orders to factories for items that are expected to last more than 3 years. Examples are major household appliances.

Employment Cost Index: An inflation indicator that measures private industry compensation including wages, salaries, and fringe benefits for full-time as well as hourly workers.

Employment Number: The number of nonfarm workers hired in a particular month.

Factory Orders: Orders for factory goods, consisting of manufacturers' plans for production of both nondurable and durable goods.

Federal Funds Rate: The rate that commercial banks charge each other when one lends excess reserve funds to another bank on an overnight basis. The federal funds rate is established by the amount of money supply added or subtracted to the banking system by the Federal Reserve Board.

Finished Goods Index: The prices of goods that have completed the final stage of the manufacturing process and are sold to retailers.

Fixed-Weight Deflator: The gross domestic product inflation indicator that measures price changes by keeping the same composition of the "market basket" of goods.

Gross Domestic Product (GDP): An inflation-adjusted measure of the nation's total output of goods and services produced only in the United States. The GDP measures consumer demand.

Help-Wanted Index: An index published by the Conference Board that surveys help-wanted classified advertising volume in 51 major newspapers throughout the United States.

Household Survey: Counts each person employed once, using a sample of 60,000 households. It helps in determining the unemployment rate.

Housing Construction: The indicator that describes the sector of the economy consisting of housing starts and housing permits for both single-family and multifamily units.

Housing Permit: The approval to build a new home or apartment complex, received from a local or state building department.

Housing Starts: The beginning of the construction phase of a new home or apartment complex.

Implicit Price Deflator: The gross domestic product inflation component that measures not only the price changes of a "market basket" of bonds and services but also changes in the composition of that market basket.

Index of Coincident Economic Indicators: An index showing current economic activity; it consists of industrial production, personal income excluding transfer payments to social security recipients and others, and manufacturing and retail sales.

Index of Consumer Sentiment: An index published by the University of Michigan's Institute for Social Research that measures consumers' opinions about both the current and future outlook for the economy as it affects their personal financial decisions. It is included in the Index of Leading Economic Indicators.

Index of Lagging Economic Indicators: The components of this index tend to rise or fall after the economy has changed direction. The index consists of capital spending, average duration of unemployment, labor cost per unit of output, commercial and industrial loans outstanding, ratio of consumer installment debt to personal income, and average prime rate charged by banks.

Index of Leading Economic Indicators: An index designed to predict the direction of economic activity in 6 to 9 months based on 11 indicators. They include (1) average work week of production workers in manufacturing; (2) average weekly claims for state unemployment insurance; (3) new factory orders for consumer goods adjusted for inflation; (4) vendor performance or the pace of delivery times of goods; (5) contracts and orders for new plant and equipment, adjusted for inflation; (6) new building permits issued; (7) durable goods orders backlog or unfilled orders; (8) change in raw materials prices; (9) stock prices as measured by the Standard & Poor's 500 stock index; (10) money supply (M2) composed of money in checking accounts and certificates of deposit; and (11) Index of Consumer Sentiment, which is measured by the University of Michigan's Institute for Social Research.

Industrial Production: An indicator that measures the production capability of U.S. factories and accounts for 25% of the nation's total business activities.

Interest Rate—Psychological: The reaction of yields to the multitude of factors that influence the movement of interest rates on a daily basis, including domestic and foreign economic, inflationary, monetary, fiscal, and political factors. Over time, the yields lead to a change in interest rates as reflected in Treasury securities, mortgage rates, and other types of interest rates.

Interest Rate—Technical: The rate of payment (1) to an individual, a business, or an institution for the use of money loaned to the issuer of a bond for a specific purpose, including funding the U.S. budget deficit, building a new school, or expanding a business; or (2) of a borrower for the use of money for a specific purpose, such as to purchase a new home (mortgage), to help pay for a college education, or to buy a home computer to write a book.

Intermediate Goods Index: The prices of partly finished goods requiring further processing or completed goods that are parts of other products. An example of the first type is a bolt of cloth made from wool, and an example of the second part is the engine for a car.

Inventories-to-Sales Ratio: A ratio that determines how long it would take to deplete the backlog of goods held on shelves at a specific monthly pace based on the amount of inventories relative to the amount of sales.

Mark: German currency.

Merchandise Trade: A component of the U.S. trade deficit that is composed of tangible items such as foodstuffs, manufactured goods, and raw materials.

NAPM: See *National Association of Purchasing Management Index.*

National Association of Purchasing Management Index: The results of a survey of 300 purchasing executives from 21 major industries, consisting of seven parts: new orders, production levels, employment, inventories, supplier delivery times, export orders not seasonally adjusted, and manufacturing prices. Called NAPM.

New Home Sales: The number of homes sold in a month.

New York Comex: The exchange located in New York City on which commodities such as gold are traded.

Payroll Survey: Part of the employment indicator that counts the number of jobs held by a person, using a sample of 340,000 businesses. It determines the monthly employment figure.

Personal Income: An inflation indicator that measures wages and salaries, factory payrolls, and transfer payments through social security.

PPI: See *Producer Price Index.*

Prime Rate: The interest rate that major banks charge their most important business customers.

Producer Price Index: An inflation indicator that estimates the prices received by domestic producers of goods from wholesalers, retailers, and distributors of goods moving off the assembly line.

Retail Sales: Measures durable goods, consisting of such items as cars and household appliances, plus nondurable goods such as clothing and accessories. Included are sales by restaurants, major department stores, and drugstores.

Service Trade Deficit: Part of the U.S. trade deficit that includes interest on dividends, technology transfers, services such as insurance, and financial transactions.

Tan Book: See *Beige Book.*

Trade Deficit: The monthly figure that shows the imbalance of payments between one country and another.

Unemployment Claims: Average weekly initial claims by unemployed workers from the service, business, and governmental sectors who obtain state unemployment insurance benefits.

Unemployment Rate: The number of persons who are unemployed, as measured by the percent of the total labor force employed.

Unfilled Orders: Defines the growth or decline in manufacturing activity.

WTIC: West Texas Intermediate Crude oil.

Yen: Japanese currency.

Yield—Technical: The total rate of return, computed mathematically, based on the coupon or interest rate, the dollar price of the bond, and the length of the maturity.

Yield—Psychological: The psychological response of a bond's yield to economic, inflation, monetary, fiscal, and political factors, both domestic and foreign.

Selected Bibliography

Newspapers

I have used hundreds of articles from various newspapers dating back to 1984, including *The New York Times, The Wall Street Journal, Investor's Business Daily,* and *Barron's.* These articles are, of course, too numerous to list here. Some of them, though, are mentioned in footnotes throughout the book.

Books

Cooner, James J. *Investing in Municipal Bonds: Balancing Risks and Rewards.* Wiley, New York, 1987.

Darst, David M. *The Complete Bond Book: A Guide to All Types of Fixed-Income Securities.* Chapter 5, Major Influences on the Level of Direction of Interest Rates, pp. 60–102. McGraw-Hill, New York, 1975.

Fabozzi, Frank J. and Greenfield, Henry J. (eds.). *Handbook of Economic and Financial Measures.* Dow Jones-Irwin, Homewood, Ill., 1984.

Greider, William. *Secrets of the Temple.* Simon & Schuster, New York, 1987.

Homer, Sidney and Leibowitz, Martin L. *Inside the Yield Book: New Tools for Bond Market Strategy.* Prentice-Hall, Englewood Cliffs, N.J., and New York Institute of Finance, New York, 1972.

Homer, Sidney and Sylla, Richard. *A History of Interest Rates: 2000 B.C. to the Present,* 3d ed. Rutgers University Press, New Brunswick, N.J., 1992.

Johnson, Haynes. *Sleepwalking through History: America in the Reagan Years.* Norton, New York, 1991.

Jones, David M. *Fed Watching and Interest Rate Projections: A Practical Guide.* New York Institute of Finance, a division of Simon & Schuster, 1986.

Kaufman, Henry. *Interest Rates, the Markets, and the New Financial World.* Times Books/Random House, New York, 1986.

Klugman, Paul. *The Age of Diminished Expectations: U.S. Economic Policy in the 1990s.* The MIT Press, Cambridge, Mass., 1990.

Lehman, Michael B. *The Dow Jones-Irwin Guide to Using The Wall Street Journal,* 3d ed. Dow Jones-Irwin, Homewood, Ill., 1990.

Maital, Shlomo. *Minds, Markets and Money: The Psychological Foundation of Economic Behavior.* Basic Books, New York, 1982.

Moore, Geoffrey H. *Leading Indicators for the 1990s.* Dow Jones-Irwin, Homewood, Ill., 1990.

Murphy, Joseph E. *The Random Character of Interest Rates.* Probus Publishing Company, Chicago, 1990.

Nelson, Charles R. *The Investor's Guide to Economic Indicators.* Wiley, New York, 1987.

Plocek, Joseph E. *Economic Indicators: How America Reads Its Financial Health.* New York Institute of Finance, New York, 1991.

Pring, Martin J. *How to Forecast Interest Rates: A Guide to Profits for Consumers, Managers, and Investors.* McGraw-Hill, New York, 1981.

Reich, Robert B. *The Work of Nations: Preparing Ourselves for 21st Century Capitalism.* Knopf, New York, 1991.

Ritter, Lawrence S. and Silber, William L. *Principles of Money, Banking, and Financial Markets,* 6th ed. Basic Books, New York, 1989.

Van Horne, James C. *Financial Market Rates and Flows,* 2d ed. Prentice-Hall, Englewood Cliffs, N.J., 1978.

Index

About the Author

John B. Schwartzman is vice president of The Bank of New York, where he is director of municipal bond research. He previously held the position of senior bond portfolio manager. In his capacities at The Bank of New York, he developed and has successfully used the interest rate tracking system described in this book.

He has also served as director of economic development for New York City's Department of Ports and Terminals, as senior planner for the New York City Planning Department, and as municipal bond analyst for a regional brokerage firm. He currently teaches a course at The American Institute of Banking on the factors and trends that influence interest rates.